BOX
WHO'S

BOXING WHO'S WHO

Ian Morrison

GUINNESS PUBLISHING

Editor: Charles Richards
Text design and layout: Amanda Sedge
Cover design: Ad Vantage Studios

Published in Great Britain by Guinness Publishing Ltd,
33 London Road, Enfield, Middlesex

Typeset in Bembo by Ace Filmsetting Ltd, Frome, Somerset

Printed and bound in Great Britain by
BPCC Hazell Books
Aylesbury, Bucks, England
Member of BPCC Ltd.

'Guinness' is a registered trademark of Guinness Publishing Ltd

British Library Cataloguing in Publication Data
Morrison, Ian 1947–
    Boxing who's who
    1. Boxing – Biographies – Collections
    I. Title
    796.830922

ISBN 0–85112–951–X

Front cover, clockwise from top left
Muhammad Ali, Henry Armstrong, Sugar Ray Robinson,
Mike Tyson, Jimmy Wilde, Barry McGuigan (*in action*)

ABOUT THE AUTHOR

Ian Morrison is an experienced sports author and statistician, whose previous books include *The Guinness World Championship Boxing Book*; *The Guinness Encyclopedia of International Sports Records and Results* (with Peter Matthews); and *The Guinness Motorcycle Sport Fact Book*, published in May 1991.

ACKNOWLEDGEMENTS

The author would like to thank the four main world boxing organisations for their assistance, in particular Alberto Aleman Jr (WBO), Dick Cole (WBC), Dr Elias Cordova Jr (WBA) and Bob Lee (IBF). He would also like to thank his daughter Tracey, who practised her word processing skills during the compilation of the manuscript!

AUTHOR'S NOTE

Boxing records have always been a minefield and with so many different organisations currently claiming 'world' champions, the job of compiling them is not getting any easier. The line has to be drawn somewhere, however, and those champions recognised by the four leading organisations – WBC, WBA, IBF and WBO – are included in this book; the likes of Intercontinental and Americas 'world' champions are excluded.

As this book is about *all* world champions – not just the present-day ones – there was also the problem of deciding who actually was a champion and who wasn't, and whether a fight was for the world title or not. There have been many claimants to world titles over the years; some valid, some dubious, and some downright outrageous!

Fortunately, I had managed to sort this area out when first compiling *Boxing: The Records* for Guinness in 1987. With some slight modification since then, I believe I now have a list of world champions and championship fights as accurate as any; and all these can be found in the pages of the *Guinness Boxing Who's Who*. All fight listings and career statistics are correct up to 12.12.90.

Ian Morrison

ABBREVIATIONS

WEIGHT DIVISIONS

H	heavyweight
C	cruiserweight (WBC/WBA/IBF)
	junior-heavyweight (WBO)
LH	light-heavyweight
SM	super-middleweight
M	middleweight
JM	junior-middleweight (WBA/IBF/ WBO); super-welterweight (WBC)
W	welterweight
JW	junior-welterweight (WBA/IBF/ WBO); super-lightweight (WBC)
L	lightweight
JL	junior-lightweight (WBA/IBF/ WBO); super-featherweight (WBC)
Fe	featherweight
JFe	junior-featherwight (WBA/IBF/ WBO); super-bantamweight (WBC)
B	bantamweight
JB	junior-bantamweight (WBA/IBF/ WBO); super-flyweight (WBC)
Fl	flyweight
JFl	junior-flyweight (WBA/IBF/WBO) light-flyweight (WBC)
S	strawweight WBC) mini-flyweight (WBA/IBF/WBO)

Letters in brackets indicate what each organisation calls the division, except where the name of the division is common to all four organisations.

BOXING AUTHORITIES

EBU	European Boxing Union
IBF	International Boxing Federation
IBU	International Boxing Union
NBA	National Boxing Association
NY	New York State Athletic Commission
WBA	World Boxing Association
WBC	World Boxing Council
WBO	World Boxing Organisation

FINAL DECISIONS

D	Drew
DEF	Default
DIS	Disqualified
KO	Knock-out
NC	No contest
ND	No decision
PTS	Points
RSF	Referee stopped fight
RTD	Retired
TD	Technical decision
TKO	Technical knock-out

MAJOR CITY VENUES
USA

US venues are identified by state in fight listings, the following major city venues excepted:

Atlanta, Georgia
Atlantic City, New Jersey
Baltimore, Maryland
Boston, Massachusetts
Buffalo, New York
Chicago, Illinois
Cincinnati, Ohio
Cleveland, Ohio
Dallas, Texas
Denver, Colorado
Detroit, Michigan
Hollywood, California
Honolulu, Hawaii
Houston, Texas
Indianapolis, Indiana
Kansas City, Missouri
Las Vegas, Nevada

Los Angeles, California
Memphis, Tennessee
Miami, Florida
Milwaukee, Wisconsin
Minneapolis, Minnesota
New Orleans, Louisiana
New York, New York
Oklahoma City, Oklahoma
Philadelphia, Pennsylvania
Pittsburgh, Pennsylvania
Phoenix, Arizona
St Louis, Missouri
Salt Lake City, Utah
San Diego, California
San Francisco, California
Seattle, Washington
Washington, DC

REST OF THE WORLD

Venues outside the US are identified by country in fight listings, the following major city venues excepted:

Accra, Ghana
Bangkok, Thailand
Barcelona, Spain
Belfast, N Ireland
Belgrade, Yugoslavia

Berlin, Germany
Birmingham, England
Bogota, Colombia
Bordeaux, France
Brasilia, Brazil

Brisbane, Australia
Buenos Aires, Argentina
Caracas, Venezuela
Cardiff, Wales
Copenhagen, Denmark
Dublin, Ireland
Durban, S Africa
Dusseldorf, Germany
Frankfurt, Germany
Geneva, Switzerland
Genoa, Italy
Glasgow, Scotland
Havana, Cuba
Helsinki, Finland
Jakarta, Indonesia
Johannesburg, S Africa
Kuala Lumpur, Malaysia
Leicester, England
Liverpool, England
London, England
Lyons, France
Madrid, Spain
Managua, Nicaragua
Manchester, England
Manila, Philippines
Marseilles, France
Melbourne, Australia
Mexico City, Mexico

Milan, Italy
Middlesbrough, England
Monte Carlo, Monaco
Montreal, Canada
Munich, Germany
Naples, Italy
Nice, France
Oslo, Norway
Panama City, Panama
Paris, France
Rio de Janeiro, Brazil
Rome, Italy
San Juan, Puerto Rico
Santiago, Chile
Santo Domingo, Dominican Republic
Seoul, S Korea
Stockholm, Sweden
Sunderland, England
Sydney, Australia
Tel Aviv, Israel
Tokyo, Japan
Toronto, Canada
Tunis, Tunisia
Turin, Italy
Valencia, Spain
Vancouver, Canada
Zurich, Switzerland

THE WORLD
CHAMPIONS

Horacio ACCAVALLO

Born: Parque Patricios, Argentina, 14 Oct 1934
World title fights: 4 (all flyweight) won 4, lost 0

1 Mar 1966	Fl (WBA)	Katsuyoshi Takayama	Tokyo	Won PTS–15
15 Jul 1966	Fl (WBA)	Hiroyuki Ebihara	Buenos Aires	Won PTS–15
10 Dec 1966	Fl (WBA)	Efren Torres	Buenos Aires	Won PTS–15
13 Aug 1967	Fl (WBA)	Hiroyuki Ebihara	Buenos Aires	Won PTS–15

Mauricio ACEVES

Born: Mexico City, Mexico, 18 Dec 1960
World title fights: 5 (1 junior-welter, 4 lightweight) won 2, drew 1, lost 2

24 Mar 1988	JW (WBC)	Roger Mayweather	Los Angeles	Lost KO–3
21 Jan 1989	L (WBO)	Amancio Castro	Monteria, Colombia	Drew 12
6 May 1989	L (WBO)	Amancio Castro	Santa Ana, California	Won PTS–12
30 Aug 1989	L (WBO)	Oscar Bejines	Los Angeles	Won RSF–10
22 Sep 1990	L (WBO)	Dingaan Thobela	Brownsville, Texas	Lost PTS–12

Pedro ADIGUE

Born: Palanas, Masbate, Philippines, 22 Dec 1943
World title fights: 2 (both junior-welter) won 1, lost 1

14 Dec 1968	JW (WBC)	Adolph Pruitt	Manila	Won PTS–15
31 Jan 1970	JW (WBC)	Bruno Arcari	Rome	Lost PTS–15

Virgil AKINS

Born: St Louis, Missouri, USA, 10 Mar 1928
World title fights: 3 (all welterweight) won 1, lost 2

DATE	WEIGHT	OPPONENT	VENUE	RESULT	
6 Jun 1958	W	Vince Martinez	St Louis	Won	RSF-4
5 Dec 1958	W	Don Jordan	Los Angeles	Lost	PTS-15
24 Apr 1959	W	Don Jordan	St Louis	Lost	PTS-15

Oscar ALBARADO

Born: Pecos, Texas, USA, 15 Sep 1948
World title fights: 3 (all junior-middle) won 2, lost 1

DATE	WEIGHT	OPPONENT	VENUE	RESULT	
4 Jun 1974	JM	Koichi Wajima	Tokyo	Won	KO-15
8 Oct 1974	JM	Ryu Sorimachi	Tokyo	Won	RSF-7
21 Jan 1975	JM	Koichi Wajima	Tokyo	Lost	PTS-15

Muhammad ALI
(formerly Cassius Clay)

Born: Louisville, Kentucky, USA, 17 Jan 1942
World title fights: 25 (all heavyweight) won 22, lost 3

DATE	WEIGHT	OPPONENT	VENUE	RESULT	
25 Feb 1964	H	Sonny Liston	Miami	Won	RTD-6
25 May 1965	H	Sonny Liston	Lewiston, Maine	Won	KO-1
22 Nov 1965	H	Floyd Patterson	Las Vegas	Won	RSF-12
29 Mar 1966	H	George Chuvalo	Toronto	Won	PTS-15
21 May 1966	H	Henry Cooper	London	Won	RSF-6
6 Aug 1966	H	Brian London	London	Won	KO-3
10 Sep 1966	H	Karl Mildenberger	Frankfurt	Won	RSF-12
14 Nov 1966	H	Cleveland Williams	Houston	Won	RSF-3
6 Feb 1967	H	Ernie Terrell	Houston	Won	PTS-15

DATE	WEIGHT	OPPONENT	VENUE	RESULT
22 Mar 1967	H	Zora Folley	New York	Won KO–7
8 Mar 1971	H	Joe Frazier	New York	Lost PTS–15
30 Oct 1974	H	George Foreman	Kinshasa, Zaire	Won KO–8
24 Mar 1975	H	Chuck Wepner	Cleveland	Won RSF–15
16 May 1975	H	Ron Lyle	Las Vegas	Won RSF–11
1 Jul 1975	H	Joe Bugner	Kuala Lumpur	Won PTS–15
1 Oct 1975	H	Joe Frazier	Manila	Won RTD–14
20 Feb 1976	H	Jean Pierre Coopman	San Juan	Won KO–5
30 Apr 1976	H	Jimmy Young	Landover, Maryland	Won PTS–15
24 May 1976	H	Richard Dunn	Munich	Won KO–5
28 Sep 1976	H	Ken Norton	New York	Won PTS–15
16 May 1977	H	Alfredo Evangelista	Landover	Won PTS–15
29 Sep 1977	H	Earnie Shavers	New York	Won PTS–15
15 Feb 1978	H	Leon Spinks	Las Vegas	Lost PTS–15
15 Sep 1978	H (WBA)	Leon Spinks	New Orleans	Won PTS–15
2 Oct 1980	H (WBC)	Larry Holmes	Las Vegas	Lost RTD–10

Terry ALLEN

Born: London, England, 18 Jun 1924
World title fights: 5 (all flyweight) won 1, lost 3, drew 1

DATE	WEIGHT	OPPONENT	VENUE	RESULT
30 Sep 1949	Fl	Rinty Monaghan	Belfast	Drew 15
25 Apr 1950	Fl	Honore Pratesi	London	Won PTS–15
1 Aug 1950	Fl	Dado Marino	Honolulu	Lost PTS–15
1 Nov 1951	Fl	Dado Marino	Honolulu	Lost PTS–15
27 Oct 1953	Fl	Yoshio Shirai	Tokyo	Lost PTS–15

DATE	WEIGHT	OPPONENT	VENUE	RESULT

Elvis ALVAREZ

Born: Medellin, Colombia, 2 Feb 1965
World title fights: 1 (flyweight) won 1, lost 0

DATE	WEIGHT	OPPONENT	VENUE	RESULT	
3 Mar 1989	Fl (WBO)	Miguel Mercedes	Medellin, Colombia	Won	PTS–12

Lou AMBERS

Born: Herkimer, New York, USA, 8 Nov 1913
World title fights: 7 (all lightweight) won 4, lost 3

DATE	WEIGHT	OPPONENT	VENUE	RESULT	
10 May 1935	L	Tony Canzoneri	New York	Lost	PTS–15
3 Sep 1936	L	Tony Canzoneri	New York	Won	PTS–15
7 May 1937	L	Tony Canzoneri	New York	Won	PTS–15
23 Sep 1937	L	Pedro Montanez	New York	Won	PTS–15
17 Aug 1938	L	Henry Armstrong	New York	Lost	PTS–15
22 Aug 1939	L	Henry Armstrong	New York	Won	PTS–15
10 May 1940	L (NY)	Lew Jenkins	New York	Lost	RSF–3

Romeo ANAYA

Born: Chiapas, Mexico, 5 Apr 1946
World title fights: 5 (all bantamweight) won 3, lost 2

DATE	WEIGHT	OPPONENT	VENUE	RESULT	
20 Jan 1973	B (WBA)	Enrique Pinder	Panama City	Won	KO–3
28 Apr 1973	B (WBA)	Rogelio Lara	Los Angeles	Won	PTS–15
18 Aug 1973	B (WBA)	Enrique Pinder	Los Angeles	Won	KO–3
3 Nov 1973	B (WBA)	Arnold Taylor	Johannesburg	Lost	KO–14
25 May 1974	B (WBC)	Rafael Herrera	Mexico City	Lost	KO–6

DATE	WEIGHT	OPPONENT	VENUE	RESULT

Dennis ANDRIES

Born: Georgetown, Guyana, 5 Nov 1953
World title fights: 7 (all light-heavy) won 5, lost 2

DATE	WEIGHT	OPPONENT	VENUE	RESULT
30 Apr 1986	LH (WBC)	J B Williamson	London	Won PTS–12
10 Sep 1986	LH (WBC)	Tony Sibson	London	Won RSF–9
7 Mar 1987	LH (WBC)	Thomas Hearns	Detroit	Lost RSF–10
22 Feb 1989	LH (WBC)	Tony Willis	Tucson, Arizona	Won RSF–5
24 Jun 1989	LH (WBC)	Jeff Harding	Atlantic City	Lost RSF–12
28 Jul 1990	LH (WBC)	Jeff Harding	Melbourne	Won KO–7
10 Oct 1990	LH (WBC)	Sergio Merani	London	Won RSF–4

Sammy ANGOTT

Born: Washington, Pennsylvania, USA, 17 Jan 1915
Died: Cleveland, 22 Oct 1980
World title fights: 5 (all lightweight) won 4, lost 1

DATE	WEIGHT	OPPONENT	VENUE	RESULT
3 May 1940	L (NBA)	Davey Day	Louisville, Kentucky	Won PTS–15
19 Dec 1941	L	Lew Jenkins	New York	Won PTS–15
15 May 1942	L	Allie Stolz	New York	Won PTS–15
27 Oct 1943	L (NBA)	Slugger White	Hollywood	Won PTS–15
8 Mar 1944	L (NBA)	Juan Zurita	Hollywood	Lost PTS–15

Vito ANTUOFERMO

Born: Bari, Italy, 9 Feb 1953
World title fights: 5 (all middleweight) won 1, lost 3, drew 1

DATE	WEIGHT	OPPONENT	VENUE	RESULT
30 Jun 1979	M	Hugo Corro	Monte Carlo	Won PTS–15
30 Nov 1979	M	Marvin Hagler	Las Vegas	Drew 15
16 Mar 1980	M	Alan Minter	Las Vegas	Lost PTS–15

DATE	WEIGHT	OPPONENT	VENUE	RESULT
28 Jun 1980	M	Alan Minter	London	Lost KO–8
13 Jun 1981	M	Marvin Hagler	Boston	Lost RTD–4

Fred APOSTOLI

Born: San Francisco, USA, 2 Feb 1913
Died: San Francisco, 29 Nov 1973
World title fights: 3 (all middleweight) won 2, lost 1

DATE	WEIGHT	OPPONENT	VENUE	RESULT
1 Apr 1938	M (NY)	Glen Lee	New York	Won PTS–15
18 Nov 1938	M (NY)	Young Corbett III	New York	Won KO–8
2 Oct 1939	M (NY)	Ceferino Garcia	New York	Lost KO–7

Lupe AQUINO

Born: Chihuahua, Mexico, 23 Jan 1963
World title fights: 3 (all junior-middle) won 1, lost 2

DATE	WEIGHT	OPPONENT	VENUE	RESULT
12 Jul 1987	JM (WBC)	Duane Thomas	Bordeaux	Won PTS–12
2 Oct 1987	JM (WBC)	Gianfranco Rosi	Perugia, Italy	Lost PTS–12
7 Dec 1988	JM (WBO)	John David Jackson	Detroit	Lost RSF–8

Bruno ARCARI

Born: Latina Latinum, Italy, 1 Jan 1942
World title fights: 10 (all junior-welter) won 10, lost 0

DATE	WEIGHT	OPPONENT	VENUE	RESULT
31 Jan 1970	JW (WBC)	Pedro Adigue	Rome	Won PTS–15
10 Jul 1970	JW (WBC)	Rene Roque	Lignano, Italy	Won DIS–6
30 Oct 1970	JW (WBC)	Raimundo Dias	Genoa	Won KO–3
6 Mar 1971	JW (WBC)	Joao Henrique	Rome	Won PTS–15
26 Jun 1971	JW (WBC)	Enrique Jana	Palermo, Italy	Won RSF–9
9 Oct 1971	JW (WBC)	Domingo Barrera	Genoa	Won KO–10

DATE	WEIGHT	OPPONENT	VENUE	RESULT

DATE	WEIGHT	OPPONENT	VENUE	RESULT
10 Jun 1972	JW (WBC)	Joao Henrique	Genoa	Won KO–12
2 Dec 1972	JW (WBC)	Everaldo Costa Azevedo	Turin	Won PTS–15
1 Nov 1973	JW (WBC)	Jorgen Hansen	Copenhagen	Won KO–5
16 Feb 1974	JW (WBC)	Tony Ortiz	Turin	Won DIS–8

Joey ARCHIBALD

Born: Providence, Rhode Island, USA, 6 Dec 1915
World title fights: 6 (all featherweight) won 4, lost 2

DATE	WEIGHT	OPPONENT	VENUE	RESULT
17 Oct 1938	Fe (NY)	Mike Belloise	New York	Won PTS–15
18 Apr 1939	Fe	Leo Rodak	Providence, Rhode Island	Won PTS–15
28 Sep 1939	Fe	Harry Jeffra	Washington DC	Won PTS–15
20 May 1940	Fe (NY)	Harry Jeffra	Baltimore	Lost PTS–15
12 May 1941	Fe (NY)	Harry Jeffra	Washington DC	Won PTS–15
11 Sep 1941	Fe (NY)	Chalky Wright	Washington DC	Lost KO–11

Alexis ARGUELLO

Born: Managua, Nicaragua, 19 Apr 1952
World title fights: 22 (6 featherweight, 9 junior-light, 5 lightweight,
2 junior-welter) won 19, lost 3

DATE	WEIGHT	OPPONENT	VENUE	RESULT
16 Feb 1974	Fe (WBA)	Ernesto Marcel	Panama City	Lost PTS–15
23 Nov 1974	Fe (WBA)	Ruben Olivares	Los Angeles	Won KO–13
15 Mar 1975	Fe (WBA)	Leonel Hernandez	Caracas	Won RSF–8
31 May 1975	Fe (WBA)	Rigoberto Riasco	Granada, Nicaragua	Won RSF–2
12 Oct 1975	Fe (WBA)	Royal Kobayashi	Tokyo	Won KO–5
19 Jun 1976	Fe (WBA)	Salvador Torres	Los Angeles	Won KO–3
28 Jan 1978	JL (WBC)	Alfredo Escalera	San Juan	Won RSF–13
29 Apr 1978	JL (WBC)	Rey Tam	Los Angeles	Won RSF–5
3 Jun 1978	JL (WBC)	Diego Alcala	San Juan	Won KO–1

DATE	WEIGHT	OPPONENT	VENUE	RESULT

DATE	WEIGHT	OPPONENT	VENUE	RESULT
10 Nov 1978	JL (WBC)	Arturo Leon	Las Vegas	Won PTS–15
4 Feb 1979	JL (WBC)	Alfredo Escalera	Rimini, Italy	Won KO–13
8 Jul 1979	JL (WBC)	Rafael Limon	New York	Won RSF–11
16 Nov 1979	JL (WBC)	Bobby Chacon	Los Angeles	Won RTD–7
20 Jan 1980	JL (WBC)	Ruben Castillo	Tucson, Arizona	Won RSF–11
27 Apr 1980	JL (WBC)	Rolando Navarrete	San Juan	Won RSF–4
20 Jun 1981	L (WBC)	Jim Watt	London	Won PTS–15
3 Oct 1981	L (WBC)	Ray Mancini	Atlantic City	Won RSF–14
21 Nov 1981	L (WBC)	Roberto Elizondo	Las Vegas	Won KO–7
13 Feb 1982	L (WBC)	James Busceme	Beaumont, Texas	Won RSF–6
22 May 1982	L (WBC)	Andy Ganigan	Las Vegas	Won KO–5
12 Nov 1982	JW (WBA)	Aaron Pryor	Miami	Lost RSF–14
9 Sep 1983	JW (WBA)	Aaron Pryor	Las Vegas	Lost KO–10

Alberto 'Baby' ARIZMENDI

Born: Coahila, Mexico, 17 Mar 1914
Died: Los Angeles, 31 Dec 1963
World title fights: 3 (1 welterweight, 2 featherweight) won 1, lost 2

DATE	WEIGHT	OPPONENT	VENUE	RESULT
24 Feb 1933	Fe (NBA)	Freddie Miller	Los Angeles	Lost PTS–10
30 Aug 1934	Fe (NBA)	Mike Belloise	New York	Won PTS–15
10 Jan 1939	W	Henry Armstrong	Los Angeles	Lost PTS–10

Henry ARMSTRONG

Born: Columbus, Mississippi, USA, 12 Dec 1912
Died: Los Angeles, 23 Oct 1988
World title fights: 26 (1 featherweight, 22 welterweight, 2 lightweight, 1 middleweight) won 22, lost 3, drew 1

DATE	WEIGHT	OPPONENT	VENUE	RESULT
29 Oct 1937	Fe	Petey Sarron	New York	Won KO–6

DATE	WEIGHT	OPPONENT	VENUE	RESULT

DATE	WEIGHT	OPPONENT	VENUE	RESULT	
31 May 1938	W	Barney Ross	New York	Won	PTS–15
17 Aug 1938	L	Lou Ambers	New York	Won	PTS–15
25 Nov 1938	W	Ceferino Garcia	New York	Won	PTS–15
5 Dec 1938	W	Al Manfredo	Cleveland	Won	KO–3
10 Jan 1939	W	Baby Arizmendi	Los Angeles	Won	PTS–10
4 Mar 1939	W	Bobby Pacho	Havana	Won	KO–4
16 Mar 1939	W	Lew Feldman	St Louis	Won	KO–1
31 Mar 1939	W	Davey Day	New York	Won	KO–12
25 May 1939	W	Ernie Roderick	London	Won	PTS–15
22 Aug 1939	L	Lou Ambers	New York	Lost	PTS–15
9 Oct 1939	W	Al Manfredo	Des Moines, Iowa	Won	KO–4
13 Oct 1939	W	Howard Scott	Minneapolis	Won	KO–2
20 Oct 1939	W	Ritchie Fontaine	Seattle	Won	KO–3
24 Oct 1939	W	Jimmy Garrison	Los Angeles	Won	PTS–10
30 Oct 1939	W	Bobby Pacho	Denver	Won	KO–4
11 Dec 1939	W	Jimmy Garrison	Cleveland	Won	KO–7
4 Jan 1940	W	Joe Ghnouly	St Louis	Won	KO–5
24 Jan 1940	W	Pedro Montanez	New York	Won	KO–9
1 Mar 1940	M (NY)	Ceferino Garcia	Los Angeles	Drew	10
26 Apr 1940	W	Paul Junior	Boston	Won	KO–7
24 May 1940	W	Ralph Zanelli	Boston	Won	KO–5
21 Jun 1940	W	Paul Junior	Portland, Maine	Won	KO–3
23 Sep 1940	W	Phil Furr	Washington DC	Won	KO–4
4 Oct 1940	W	Fritzie Zivic	New York	Lost	PTS–15
17 Jan 1941	W	Fritzie Zivic	New York	Lost	KO–12

DATE	WEIGHT	OPPONENT	VENUE	RESULT

Rene ARREDONDO

Born: Apatzingan, Mexico, 15 Jun 1961
World title fights: 4 (all junior-welter) won 2, lost 2

DATE	WEIGHT	OPPONENT	VENUE	RESULT	
5 May 1986	JW (WBC)	Lonnie Smith	Los Angeles	Won	KO-5
24 Jul 1986	JW (WBC)	Tsuyoshi Hamada	Tokyo	Lost	KO-1
22 Jul 1987	JW (WBC)	Tsuyoshi Hamada	Tokyo	Won	RSF-6
12 Nov 1987	JW (WBC)	Roger Mayweather	Los Angeles	Lost	KO-6

Ricardo ARREDONDO

Born: Apatzingan, Mexico, 26 May 1949
World title fights: 8 (all junior-light) won 6, lost 2

DATE	WEIGHT	OPPONENT	VENUE	RESULT	
4 Mar 1971	JL (WBA)	Hiroshi Kobayashi	Utsonomija, Japan	Lost	PTS-15
10 Oct 1971	JL (WBC)	Yoshiaki Numata	Sendai, Japan	Won	KO-10
29 Jan 1972	JL (WBC)	Jose Isaac Marin	San Jose, Costa Rica	Won	PTS-15
22 Apr 1972	JL (WBC)	William Martinez	Mexico City	Won	KO-5
15 Sep 1972	JL (WBC)	Susumu Okabe	Tokyo	Won	KO-12
6 Mar 1973	JL (WBC)	Apollo Yoshio	Fukuoka, Japan	Won	PTS-15
1 Sep 1973	JL (WBC)	Morito Kashiwaba	Tokyo	Won	RSF-6
28 Feb 1974	JL (WBC)	Kuniaki Shibata	Tokyo	Lost	PTS-15

Harry ARROYO

Born: Youngstown, Ohio, USA, 25 Oct 1957
World title fights: 4 (all lightweight) won 3, lost 1

DATE	WEIGHT	OPPONENT	VENUE	RESULT	
15 Apr 1984	L (IBF)	Charlie 'Choo Choo' Brown	Atlantic City	Won	RSF-14
1 Sep 1984	L (IBF)	Charlie 'White Lightning' Brown	Youngstown, Ohio	Won	RSF-8
12 Jan 1985	L (IBF)	Terrence Alli	Atlantic City	Won	RSF-11
6 Apr 1985	L (IBF)	Jimmy Paul	Atlantic City	Lost	PTS-15

Abe ATTELL

Born: San Francisco, USA, 22 Feb 1884
Died: New Paltz, New York, 7 Feb 1970
World title fights: 14 (all featherweight) won 10, lost 1, drew 3

DATE	WEIGHT	OPPONENT	VENUE	RESULT
1 Feb 1904	Fe	Harry Forbes	St Louis	Won KO–5
22 Feb 1905	Fe	Kid Goodman	Boston	Drew 15
4 Jul 1906	Fe	Frankie Neil	Los Angeles	Won PTS–20
30 Oct 1906	Fe	Harry Baker	Los Angeles	Won PTS–20
7 Dec 1906	Fe	Jimmy Walsh	Los Angeles	Won KO–8
18 Jan 1907	Fe	Harry Baker	Los Angeles	Won KO–8
24 May 1907	Fe	Kid Solomon	Los Angeles	Won PTS–20
29 Oct 1907	Fe	Freddie Weekes	Los Angeles	Won KO–4
1 Jan 1908	Fe	Owen Moran	San Francisco	Drew 25
30 Apr 1908	Fe	Tommy Sullivan	San Francisco	Won KO–4
7 Sep 1908	Fe	Owen Moran	San Francisco	Drew 23
26 Mar 1909	Fe	Frankie White	Dayton, Ohio	Won KO–8
28 Feb 1910	Fe	Harry Forbes	New York	Won KO–6
22 Feb 1912	Fe	Johnny Kilbane	Vernon, California	Lost PTS–20

Antonio AVELAR

Born: Jalisco, Mexico, 25 Aug 1958
World title fights: 4 (all flyweight) won 2, lost 2

DATE	WEIGHT	OPPONENT	VENUE	RESULT
10 Feb 1979	Fl (WBC)	Miguel Canto	Merida, Mexico	Lost PTS–15
12 May 1981	Fl (WBC)	Shoji Oguma	Tokyo	Won KO–7
30 Aug 1981	Fl (WBC)	Tae-Shik Kim	Seoul	Won KO–2
20 Mar 1982	Fl (WBC)	Prudencio Cardona	Tampico, Mexico	Lost KO–1

Billy BACKUS

Born: Canastota, New York, USA, 5 Mar 1943
World title fights: 3 (all welterweight) won 1, lost 2

DATE	WEIGHT	OPPONENT	VENUE	RESULT	
3 Dec 1970	W	Jose Napoles	Syracuse, New York	Won	RSF–4
4 Jun 1971	W	Jose Napoles	Los Angeles	Lost	TKO–4
20 May 1978	W (WBA)	Pipino Cuevas	Los Angeles	Lost	RSF–2

In-Chul BAEK

Born: Chun-Nam, South Korea, 20 Dec 1961
World title fights: 5 (1 junior-middle, 4 super-middle) won 3, lost 2

DATE	WEIGHT	OPPONENT	VENUE	RESULT	
21 Nov 1987	JM (WBA)	Julian Jackson	Las Vegas	Lost	RSF–3
27 May 1989	SM (WBA)	Fulgencio Obelmejias	Seoul	Won	RSF–11
8 Oct 1989	SM (WBA)	Ron Essett	Seoul	Won	RSF–11
13 Jan 1990	SM (WBA)	Yoshiaki Tajima	Ulsan, S Korea	Won	RTD–7
30 Mar 1990	SM (WBA)	Christophe Tiozzo	Lyons	Lost	RSF–10

Max BAER

Born: Omaha, Nebraska, USA, 11 Feb 1909
Died: Hollywood, 21 Nov 1959
World title fights: 2 (both heavyweight) won 1, lost 1

DATE	WEIGHT	OPPONENT	VENUE	RESULT	
14 Jun 1934	H	Primo Carnera	Long Island, New York	Won	KO–11
13 Jun 1935	H	Jim Braddock	Long Island	Lost	PTS–15

Gustavo BALLAS

Born: Cordoba, Argentina, 10 Feb 1958
World title fights: 4 (all junior-bantam) won 1, lost 3

DATE	WEIGHT	OPPONENT	VENUE	RESULT	
12 Sep 1981	JB (WBA)	Suk-Chul Bae	Buenos Aires	Won	RSF–8
5 Dec 1981	JB (WBA)	Rafael Pedroza	Panama City	Lost	PTS–15
29 Jul 1982	JB (WBA)	Jiro Watanabe	Osaka, Japan	Lost	RSF–9
24 Oct 1987	JB (WBC)	Baby Rojas	Miami	Lost	RSF–4

Mike BALLERINO

Born: Bayonne, New Jersey, USA, 10 Apr 1901
Died: Tampa, Florida, 4 Apr 1965
World title fights: 3 (all junior-light) won 1, lost 2

DATE	WEIGHT	OPPONENT	VENUE	RESULT	
15 Oct 1924	JL	Steve 'Kid' Sullivan	New York	Lost	KO–5
1 Apr 1925	JL	Steve 'Kid' Sullivan	Philadelphia	Won	PTS–10
2 Dec 1925	JL	Tod Morgan	Los Angeles	Lost	KO–10

Paul BANKE

Born: Azusa, California, USA, 1 Mar 1964
World title fights: 4 (all junior-feather) won 2, lost 2

DATE	WEIGHT	OPPONENT	VENUE	RESULT	
24 Jun 1989	JFe (WBC)	Daniel Zaragoza	Los Angeles	Lost	PTS–12
23 Apr 1990	JFe (WBC)	Daniel Zaragoza	Los Angeles	Won	RSF–9
17 Aug 1990	JFe (WBC)	Ki-Jun Lee	Seoul	Won	RSF–12
5 Nov 1990	JFe (WBC)	Pedro Decima	Inglewood, California	Lost	RSF–4

Iran BARKLEY

Born: Bronx, New York, USA, 9 May 1960
World title fights: 5 (all middleweight) won 1, lost 4

DATE	WEIGHT	OPPONENT	VENUE	RESULT	
23 Oct 1987	M (WBA)	Sumbu Kalambay	Livorno, Italy	Lost	PTS–15
6 Jun 1988	M (WBC)	Thomas Hearns	Las Vegas	Won	RSF–3
24 Feb 1989	M (WBC)	Roberto Duran	Atlantic City	Lost	PTS–12
19 Aug 1989	M (IBF)	Michael Nunn	Reno, Nevada	Lost	PTS–12
18 Aug 1990	M (WBO)	Nigel Benn	Las Vegas	Lost	RSF–1

Rene BARRIENTOS

Born: Balite, Philippines, Feb 1942
World title fights: 4 (all junior-light) won 1, lost 2, drew 1

DATE	WEIGHT	OPPONENT	VENUE	RESULT	
30 Mar 1968	JL	Hiroshi Kobayashi	Tokyo	Drew	15
15 Feb 1969	JL (WBC)	Ruben Navarro	Manila	Won	PTS–15
5 Apr 1970	JL (WBC)	Yoshiaki Numata	Tokyo	Lost	PTS–15
3 Jan 1971	JL (WBC)	Yoshiaki Numata	Shizuoka, Japan	Lost	PTS–15

Jimmy BARRY

Born: Chicago, USA, 7 Mar 1870
Died: Chicago, 4 Apr 1943
World title fights: 3 (all bantamweight) won 1, drew 2

DATE	WEIGHT	OPPONENT	VENUE	RESULT	
6 Dec 1897	B	Walter Croot	London	Won	KO–20
30 May 1898	B	Casper Leon	New York	Drew	20
29 Dec 1898	B	Casper Leon	Davenport, Iowa	Drew	20

Sal BARTOLO

Born: Boston, USA, 5 Nov 1917
World title fights: 6 (all featherweight) won 4, lost 2

DATE	WEIGHT	OPPONENT	VENUE	RESULT
8 Jun 1943	Fe (NY)	Willie Pep	Boston	Lost PTS-15
10 Mar 1944	Fe (NBA)	Phil Terranova	Boston	Won PTS-15
5 May 1944	Fe (NBA)	Phil Terranova	Boston	Won PTS-15
15 Dec 1944	Fe (NBA)	Willie Roche	Boston	Won PTS-15
3 May 1946	Fe (NBA)	Spider Armstrong	Boston	Won KO-6
7 Jun 1946	Fe	Willie Pep	New York	Lost KO-12

Carmen BASILIO

Born: Canastota, New York, USA, 2 Apr 1927
World title fights: 11 (6 welterweight, 5 middleweight) won 5, lost 6

DATE	WEIGHT	OPPONENT	VENUE	RESULT
18 Sep 1953	W	Kid Gavilan	Syracuse, New York	Lost PTS-15
10 Jun 1955	W	Tony DeMarco	Syracuse	Won RSF-12
30 Nov 1955	W	Tony DeMarco	Boston	Won KO-12
14 Mar 1956	W	Johnny Saxton	Chicago	Lost PTS-15
12 Sep 1956	W	Johnny Saxton	Syracuse	Won KO-9
22 Feb 1957	W	Johnny Saxton	Cleveland	Won KO-2
23 Sep 1957	M	Sugar Ray Robinson	New York	Won PTS-15
25 Mar 1958	M	Sugar Ray Robinson	Chicago	Lost PTS-15
28 Aug 1959	M (NBA)	Gene Fullmer	San Francisco	Lost KO-14
29 Jun 1960	M (NBA)	Gene Fullmer	Salt Lake City	Lost KO-12
22 Apr 1961	M	Paul Pender	Boston	Lost PTS-15

DATE	WEIGHT	OPPONENT	VENUE	RESULT

Benny BASS

Born: Kiev, Russia, 4 Dec 1904
Died: Philadelphia, 25 Jun 1925
World title fights: 4 (2 featherweight, 2 junior-light) won 2, lost 2

DATE	WEIGHT	OPPONENT	VENUE	RESULT	
19 Sep 1927	Fe	Red Chapman	Philadelphia	Won	PTS–10
10 Feb 1928	Fe	Tony Canzoneri	New York	Lost	PTS–15
19 Dec 1929	JL	Tod Morgan	New York	Won	KO–2
15 Jul 1931	JL	Kid Chocolate	Philadelphia	Lost	RSF–7

Fidel BASSA

Born: El Reten-Magdalena, Colombia, 18 Dec 1962
World title fights: 8 (all flyweight) won 6, lost 1, drew 1

DATE	WEIGHT	OPPONENT	VENUE	RESULT	
13 Feb 1987	Fl (WBA)	Hilario Zapata	Barranquilla, Colombia	Won	PTS–15
25 Apr 1987	Fl (WBA)	Dave McAuley	Belfast	Won	RSF–13
15 Aug 1987	Fl (WBA)	Hilario Zapata	Panama City	Drew	15
18 Dec 1987	Fl (WBA)	Felix Marti	Cartagena, Colombia	Won	PTS–12
26 Mar 1988	Fl (WBA)	Dave McAuley	Belfast	Won	PTS–12
2 Oct 1988	Fl (WBA)	Ray Medel	San Antonio, Texas	Won	PTS–12
15 Apr 1989	Fl (WBA)	Julio Gudino	Barranquilla	Won	RSF–6
30 Sep 1989	Fl (WBA)	Jesus Rojas	Barranquilla	Lost	PTS–12

Hogan 'Kid' BASSEY

Born: Calabar, Nigeria, 3 Jun 1932
World title fights: 4 (all featherweight) won 2, lost 2

DATE	WEIGHT	OPPONENT	VENUE	RESULT	
24 Jun 1957	Fe	Cherif Hamia	Paris	Won	RSF–10
1 Apr 1958	Fe	Ricardo Moreno	Los Angeles	Won	KO–3
18 Mar 1959	Fe	Davey Moore	Los Angeles	Lost	RTD–13
19 Aug 1959	Fe	Davey Moore	Los Angeles	Lost	RTD–10

Battling BATTALINO

Born: Hartford, Connecticut, USA, 18 Feb 1908
Died: Hartford, 25 Jul 1977
World title fights: 6 (all featherweight) won 6, lost 0

DATE	WEIGHT	OPPONENT	VENUE	RESULT
23 Sep 1929	Fe	Andre Routis	Hartford, Connecticut	Won PTS-15
12 Dec 1930	Fe	Kid Chocolate	New York	Won PTS-15
23 May 1931	Fe	Fidel La Barba	New York	Won PTS-15
1 Jul 1931	Fe	Irish Bobby Brady	Jersey City, New Jersey	Won PTS-10
23 Jul 1931	Fe	Freddie Miller	Cincinnati	Won PTS-10
4 Nov 1931	Fe	Eddie Mastro	Chicago	Won PTS-10

Joe BECERRA

Born: Guadalajara, Mexico, 15 Apr 1936
World title fights: 3 (all bantamweight) won 3, lost 0

DATE	WEIGHT	OPPONENT	VENUE	RESULT
8 Jul 1959	B	Alphonse Halimi	Los Angeles	Won KO-8
4 Feb 1960	B	Alphonse Halimi	Los Angeles	Won KO-9
23 May 1960	B	Kenji Yonekura	Tokyo	Won PTS-15

Albert 'Frenchie' BELANGER

Born: Toronto, Canada, 17 May 1906
Died: Toronto, 27 May 1969
World title fights: 5 (all flyweight) won 2, lost 3

DATE	WEIGHT	OPPONENT	VENUE	RESULT
28 Nov 1927	FL (NBA)	Frankie Genaro	Toronto	Won PTS-10
19 Dec 1927	Fl (NBA)	Ernie Jarvis	Toronto	Won PTS-10
6 Feb 1928	Fl (NBA)	Frankie Genaro	Toronto	Lost PTS-10
12 Mar 1929	Fl (NY)	Izzy Schwartz	Toronto	Lost PTS-12
10 Jun 1930	Fl (NBA)	Frankie Genaro	Toronto	Lost PTS-10

Toufik BELBOULI

Born: Bovenzi, Mauritania, 10 Dec 1954
World title fights: 2 (both cruiserweight) won 1, drew 1

DATE	WEIGHT	OPPONENT	VENUE	RESULT	
25 Mar 1989	C (WBA)	Michael Greer	Casablanca, Morocco	Won	RSF–8
23 Nov 1990	C (WBA)	Robert Daniels	Madrid	Drew	12

Mike BELLOISE

Born: New York City, USA, 18 Feb 1911
Died: New York City, 2 Jun 1969
World title fights: 2 (both featherweight) won 1, lost 1

DATE	WEIGHT	OPPONENT	VENUE	RESULT	
4 Sep 1936	Fe (NY)	Dave Crowley	New York	Won	KO–9
17 Oct 1938	Fe (NY)	Joey Archibald	New York	Lost	PTS–15

Fabrice BENICHOU

Born: Madrid, Spain, 5 Apr 1965
World title fights: 6 (all junior-feather) won 3, lost 3

DATE	WEIGHT	OPPONENT	VENUE	RESULT	
26 Sep 1988	JFe (IBF)	Jose Sanabria	Nogent-sur-Marne, France	Lost	RSF–10
10 Mar 1989	JFe (IBF)	Jose Sanabria	Limoges, France	Won	PTS–12
11 Jun 1989	JFe (IBF)	Cornelius Badenhorst	Frosinone, Italy	Won	KO–5
7 Oct 1989	JFe (IBF)	Ramon Cruz	Bordeaux	Won	PTS–12
10 Mar 1990	JFe (IBF)	Welcome Ncita	Tel Aviv	Lost	PTS–12
18 Oct 1990	JFe (WBA)	Luis Mendoza	Paris	Lost	PTS–12

Wilfred BENITEZ
(formerly Wilfredo Benitez)

Born: Bronx, New York, USA, 12 Sep 1958
World title fights: 10 (3 junior-welter, 3 welterweight, 4 junior-middle)
won 8, lost 2

DATE	WEIGHT	OPPONENT	VENUE	RESULT	
6 Mar 1976	JW (WBA)	Antonio Cervantes	San Juan	Won	PTS–15
31 May 1976	JW (WBA)	Emiliano Villa	San Juan	Won	PTS–15
16 Oct 1976	JW (WBA)	Tony Petronelli	San Juan	Won	RSF–3
14 Jan 1979	W (WBC)	Carlos Palomino	San Juan	Won	PTS–15
25 Mar 1979	W (WBC)	Harold Weston	San Juan	Won	PTS–15
30 Nov 1979	W (WBC)	Sugar Ray Leonard	Las Vegas	Lost	RSF–15
23 May 1981	JM (WBC)	Maurice Hope	Las Vegas	Won	KO–12
14 Nov 1981	JM (WBC)	Carlos Santos	Las Vegas	Won	PTS–15
30 Jan 1982	JM (WBC)	Roberto Duran	Las Vegas	Won	PTS–15
3 Dec 1982	JM (WBC)	Thomas Hearns	New Orleans	Lost	PTS–15

Nigel BENN

Born: Ilford, Essex, England, 22 Jan 1964
World title fights: 3 (all middleweight) won 2, lost 1

DATE	WEIGHT	OPPONENT	VENUE	RESULT	
29 Apr 1990	M (WBO)	Doug De Witt	Atlantic City	Won	RSF–8
18 Aug 1990	M (WBO)	Iran Barkley	Las Vegas	Won	RSF–1
18 Nov 1990	M (WBO)	Chris Eubank	Birmingham	Lost	RSF–9

Bernard BENTON

Born: Toledo, Ohio, USA, 6 Jan 1957
World title fights: 2 (both cruiserweight) won 1, lost 1

DATE	WEIGHT	OPPONENT	VENUE	RESULT	
22 Sep 1985	C (WBC)	Alfonzo Ratliff	Las Vegas	Won	PTS–12
22 Mar 1986	C (WBC)	Carlos DeLeon	Las Vegas	Lost	PTS–12

DATE	WEIGHT	OPPONENT	VENUE	RESULT

Nino BENVENUTI

Born: Trieste, Italy, 26 Apr 1938
World title fights: 12 (3 junior-middle, 9 middleweight) won 8, lost 4

DATE	WEIGHT	OPPONENT	VENUE	RESULT
18 Jun 1965	JM	Sandro Mazzinghi	Milan	Won KO–6
17 Dec 1965	JM	Sandro Mazzinghi	Rome	Won PTS–15
25 Jun 1966	JM	Ki-Soo Kim	Seoul	Lost PTS–15
17 Apr 1967	M	Emile Griffith	New York	Won PTS–15
29 Sep 1967	M	Emile Griffith	New York	Lost PTS–15
4 Mar 1968	M	Emile Griffith	New York	Won PTS–15
14 Dec 1968	M	Don Fullmer	San Remo, Italy	Won PTS–15
4 Oct 1969	M	Fraser Scott	Naples	Won DIS–7
22 Nov 1969	M	Luis Rodriguez	Rome	Won KO–11
23 May 1970	M	Tom Bethea	Umag, Yugoslavia	Won KO–8
7 Nov 1970	M	Carlos Monzon	Rome	Lost KO–12
8 May 1971	M	Carlos Monzon	Monte Carlo	Lost RSF–3

Trevor BERBICK

Born: Port Anthony, Jamaica, 1 Aug 1952
World title fights: 3 (all heavyweight) won 1, lost 2

DATE	WEIGHT	OPPONENT	VENUE	RESULT
11 Apr 1981	H (WBC)	Larry Holmes	Las Vegas	Lost PTS–15
22 Mar 1986	H (WBC)	Pinklon Thomas	Las Vegas	Won PTS–12
22 Nov 1986	H (WBC)	Mike Tyson	Las Vegas	Lost RSF–2

Jack 'Kid' BERG

Born: London, England, 28 Jun 1909
World title fights: 6 (4 junior-welter, 1 lightweight/junior-welter, 1 lightweight)
won 4, lost 2

DATE	WEIGHT	OPPONENT	VENUE	RESULT	
18 Feb 1930	JW (NY)	Mushy Callahan	London	Won	RTD–10
12 Jun 1930	JW (NY)	Herman Perlick	New York	Won	RSF–10
3 Sep 1930	JW (NY)	Buster Brown	Newark, New Jersey	Won	PTS–10
23 Jan 1931	JW	Goldie Hess	Chicago	Won	PTS–10
23 Apr 1931	L/JW	Tony Canzoneri	Chicago	Lost	KO–3
10 Sep 1931	L	Tony Canzoneri	New York	Lost	PTS–15

Paul BERLENBACH

Born: New York City, USA, 18 Feb 1901
Died: Port Jefferson, New York, 30 Sep 1985
World title fights: 5 (all light-heavy) won 4, lost 1

DATE	WEIGHT	OPPONENT	VENUE	RESULT	
31 May 1925	LH	Mike McTigue	New York	Won	PTS–15
11 Sep 1925	LH	Jimmy Slattery	New York	Won	RSF–11
11 Dec 1925	LH	Jack Delaney	New York	Won	PTS–15
10 Jun 1926	LH	Young Stribling	New York	Won	PTS–15
16 Jul 1926	LH	Jack Delaney	New York	Lost	PTS–15

Bobby BERNA

Born: Philippines, 19 May 1961
World title fights: 4 (all junior-feather) won 1, lost 3

DATE	WEIGHT	OPPONENT	VENUE	RESULT	
15 Jun 1983	JFe (WBC)	Jaime Garza	Los Angeles	Lost	RSF–2
4 Dec 1983	JFe (IBF)	Seung-Il Suh	Seoul	Won	KO–9
15 Apr 1984	JFe (IBF)	Seung-Il Suh	Seoul	Lost	KO–10
28 Jun 1985	JFe (IBF)	Chi-Won Kim	Pusan, S Korea	Lost	KO–4

Gabriel BERNAL

Born: Guerrero, Mexico, 24 Mar 1956
World title fights: 5 (all flyweight) won 2, lost 2, drew 1

DATE	WEIGHT	OPPONENT	VENUE	RESULT
9 Apr 1984	Fl (WBC)	Koji Kobayashi	Tokyo	Won RSF–2
1 Jun 1984	Fl (WBC)	Antoine Montero	Nimes, France	Won RSF–11
8 Oct 1984	Fl (WBC)	Sot Chitalada	Bangkok	Lost PTS–12
22 Jun 1985	Fl (WBC)	Sot Chitalada	Bangkok	Drew 12
10 Dec 1986	Fl (WBC)	Sot Chitalada	Bangkok	Lost PTS–12

Jack BERNSTEIN

Born: New York City, USA, 5 Nov 1899
Died: Yonkers, New York, 26 Dec 1945
World title fights: 2 (both junior-light) won 1, lost 1

DATE	WEIGHT	OPPONENT	VENUE	RESULT
30 May 1923	JL	Johnny Dundee	New York	Won PTS–15
17 Dec 1923	JL	Johnny Dundee	New York	Lost PTS–15

Melio BETTINA

Born: Bridgeport, Connecticut, USA, 18 Nov 1916
World title fights: 4 (all light-heavy) won 1, lost 3

DATE	WEIGHT	OPPONENT	VENUE	RESULT
3 Feb 1939	LH (NY)	Tiger Jack Fox	New York	Won RSF–9
13 Jul 1939	LH	Billy Conn	New York	Lost PTS–15
25 Sep 1939	LH	Billy Conn	Pittsburgh	Lost PTS–15
13 Jan 1941	LH (NBA)	Anton Christoforidis	Cleveland	Lost PTS–15

Maurice BLOCKER

Born: Washington, USA, 15 May 1963
World title fights: 2 (both welterweight) won 1, lost 1

18 Apr 1987	W (WBC/IBF)	Lloyd Honeyghan	London	Lost	PTS–12
19 Aug 1990	W (WBC)	Marlon Starling	Reno, Nevada	Won	PTS–12

Rolando BOHOL

Born: Philippines, 25 Dec 1966
World title fights: 3 (all flyweight) won 2, lost 1

16 Jan 1988	Fl (IBF)	Chang-Ho Choi	Manila	Won	PTS–15
6 May 1988	Fl (IBF)	Cho-Woon Park	Manila	Won	PTS–15
5 Oct 1988	Fl (IBF)	Duke McKenzie	London	Lost	KO–11

Venice BORKORSOR

Born: Thailand, 1950
World title fights: 4 (2 flyweight, 2 bantamweight) won 2, lost 2

29 Sep 1972	Fl (WBC)	Betulio Gonzalez	Bangkok	Won	RTD–10
9 Feb 1973	Fl (WBC)	Erbito Salavarria	Bangkok	Won	PTS–15
13 Oct 1973	B (WBC)	Rafael Herrera	Los Angeles	Lost	PTS–15
30 Jan 1976	B (WBC)	Rodolfo Martinez	Bangkok	Lost	PTS–15

Carmelo BOSSI

Born: Milan, Italy, 15 Oct 1939
World title fights: 3 (all junior-middle) won 1, lost 1, drew 1

9 Jul 1970	JM	Fred Little	Monza, Italy	Won	PTS–15
29 Apr 1971	JM	Jose Hernandez	Madrid	Drew	15
31 Oct 1971	JM	Koichi Wajima	Tokyo	Lost	PTS–15

Kamel BOU-ALI

Born: Tunisia, 6 Dec 1958
World title fights: 3 (all junior-light) won 1, lost 1, NC 1

DATE	WEIGHT	OPPONENT	VENUE	RESULT
26 Jan 1985	JL (WBA)	Rocky Lockridge	Riva Del Garda, Italy	Lost RSF–6
9 Dec 1989	JL (WBO)	Antonio Rivera	Teramo, Italy	Won KO–8
20 Oct 1990	JL (WBO)	Pedro Florindo Villegas	Cesena, Italy	NC–2

Joe BOWKER

Born: Salford, England, 20 Jul 1883
Died: London, 22 Oct 1955
World title fights: 1 (bantamweight) won 1, lost 0

DATE	WEIGHT	OPPONENT	VENUE	RESULT
17 Oct 1904	B	Frankie Neil	London	Won PTS–20

Cornelius BOZA-EDWARDS

Born: Kampala, Uganda, 27 May 1956
World title fights: 6 (4 junior-light, 2 lightweight) won 2, lost 4

DATE	WEIGHT	OPPONENT	VENUE	RESULT
8 Mar 1981	JL (WBC)	Rafael Limon	Stockton, California	Won PTS–15
30 May 1981	JL (WBC)	Bobby Chacon	Las Vegas	Won RTD–13
29 Aug 1981	JL (WBC)	Rolando Navarrete	Via Reggio, Italy	Lost KO–5
15 May 1983	JL (WBC)	Bobby Chacon	Las Vegas	Lost PTS–12
26 Sep 1986	L (WBC)	Hector Camacho	Miami	Lost PTS–12
10 Oct 1987	L (WBC)	Jose-Luis Ramirez	Paris	Lost KO–5

James J BRADDOCK

Born: New York City, USA, 7 Jun 1906
Died: North Bergen, New Jersey, 29 Nov 1974
World title fights: 3 (1 light-heavy, 2 heavyweight) won 1, lost 2

DATE	WEIGHT	OPPONENT	VENUE	RESULT	
18 Jul 1929	LH	Tommy Loughran	New York	Lost	PTS–15
13 Jun 1935	H	Max Baer	Long Island, New York	Won	PTS–15
22 Jun 1937	H	Joe Louis	Chicago	Lost	KO–8

Livingstone BRAMBLE

Born: St Kitts, Windward Islands, 3 Mar 1960
World title fights: 4 (all lightweight) won 3, lost 1

DATE	WEIGHT	OPPONENT	VENUE	RESULT	
1 Jun 1984	L (WBA)	Ray Mancini	Buffalo	Won	RSF–14
16 Feb 1985	L (WBA)	Ray Mancini	Reno, Nevada	Won	PTS–15
16 Feb 1986	L (WBA)	Tyrone Crawley	Reno, Nevada	Won	RSF–13
26 Sep 1986	L (WBA)	Edwin Rosario	Miami	Lost	KO–2

Johnny BRATTON

Born: Little Rock, Arkansas, USA, 9 Sep 1927
World title fights: 3 (all welterweight) won 1, lost 2

DATE	WEIGHT	OPPONENT	VENUE	RESULT	
14 Mar 1951	W (NBA)	Charley Fusari	Chicago	Won	PTS–15
18 May 1951	W	Kid Gavilan	New York	Lost	PTS–15
13 Nov 1953	W	Kid Gavilan	Chicago	Lost	PTS–15

Dwight BRAXTON
see Dwight Muhammad QAWI

Mark BRELAND

Born: Brooklyn, New York, USA, 11 May 1963
World title fights: 9 (all welterweight) won 6, lost 2, drew 1

DATE	WEIGHT	OPPONENT	VENUE	RESULT	
6 Feb 1987	W (WBA)	Harold Volbrecht	Atlantic City	Won	KO–7
22 Aug 1987	W (WBA)	Marlon Starling	Columbia, South Carolina	Lost	RSF–11
16 Apr 1988	W (WBA)	Marlon Starling	Las Vegas	Drew	12
4 Feb 1989	W (WBA)	Seung-Soon Lee	Las Vegas	Won	RSF–1
22 Apr 1989	W (WBA)	Rafael Pineda	Atlantic City	Won	RTD–5
13 Oct 1989	W (WBA)	Mauro Martelli	Geneva	Won	RSF–2
10 Dec 1989	W (WBA)	Fujio Ozaki	Tokyo	Won	RSF–4
3 Mar 1990	W (WBA)	Lloyd Honeyghan	London	Won	RSF–3
9 Jul 1990	W (WBA)	Aaron Davis	Reno, Nevada	Lost	KO–9

Jack BRITTON

Born: Clinton, New York, USA, 14 Oct 1885
Died: Miami, 27 Mar 1962
World title fights: 12 (all welterweight) won 6, lost 4, drew 2

DATE	WEIGHT	OPPONENT	VENUE	RESULT	
31 Aug 1915	W	Ted 'Kid' Lewis	Boston	Lost	PTS–12
27 Sep 1915	W	Ted 'Kid' Lewis	Boston	Lost	PTS–12
24 Apr 1916	W	Ted 'Kid' Lewis	New Orleans	Won	PTS–20
25 Jun 1917	W	Ted 'Kid' Lewis	Dayton, Ohio	Lost	PTS–20
17 Mar 1919	W	Ted 'Kid' Lewis	Canton, Ohio	Won	KO–9
5 May 1919	W	Johnny Griffiths	Buffalo	Won	PTS–15
31 May 1920	W	Johnny Griffiths	Akron, Ohio	Won	PTS–15
23 Aug 1920	W	Lou Bogash	Bridgeport, Connecticut	Drew	12
7 Feb 1921	W	Ted 'Kid' Lewis	New York	Won	PTS–15
17 Feb 1922	W	Dave Shade	New York	Drew	15
26 Jun 1922	W	Benny Leonard	New York	Won	DIS–13
1 Nov 1922	W	Mickey Walker	New York	Lost	PTS–15

Lou BROUILLARD

Born: St Eugene, Quebec, Canada, 23 May 1911
Died: Taunton, Massachusetts, 14 Sep 1984
World title fights: 5 (2 welterweight, 3 middleweight) won 2, lost 3

DATE	WEIGHT	OPPONENT	VENUE	RESULT	
23 Oct 1931	W	Young Jack Thompson	Boston	Won	PTS–15
28 Jan 1932	W	Jackie Fields	Chicago	Lost	PTS–10
9 Aug 1933	M (NY)	Ben Jeby	New York	Won	KO–7
30 Oct 1933	M (NY)	Vince Dundee	Boston	Lost	PTS–15
20 Jan 1936	M (NBA)	Marcel Thil	Paris	Lost	DIS–4

Charlie 'Choo Choo' BROWN

Born: Philadelphia, USA, 16 Apr 1958
World title fights: 2 (both lightweight) won 1, lost 1

DATE	WEIGHT	OPPONENT	VENUE	RESULT	
30 Jan 1984	L (IBF)	Melvin Paul	Atlantic City	Won	PTS–15
15 Apr 1984	L (IBF)	Harry Arroyo	Atlantic City	Lost	RSF–14

Jackie BROWN

Born: Manchester, England, 29 Nov 1909
Died: Manchester, 15 Mar 1971
World title fights: 6 (all flyweight) won 4, lost 1, drew 1

DATE	WEIGHT	OPPONENT	VENUE	RESULT	
31 Oct 1932	Fl (NBA)	Young Victor Perez	Manchester	Won	RSF–13
12 Jun 1933	Fl (NBA)	Valentin Angelmann	London	Won	PTS–15
11 Sep 1933	Fl (NBA)	Valentin Angelmann	Manchester	Won	PTS–15
11 Dec 1933	Fl (NBA)	Ginger Foran	Manchester	Won	PTS–15
18 Jun 1934	Fl (NBA)	Valentin Angelmann	Manchester	Drew	15
9 Sep 1935	Fl (NBA)	Benny Lynch	Manchester	Lost	RTD–2

Joe BROWN

Born: New Orleans, USA, 18 May 1926
World title fights: 13 (all lightweight) won 12, lost 1

DATE	WEIGHT	OPPONENT	VENUE	RESULT	
24 Aug 1956	L	Wallace Bud Smith	New Orleans	Won	PTS–15
13 Feb 1957	L	Wallace Bud Smith	Miami	Won	KO–11
19 Jun 1957	L	Orlando Zulueta	Denver	Won	RSF–15
4 Dec 1957	L	Joey Lopez	Chicago	Won	RSF–11
7 May 1958	L	Ralph Dupas	Houston	Won	RSF–8
23 Jul 1958	L	Kenny Lane	Houston	Won	PTS–15
11 Feb 1959	L	Johnny Busso	Houston	Won	PTS–15
3 Jun 1959	L	Paolo Rosi	Washington DC	Won	RTD–8
2 Dec 1959	L	Dave Charnley	Houston	Won	RTD–5
28 Oct 1960	L	Cisco Andrade	Los Angeles	Won	PTS–15
18 Apr 1961	L	Dave Charnley	London	Won	PTS–15
28 Oct 1961	L	Bert Somodio	Manila	Won	PTS–15
21 Apr 1962	L	Carlos Ortiz	Las Vegas	Lost	PTS–15

Panama Al BROWN

Born: Colon, Panama, 5 Jul 1902
Died: New York City, 11 Apr 1951
World title fights: 12 (all bantamweight) won 11, lost 1

DATE	WEIGHT	OPPONENT	VENUE	RESULT	
18 Jun 1929	B	Vidal Gregorio	New York	Won	PTS–15
4 Oct 1930	B	Eugene Huat	Paris	Won	PTS–15
11 Feb 1931	B	Nick Bensa	Paris	Won	PTS–10
25 Aug 1931	B	Pete Sanstol	Montreal	Won	PTS–15
27 Oct 1931	B	Eugene Huat	Montreal	Won	PTS–15
10 Jul 1932	B	Kid Francis	Marseilles	Won	PTS–15
19 Sep 1932	B	Emile Pladner	Toronto	Won	KO–1

DATE	WEIGHT	OPPONENT	VENUE	RESULT
18 Mar 1933	B	Dom Bernasconi	Milan	Won PTS–12
3 Jul 1933	B	Johnny King	Manchester	Won PTS–15
19 Feb 1934	B	Young Victor Perez	Paris	Won PTS–15
1 Nov 1934	B	Young Victor Perez	Tunis	Won KO–10
1 Jun 1935	B (NY)	Baltasar Sangchili	Valencia	Lost PTS–15

Simon BROWN

Born: Jamaica, 15 Aug 1963
World title fights: 8 (all welterweight) won 8, lost 0

DATE	WEIGHT	OPPONENT	VENUE	RESULT
23 Apr 1988	W (IBF)	Tyrone Trice	Berck-sur-Mer, France	Won RSF–14
16 Jul 1988	W (IBF)	Jorge Vaca	Kingston, Jamaica	Won RSF–3
14 Oct 1988	W (IBF)	Mauro Martelli	Lausanne, Switzerland	Won PTS–12
18 Feb 1989	W (IBF)	Jorge Maysonet	Atlantic City	Won RTD–5
25 Apr 1989	W (IBF)	Al Long	Washington DC	Won RSF–7
20 Sep 1989	W (IBF)	Bobby Joe Young	New York	Won KO–2
9 Nov 1989	W (IBF)	Luis Santana	Springfield, Massachusetts	Won PTS–12
1 Apr 1990	W (IBF)	Tyrone Trice	Washington DC	Won TKO–10

Ken BUCHANAN

Born: Edinburgh, Scotland, 28 Jun 1945
World title fights: 5 (all lightweight) won 3, lost 2

DATE	WEIGHT	OPPONENT	VENUE	RESULT
26 Sep 1970	L	Ismael Laguna	San Juan	Won PTS–15
12 Feb 1971	L	Ruben Navarro	Los Angeles	Won PTS–15
13 Sep 1971	L	Ismael Laguna	New York	Won PTS–15
26 Jun 1972	L (WBA)	Roberto Duran	New York	Lost RSF–13
27 Feb 1975	L (WBC)	Guts Ishimatsu	Tokyo	Lost PTS–15

DATE	WEIGHT	OPPONENT	VENUE	RESULT

Johnny BUFF

Born: Perth Amboy, New Jersey, USA, 12 Jun 1888
Died: East Grange, New Jersey, 14 Jan 1955
World title fights: 3 (all bantamweight) won 2, lost 1

DATE	WEIGHT	OPPONENT	VENUE	RESULT	
23 Sep 1921	B	Pete Herman	New York	Won	PTS–15
10 Nov 1921	B	Little Jack Sharkey	New York	Won	PTS–15
10 Jul 1922	B	Joe Lynch	New York	Lost	RTD–14

Johnny BUMPHUS

Born: Tacoma, Washington, USA, 17 Aug 1960
World title fights: 3 (2 junior-welter, 1 welterweight) won 1, lost 2

DATE	WEIGHT	OPPONENT	VENUE	RESULT	
21 Jan 1984	JW (WBA)	Lorenzo Garcia	Atlantic City	Won	PTS–15
1 Jun 1984	JW (WBA)	Gene Hatcher	Buffalo	Lost	RSF–11
22 Feb 1987	W (WBC/IBF)	Lloyd Honeyghan	London	Lost	RSF–2

Tommy BURNS

Born: Chesley, Ontario, Canada, 17 Jun 1881
Died: Vancouver, 10 May 1955
World title fights: 13 (1 heavyweight/light-heavy, 12 heavyweight) won 11,
lost 1, drew 1

DATE	WEIGHT	OPPONENT	VENUE	RESULT	
23 Feb 1906	H	Marvin Hart	Los Angeles	Won	PTS–20
2 Oct 1906	H	Jim Flynn	Los Angeles	Won	KO–12
28 Nov 1906	H/LH	Philadelphia Jack O'Brien	Los Angeles	Drew	20
8 May 1907	H	Philadelphia Jack O'Brien	Los Angeles	Won	PTS–20
4 Jul 1907	H	Bill Squires	Colma, California	Won	KO–1
2 Dec 1907	H	Gunner Moir	London	Won	KO–10
10 Feb 1908	H	Jack Palmer	London	Won	KO–4
17 Mar 1908	H	Jem Roche	Dublin	Won	KO–1

DATE	WEIGHT	OPPONENT	VENUE	RESULT

DATE	WEIGHT	OPPONENT	VENUE	RESULT
18 Apr 1908	H	Jewey Smith	Paris	Won KO–5
13 Jun 1908	H	Bill Squires	Paris	Won KO–8
24 Aug 1908	H	Bill Squires	Sydney	Won KO–13
2 Sep 1908	H	Bill Lang	Sydney	Won KO–6
26 Dec 1908	H	Jack Johnson	Sydney	Lost RSF–14

Salvatore BURRUNI

Born: Sardinia, Italy, 11 Apr 1933
World title fights: 3 (all flyweight) won 2, lost 1

DATE	WEIGHT	OPPONENT	VENUE	RESULT
23 Apr 1965	Fl	Pone Kingpetch	Rome	Won PTS–15
2 Dec 1965	Fl	Rocky Gattellari	Sydney	Won KO–13
14 Jun 1966	Fl (WBC)	Walter McGowan	London	Lost PTS–15

Johnny CALDWELL

Born: Belfast, Northern Ireland, 7 May 1938
World title fights: 3 (all bantamweight) won 2, lost 1

DATE	WEIGHT	OPPONENT	VENUE	RESULT
27 May 1961	B (EBU)	Alphonse Halimi	London	Won PTS–15
31 Oct 1961	B (EBU)	Alphonse Halimi	London	Won PTS–15
18 Jan 1962	B	Eder Jofre	Sao Paulo, Brazil	Lost RTD–10

Mushy CALLAHAN

Born: New York City, USA, 3 Nov 1905
Died: Los Angeles, 16 Jun 1986
World title fights: 2 (both junior-welter) won 1, lost 1

DATE	WEIGHT	OPPONENT	VENUE	RESULT
21 Sep 1926	JW	Pinkey Mitchell	Vernon, California	Won PTS–10
18 Feb 1930	JW (NY)	Jack Berg	London	Lost RTD–10

Victor CALLEJAS

Born: Guaynabo, Puerto Rico, 12 Nov 1960
World title fights: 4 (3 junior-feather, 1 featherweight) won 3, lost 1

DATE	WEIGHT	OPPONENT	VENUE	RESULT	
26 May 1984	JFe (WBA)	Loris Stecca	Guaynabo, Puerto Rico	Won	KO–8
2 Feb 1985	JFe (WBA)	Seung-Hoon Lee	San Juan	Won	PTS–15
8 Nov 1985	JFe (WBA)	Loris Stecca	Rimini, Italy	Won	TKO–7
7 Mar 1988	Fe (WBC)	Jeff Fenech	Sydney	Lost	RSF–10

Jackie CALLURA

Born: Hamilton, Ontario, Canada, 24 Sep 1917
World title fights: 4 (all featherweight) won 2, lost 2

DATE	WEIGHT	OPPONENT	VENUE	RESULT	
18 Jan 1943	Fe (NBA)	Jackie Wilson	Providence, Rhode Island	Won	PTS–15
18 Mar 1943	Fe (NBA)	Jackie Wilson	Boston	Won	PTS–15
16 Aug 1943	Fe (NBA)	Phil Terranova	New Orleans	Lost	KO–8
27 Dec 1943	Fe (NBA)	Phil Terranova	New Orleans	Lost	KO–6

Hector CAMACHO

Born: Bayamon, Puerto Rico, 24 May 1962
World title fights: 8 (2 junior-light, 3 lightweight, 3 junior-welter) won 8, lost 0

DATE	WEIGHT	OPPONENT	VENUE	RESULT	
8 Aug 1983	JL (WBC)	Rafael Limon	San Juan	Won	RSF–5
18 Nov 1983	JL (WBC)	Rafael Solis	San Juan	Won	KO–5
10 Aug 1985	L (WBC)	Jose Luis Ramirez	Las Vegas	Won	PTS–12
13 Jun 1986	L (WBC)	Edwin Rosario	New York	Won	PTS–12
26 Sep 1986	L (WBC)	Cornelius Boza-Edwards	Miami	Won	PTS–12
6 Mar 1989	JW (WBO)	Ray Mancini	Reno, Nevada	Won	PTS–12
3 Feb 1990	JW (WBO)	Vinnie Pazienza	Atlantic City	Won	PTS–12
11 Aug 1990	JW (WBO)	Tony Baltazar	Lake Tahoe, Nevada	Won	PTS–12

Marvin CAMEL

Born: Missoula, Montana, USA, 24 Dec 1951
World title fights: 6 (all cruiserweight) won 2, lost 3, drew 1

DATE	WEIGHT	OPPONENT	VENUE	RESULT
8 Dec 1979	C (WBC)	Mate Parlov	Split, Yugoslavia	Drew 15
31 Mar 1980	C (WBC)	Mate Parlov	Las Vegas	Won PTS–15
25 Nov 1980	C (WBC)	Carlos DeLeon	New Orleans	Lost PTS–15
24 Feb 1982	C (WBC)	Carlos DeLeon	Atlantic City	Lost RSF–7
13 Dec 1983	C (IBF)	Roddy McDonald	Halifax, Canada	Won KO–5
6 Oct 1984	C (IBF)	Lee Roy Murphy	Billings, Montana	Lost RSF–14

Gaby CANIZALES

Born: Laredo, Texas, USA, 1 May 1960
World title fights: 4 (all bantamweight) won 1, lost 3

DATE	WEIGHT	OPPONENT	VENUE	RESULT
13 Mar 1983	B (WBA)	Jeff Chandler	Atlantic City	Lost PTS–15
10 Mar 1986	B (WBA)	Richard Sandoval	Las Vegas	Won KO–7
4 Jun 1986	B (WBA)	Bernardo Pinango	East Rutherford, New Jersey	Lost PTS–15
22 Jan 1990	B (WBC)	Raul Perez	Los Angeles	Lost PTS–12

Orlando CANIZALES

Born: Laredo, Texas, USA, 25 Nov 1965
World title fights: 6 (all bantamweight) won 6, lost 0

DATE	WEIGHT	OPPONENT	VENUE	RESULT
9 Jul 1988	B (IBF)	Kelvin Seabrooks	Atlantic City	Won RSF–15
29 Nov 1988	B (IBF)	Jimmy Navarro	San Antonio, Texas	Won KO–1
24 Jun 1989	B (IBF)	Kelvin Seabrooks	Atlantic City	Won RSF–11
27 Jan 1990	B (IBF)	Bill Hardy	Sunderland	Won PTS–12
10 Jun 1990	B (IBF)	Paul Gonzalez	El Paso, Texas	Won RSF–2
14 Aug 1990	B (IBF)	Eddie Rangel	New York	Won RSF–5

DATE	WEIGHT	OPPONENT	VENUE	RESULT

Miguel CANTO

Born: Yucatan, Mexico, 30 Jan 1949
World title fights: 18 (all flyweight) won 15, lost 2, drew 1

DATE	WEIGHT	OPPONENT	VENUE	RESULT
4 Aug 1973	Fl (WBC)	Betulio Gonzalez	Maracaibo, Venezuela	Lost PTS–15
8 Jan 1975	Fl (WBC)	Shoji Oguma	Sendai, Japan	Won PTS–15
24 May 1975	Fl (WBC)	Betulio Gonzalez	Monterrey, Mexico	Won PTS–15
23 Aug 1975	Fl (WBC)	Jiro Takada	Merida, Mexico	Won RSF–11
13 Dec 1975	Fl (WBC)	Ignacio Espinal	Merida	Won PTS–15
15 May 1976	Fl (WBC)	Susumu Hanagata	Merida	Won PTS–15
3 Oct 1976	Fl (WBC)	Betulio Gonzalez	Caracas	Won PTS–15
19 Nov 1976	Fl (WBC)	Orlando Javierto	Los Angeles	Won PTS–15
24 Apr 1977	Fl (WBC)	Reyes Arnal	Caracas	Won PTS–15
15 Jun 1977	Fl (WBC)	Kimio Furesawa	Tokyo	Won PTS–15
17 Sep 1977	Fl (WBC)	Martin Vargas	Merida	Won PTS–15
30 Nov 1977	Fl (WBC)	Martin Vargas	Santiago	Won PTS–15
4 Jan 1978	Fl (WBC)	Shoji Oguma	Koriyama, Japan	Won PTS–15
18 Apr 1978	Fl (WBC)	Shoji Oguma	Tokyo	Won PTS–15
20 Nov 1978	Fl (WBC)	Tacomron Viboonchai	Houston	Won PTS–15
10 Feb 1979	Fl (WBC)	Antonio Avelar	Merida	Won PTS–15
18 Mar 1979	Fl (WBC)	Chan-Hee Park	Pusan, S Korea	Lost PTS–15
9 Sep 1979	Fl (WBC)	Chan-Hee Park	Seoul	Drew 15

Tony CANZONERI

Born: Slidell, Louisiana, USA, 6 Nov 1908
Died: New York City, 9 Dec 1959
World title fights: 22 (2 bantamweight, 3 featherweight, 9 lightweight,
3 junior-welter/lightweight, 5 junior-welter) won 12, lost 9, drew 1

DATE	WEIGHT	OPPONENT	VENUE	RESULT
26 Mar 1927	B (NBA)	Bud Taylor	Chicago	Drew 10

DATE	WEIGHT	OPPONENT	VENUE	RESULT
24 Jun 1927	B (NBA)	Bud Taylor	Chicago	Lost PTS–10
24 Oct 1927	Fe (NY)	Johnny Dundee	New York	Won PTS–15
10 Feb 1928	Fe	Benny Bass	New York	Won PTS–15
28 Sep 1928	Fe	Andre Routis	New York	Lost PTS–15
2 Aug 1929	L	Sammy Mandell	Chicago	Lost PTS–10
14 Nov 1930	L	Al Singer	New York	Won KO–1
23 Apr 1931	JW/L	Jack Berg	Chicago	Won KO–3
13 Jul 1931	JW	Cecil Payne	Los Angeles	Won PTS–10
10 Sep 1931	L	Jack Berg	New York	Won PTS–15
29 Oct 1931	JW	Phillie Griffin	Newark, New Jersey	Won PTS–10
20 Nov 1931	JW/L	Kid Chocolate	New York	Won PTS–15
18 Jan 1932	JW	Johnny Jadick	Philadelphia	Lost PTS–10
18 Jul 1932	JW	Johnny Jadick	Philadelphia	Lost PTS–10
4 Nov 1932	L	Billy Petrole	New York	Won PTS–15
21 May 1933	JW	Battling Shaw	New Orleans	Won PTS–10
23 Jun 1933	JW/L	Barney Ross	Chicago	Lost PTS–10
12 Sep 1933	L	Barney Ross	New York	Lost PTS–15
10 May 1935	L	Lou Ambers	New York	Won PTS–15
4 Oct 1935	L	Al Roth	New York	Won PTS–15
3 Sep 1936	L	Lou Ambers	New York	Lost PTS–15
7 May 1937	L	Lou Ambers	New York	Lost PTS–15

Michael CARBAJAL

Born: Phoenix, Arizona, USA, 17 Sep 1967
World title fights: 2 (both junior-fly) won 2, lost 0

DATE	WEIGHT	OPPONENT	VENUE	RESULT
29 Jul 1990	JFl (IBF)	Muangchai Kittikasem	Phoenix	Won RSF–7
8 Dec 1990	JFl (IBF)	Leon Salazar	Scottsdale, Arizona	Won KO–4

DATE	WEIGHT	OPPONENT	VENUE	RESULT

Prudencio CARDONA

Born: Bolivar, Colombia, 22 Dec 1951
World title fights: 3 (all flyweight) won 1, lost 2

DATE	WEIGHT	OPPONENT	VENUE	RESULT	
20 Mar 1982	Fl (WBC)	Antonio Avelar	Tampico, Mexico	Won	KO–1
25 Jul 1982	Fl (WBC)	Freddie Castillo	Merida, Mexico	Lost	PTS–15
15 Sep 1984	Fl (WBA)	Santos Laciar	Cordoba, Argentina	Lost	KO–10

Ricardo CARDONA

Born: Bolivar, Colombia, 9 Nov 1952
World title fights: 8 (all junior-feather) won 6, lost 2

DATE	WEIGHT	OPPONENT	VENUE	RESULT	
6 May 1978	JFe (WBA)	Soo-Hwan Hong	Seoul	Won	RSF–12
2 Sep 1978	JFe (WBA)	Ruben Valdez	Cartagena, Colombia	Won	PTS–15
12 Nov 1978	JFe (WBA)	Soo-Hyun Chung	Seoul	Won	PTS–15
23 Jun 1979	JFe (WBA)	Soo-Hyun Chung	Seoul	Won	PTS–15
6 Sep 1979	JFe (WBA)	Yukio Segawa	Hachinohe, Japan	Won	PTS–15
15 Dec 1979	JFe (WBA)	Sergio Palma	Barranquilla, Colombia	Won	PTS–15
4 May 1980	JFe (WBA)	Leo Randolph	Seattle	Lost	RSF–15
15 Aug 1981	JFe (WBA)	Sergio Palma	Buenos Aires	Lost	RSF–12

Erubey 'Chango' CARMONA

Born: Mexico City, Mexico, 29 Sep 1944
World title fights: 2 (both lightweight) won 1, lost 1

DATE	WEIGHT	OPPONENT	VENUE	RESULT	
15 Sep 1972	L (WBC)	Mando Ramos	Los Angeles	Won	RSF–8
10 Nov 1972	L (WBC)	Rodolfo Gonzalez	Los Angeles	Lost	RTD–12

Primo CARNERA

Born: Sequals, Italy, 26 Oct 1906
Died: Sequals, 29 Jun 1967
World title fights: 4 (all heavyweight) won 3, lost 1

DATE	WEIGHT	OPPONENT	VENUE	RESULT
29 Jun 1933	H	Jack Sharkey	Long Island, New York	Won KO–6
22 Oct 1933	H	Paolino Uzcudun	Rome	Won PTS–15
1 Mar 1934	H	Tommy Loughran	Miami	Won PTS–15
14 Jun 1934	H	Max Baer	Long Island	Lost KO–11

Georges CARPENTIER

Born: Lens, France, 12 Jan 1894
Died: Paris, 28 Oct 1975
World title fights: 5 (1 middleweight, 3 light-heavy, 1 heavyweight) won 2, lost 3

DATE	WEIGHT	OPPONENT	VENUE	RESULT
23 Oct 1912	M	Billy Papke	Paris	Lost RTD–17
12 Oct 1920	LH	Battling Levinsky	Jersey City, New Jersey	Won KO–4
2 Jul 1921	H	Jack Dempsey	Jersey City	Lost KO–4
11 May 1922	LH	Ted 'Kid' Lewis	London	Won KO–1
24 Sep 1922	LH	Battling Siki	Paris	Lost KO–6

Pedro CARRASCO

Born: Huelva, Spain, 11 Jul 1943
World title fights: 3 (all lightweight) won 1, lost 2

DATE	WEIGHT	OPPONENT	VENUE	RESULT
5 Nov 1971	L (WBC)	Mando Ramos	Madrid	Won DIS–11
18 Feb 1972	L (WBC)	Mando Ramos	Los Angeles	Lost PTS–15
28 Jun 1972	L (WBC)	Mando Ramos	Madrid	Lost PTS–15

Jimmy CARRUTHERS

Born: Paddington, New South Wales, Australia, 5 Jul 1929
World title fights: 4 (all bantamweight) won 4, lost 0

DATE	WEIGHT	OPPONENT	VENUE	RESULT
15 Nov 1952	B	Vic Toweel	Johannesburg	Won KO-1
21 Mar 1953	B	Vic Toweel	Johannesburg	Won KO-10
13 Nov 1953	B	Henry Pappy Gault	Sydney	Won PTS-15
2 May 1954	B	Chamrern Songkitrat	Bangkok	Won PTS-12

Jimmy CARTER

Born: Aiken, South Carolina, USA, 15 Dec 1923
World title fights: 12 (all lightweight) won 8, lost 4

DATE	WEIGHT	OPPONENT	VENUE	RESULT
25 May 1951	L	Ike Williams	New York	Won RSF-14
14 Nov 1951	L	Art Aragon	Los Angeles	Won PTS-15
1 Apr 1952	L	Lauro Salas	Los Angeles	Won PTS-15
14 May 1952	L	Lauro Salas	Los Angeles	Lost PTS-15
15 Oct 1952	L	Lauro Salas	Chicago	Won PTS-15
24 Apr 1953	L	Tommy Collins	Boston	Won RSF-4
12 Jun 1953	L	George Araujo	New York	Won RSF-15
11 Nov 1953	L	Armand Savoie	Montreal	Won KO-5
5 Mar 1954	L	Paddy DeMarco	New York	Lost PTS-15
17 Nov 1954	L	Paddy DeMarco	San Francisco	Won RSF-15
29 Jun 1955	L	Wallace 'Bud' Smith	Boston	Lost PTS-15
19 Oct 1955	L	Wallace 'Bud' Smith	Cincinnati	Lost PTS-15

Miguel Angel CASTELLINI

Born: Santa Rosa, La Pampa, Argentina, 26 Jan 1947
World title fights: 2 (both junior-middle) won 1, lost 1

DATE	WEIGHT	OPPONENT	VENUE	RESULT	
8 Oct 1976	JM (WBA)	Jose Duran	Madrid	Won	PTS–15
6 Mar 1977	JM (WBA)	Eddie Gazo	Managua	Lost	PTS–15

Freddie CASTILLO

Born: Yucatan, Mexico, 15 Jun 1955
World title fights: 5 (2 junior-fly, 3 flyweight) won 2, lost 3

DATE	WEIGHT	OPPONENT	VENUE	RESULT	
19 Feb 1978	JFl (WBC)	Luis Estaba	Caracas	Won	RSF–14
6 May 1978	JFl (WBC)	Netrnoi Vorasingh	Bangkok	Lost	PTS–15
25 Jul 1982	Fl (WBC)	Prudencio Cardona	Merida, Mexico	Won	PTS–15
7 Nov 1982	Fl (WBC)	Eleoncio Mercedes	Los Angeles	Lost	PTS–15
22 Feb 1986	Fl (WBC)	Sot Chitalada	Kuwait	Lost	PTS–12

Jesus 'Chucho' CASTILLO

Born: Nuevo Valle de Moreno, Mexico, 17 Jun 1944
World title fights: 4 (all bantamweight) won 1, lost 3

DATE	WEIGHT	OPPONENT	VENUE	RESULT	
6 Dec 1968	B	Lionel Rose	Los Angeles	Lost	PTS–15
18 Apr 1970	B	Ruben Olivares	Los Angeles	Lost	PTS–15
16 Oct 1970	B	Ruben Olivares	Los Angeles	Won	RSF–14
2 Apr 1971	B	Ruben Olivares	Los Angeles	Lost	PTS–15

Frank CEDENO

Born: Cebu, Philippines, 16 Mar 1958
World title fights: 3 (2 flyweight, 1 junior-bantam) won 1, lost 2

DATE	WEIGHT	OPPONENT	VENUE	RESULT	
27 Sep 1983	Fl (WBC)	Charlie Magri	London	Won	RSF–6

DATE	WEIGHT	OPPONENT	VENUE	RESULT	
18 Jan 1984	Fl (WBC)	Koji Kobayashi	Tokyo	Lost	RSF–2
19 Mar 1987	JB (WBC)	Gilberto Roman	Mexicali, Mexico	Lost	PTS–12

Marcel CERDAN

Born: Sidi Bel-Abbes, Algeria, 22 Jul 1916
Died: Azores, 27 Oct 1949
World title fights: 2 (both middleweight) won 1, lost 1

DATE	WEIGHT	OPPONENT	VENUE	RESULT	
21 Sep 1948	M	Tony Zale	Jersey City, New Jersey	Won	KO–12
16 Jun 1949	M	Jake La Motta	Detroit	Lost	RTD–10

Antonio CERVANTES

Born: San Basilio de Palenque, Bolivar, Colombia, 23 Dec 1945
World title fights: 21 (all junior-welter) won 18, lost 3

DATE	WEIGHT	OPPONENT	VENUE	RESULT	
11 Dec 1971	JW (WBA)	Nicolino Loche	Buenos Aires	Lost	PTS–15
29 Oct 1972	JW (WBA)	Alfonzo Frazer	Panama City	Won	KO–10
15 Feb 1973	JW (WBA)	Jose Marquez	San Juan	Won	PTS–15
17 Mar 1973	JW (WBA)	Nicolino Loche	Maracay, Venezuela	Won	RTD–9
19 May 1973	JW (WBA)	Alfonzo Frazer	Panama City	Won	RSF–5
8 Sep 1973	JW (WBA)	Carlos Gimenez	Bogota	Won	RSF–5
5 Dec 1973	JW (WBA)	Tetsuo Lion Furuyama	Panama City	Won	PTS–15
2 Mar 1974	JW (WBA)	Kil-Lee Chang	Cartagena, Colombia	Won	KO–6
27 Jul 1974	JW (WBA)	Victor Ortiz	Cartagena	Won	KO–2
26 Oct 1974	JW (WBA)	Yasukai Kadoto	Tokyo	Won	KO–8
17 May 1975	JW (WBA)	Esteban De Jesus	Panama City	Won	PTS–15
15 Nov 1975	JW (WBA)	Hector Thompson	Panama City	Won	RTD–7
6 Mar 1976	JW (WBA)	Wilfredo Benitez	San Juan	Lost	PTS–15
25 Jun 1977	JW (WBA)	Carlos Gimenez	Maracaibo, Venezuela	Won	RSF–5
5 Nov 1977	JW (WBA)	Adriano Marrero	Maracay	Won	PTS–15

DATE	WEIGHT	OPPONENT	VENUE	RESULT

DATE	WEIGHT	OPPONENT	VENUE	RESULT
28 Apr 1978	JW (WBA)	Tongta Kiatvayupak	Udon-Thani, Thailand	Won KO–6
26 Aug 1978	JW (WBA)	Norman Sekgapane	Mabatho, S Africa	Won KO–9
18 Jan 1979	JW (WBA)	Miguel Montilla	New York	Won PTS–15
25 Aug 1979	JW (WBA)	Kwang-Min Kim	Seoul	Won PTS–15
29 Mar 1980	JW (WBA)	Miguel Montilla	Cartagena	Won RSF–7
2 Aug 1980	JW (WBA)	Aaron Pryor	Cincinnati	Lost KO–4

Bobby CHACON

Born: Los Angeles, USA, 28 Nov 1951
World title fights: 8 (3 featherweight, 4 junior-light, 1 lightweight) won 4, lost 4

DATE	WEIGHT	OPPONENT	VENUE	RESULT
7 Sep 1974	Fe (WBC)	Alfredo Marcano	Los Angeles	Won RSF–9
1 Mar 1975	Fe (WBC)	Jesus Estrada	Los Angeles	Won KO–2
20 Jun 1975	Fe (WBC)	Ruben Olivares	Los Angeles	Lost RSF–2
16 Nov 1979	JL (WBC)	Alexis Arguello	Los Angeles	Lost RTD–7
30 May 1981	JL (WBC)	Cornelius Boza-Edwards	Las Vegas	Lost RTD–13
11 Dec 1982	JL (WBC)	Rafael Limon	Sacramento, California	Won PTS–15
15 May 1983	JL (WBC)	Cornelius Boza-Edwards	Las Vegas	Won PTS–12
14 Jan 1984	L (WBA)	Ray Mancini	Reno, Nevada	Lost RSF–3

Jeff CHANDLER

Born: Philadelphia, USA, 3 Sep 1956
World title fights: 12 (all bantamweight) won 10, lost 1, drew 1

DATE	WEIGHT	OPPONENT	VENUE	RESULT
14 Nov 1980	B (WBA)	Julian Solis	Miami	Won RSF–14
31 Jan 1981	B (WBA)	Jorge Lujan	Philadelphia	Won PTS–15
4 Apr 1981	B (WBA)	Eijiro Murata	Tokyo	Drew 15
25 Jul 1981	B (WBA)	Julian Solis	Atlantic City	Won KO–7
10 Dec 1981	B (WBA)	Eijiro Murata	Atlantic City	Won RSF–13
27 Jan 1982	B (WBA)	Johnny Carter	Philadelphia	Won RSF–6

DATE	WEIGHT	OPPONENT	VENUE	RESULT

DATE	WEIGHT	OPPONENT	VENUE	RESULT
27 Mar 1982	B (WBA)	Johnny Carter	Philadelphia	Won RSF–6
27 Oct 1982	B (WBA)	Miguel Iriarte	Atlantic City	Won RSF–9
13 Mar 1983	B (WBA)	Gaby Canizales	Atlantic City	Won PTS–15
10 Sep 1983	B (WBA)	Eijiro Murata	Tokyo	Won RSF–10
17 Dec 1983	B (WBA)	Oscar Muniz	Atlantic City	Won RSF–7
7 Apr 1984	B (WBA)	Richard Sandoval	Atlantic City	Lost RSF–15

Jung-Koo CHANG

Born: Pusan, South Korea, 4 Feb 1963
World title fights: 19 (all junior-fly) won 16, lost 3

DATE	WEIGHT	OPPONENT	VENUE	RESULT
18 Sep 1982	JFl (WBC)	Hilario Zapata	Seoul	Lost PTS–15
26 Mar 1983	JFl (WBC)	Hilario Zapata	Seoul	Won RSF–3
11 Jun 1983	JFl (WBC)	Masaharu Iha	Taegu, S Korea	Won RSF–2
10 Sep 1983	JFl (WBC)	German Torres	Taejon, S Korea	Won PTS–12
31 Mar 1984	JFl (WBC)	Sot Chitalada	Pusan, S Korea	Won PTS–12
18 Aug 1984	JFl (WBC)	Katsuo Tokashiki	Pohang, S Korea	Won RSF–9
15 Dec 1984	JFl (WBC)	Tadashi Kuramochi	Pusan	Won PTS–12
27 Apr 1985	JFl (WBC)	German Torres	Ulsan, S Korea	Won PTS–12
4 Aug 1985	JFl (WBC)	Francisco Montiel	Seoul	Won PTS–12
10 Nov 1985	JFl (WBC)	Jorge Cano	Taejon	Won PTS–12
13 Apr 1986	JFl (WBC)	German Torres	Seoul	Won PTS–12
13 Sep 1986	JFl (WBC)	Francisco Montiel	Seoul	Won PTS–12
14 Dec 1986	JFl (WBC)	Hideyuki Ohashi	Inchon, S Korea	Won RSF–5
19 Apr 1987	JFl (WBC)	Efren Pinto	Seoul	Won RSF–6
28 Jun 1987	JFl (WBC)	Agustin Garcia	Inchon	Won KO–10
13 Dec 1987	JFl (WBC)	Isidro Perez	Pohang	Won PTS–12
27 Jun 1988	JFl (WBC)	Hideyuki Ohashi	Tokyo	Won RSF–8
9 Dec 1989	JFl (WBC)	Humberto Gonzalez	Seoul	Lost PTS–12
24 Nov 1990	Fl (WBC)	Sot Chitalada	Seoul	Lost PTS–12

DATE	WEIGHT	OPPONENT	VENUE	RESULT

Tae-Il CHANG

Born: Damyang-Kun, South Korea, 10 Apr 1965
World title fights: 3 (all junior-bantam) won 1, lost 2

DATE	WEIGHT	OPPONENT	VENUE	RESULT	
17 May 1987	JB (IBF)	Kwon-Sun Chon	Seoul	Won	PTS–15
17 Oct 1987	JB (IBF)	Ellyas Pical	Jakarta	Lost	PTS–15
15 Jan 1989	JB (WBA)	Kaosai Galaxy	Bangkok	Lost	KO–2

Ezzard CHARLES

Born: Lawrenceville, Georgia, USA, 7 Jul 1921
Died: Chicago, 27 May 1975
World title fights: 13 (all heavyweight) won 9, lost 4

DATE	WEIGHT	OPPONENT	VENUE	RESULT	
22 Jun 1949	H (NBA)	Jersey Joe Walcott	Chicago	Won	PTS–15
10 Aug 1949	H (NBA)	Gus Lesnevich	New York	Won	RSF–7
14 Oct 1949	H (NBA)	Pat Valentino	San Francisco	Won	KO–8
15 Aug 1950	H (NBA)	Freddy Beshore	Buffalo	Won	RSF–14
27 Sep 1950	H	Joe Louis	New York	Won	PTS–15
5 Dec 1950	H	Nick Baronne	Cincinnati	Won	KO–11
12 Jan 1951	H	Lee Oma	New York	Won	RSF–10
7 Mar 1951	H	Jersey Joe Walcott	Detroit	Won	PTS–15
30 May 1951	H	Joey Maxim	Chicago	Won	PTS–15
18 Jul 1951	H	Jersey Joe Walcott	Pittsburgh	Lost	KO–7
5 Jun 1952	H	Jersey Joe Walcott	Philadelphia	Lost	PTS–15
17 Jun 1954	H	Rocky Marciano	New York	Lost	PTS–15
17 Sep 1954	H	Rocky Marciano	New York	Lost	KO–8

Berkrerk CHARTVANCHAI

Born: Bangkok, Thailand, 1946
World title fights: 2 (both flyweight) won 1, lost 1

DATE	WEIGHT	OPPONENT	VENUE	RESULT	
14 Apr 1970	Fl (WBA)	Bernabe Villacampo	Bangkok	Won	PTS–15
22 Oct 1970	Fl (WBA)	Masao Ohba	Tokyo	Lost	RSF–13

Eric CHAVEZ

Born: Talisay Cebu, Philippines, 9 Apr 1962
World title fights: 3 (all strawweight) won 1, lost 2

DATE	WEIGHT	OPPONENT	VENUE	RESULT	
21 Sep 1989	S (IBF)	Nico Thomas	Jakarta	Won	KO–4
21 Feb 1990	S (IBF)	Falan Lookmingkwan	Bangkok	Lost	RSF–7
15 Aug 1990	S (IBF)	Falan Lookmingkwan	Bangkok	Lost	PTS–12

Julio Cesar CHAVEZ

Born: Ciudad Obregon, Mexico, 12 Jul 1962
World title fights: 18 (10 junior-light, 3 lightweight, 5 junior-welter)
won 18, lost 0

DATE	WEIGHT	OPPONENT	VENUE	RESULT	
13 Sep 1984	JL (WBC)	Mario Martinez	Los Angeles	Won	RSF–8
19 Apr 1985	JL (WBC)	Ruben Castillo	Los Angeles	Won	RSF–6
7 Jul 1985	JL (WBC)	Roger Mayweather	Las Vegas	Won	RSF–2
20 Sep 1985	JL (WBC)	Dwight Pratchett	Las Vegas	Won	PTS–12
15 May 1986	JL (WBC)	Faustino Barrios	Paris	Won	RSF–5
13 Jun 1986	JL (WBC)	Raul Rojas	New York	Won	RSF–7
3 Aug 1986	JL (WBC)	Rocky Lockridge	Monte Carlo	Won	PTS–12
12 Dec 1986	JL (WBC)	Juan LaPorte	New York	Won	PTS–12
18 Apr 1987	JL (WBC)	Francisco da Cruz	Nimes, France	Won	RSF–4
21 Aug 1987	JL (WBC)	Danilo Cabrera	Tijuana, Mexico	Won	PTS–12

DATE	WEIGHT	OPPONENT	VENUE	RESULT
22 Nov 1987	L (WBA)	Edwin Rosario	Las Vegas	Won RSF–11
16 Apr 1988	L (WBA)	Rodolfo Aguilar	Las Vegas	Won RSF–6
29 Oct 1988	L (WBA/WBC)	Jose Luis Ramirez	Las Vegas	Won TD–11
13 May 1989	JW (WBC)	Roger Mayweather	Los Angeles	Won RSF–10
18 Nov 1989	JW (WBC)	Sammy Fuentes	Las Vegas	Won RTD–10
16 Dec 1989	JW (WBC)	Alberto Cortes	Mexico City	Won KO–3
17 Mar 1990	JW (WBC/IBF)	Meldrick Taylor	Las Vegas	Won RSF–12
8 Dec 1990	JW (WBC/IBF)	Kyung-Duk Ahn	Atlantic City	Won RSF–3

Chartchai CHIONOI

Born: Bangkok, Thailand, 10 Oct 1942
World title fights: 13 (all flyweight) won 9, lost 4

DATE	WEIGHT	OPPONENT	VENUE	RESULT
30 Dec 1966	Fl (WBC)	Walter McGowan	Bangkok	Won RSF–9
26 Jul 1967	Fl (WBC)	Puntip Keosuriya	Bangkok	Won KO–3
19 Sep 1967	Fl (WBC)	Walter McGowan	London	Won RSF–7
28 Jan 1968	Fl (WBC)	Efren Torres	Mexico City	Won RSF–13
10 Nov 1968	Fl (WBC)	Bernabe Villacampo	Bangkok	Won PTS–15
23 Feb 1969	Fl (WBC)	Efren Torres	Mexico City	Lost RSF–8
20 Mar 1970	Fl (WBC)	Efren Torres	Bangkok	Won PTS–15
7 Dec 1970	Fl (WBC)	Erbito Salavarria	Bangkok	Lost RSF–2
2 Jan 1973	Fl (WBA)	Masao Ohba	Tokyo	Lost RSF–12
17 May 1973	Fl (WBA)	Fritz Chervet	Bangkok	Won RSF–4
27 Oct 1973	Fl (WBA)	Susumu Hanagata	Bangkok	Won PTS–15
27 Apr 1974	Fl (WBA)	Fritz Chervet	Zurich	Won PTS–15
18 Oct 1974	Fl (WBA)	Susumu Hanagata	Yokohama, Japan	Lost RSF–6

DATE	WEIGHT	OPPONENT	VENUE	RESULT

George CHIP

Born: Scranton, Pennsylvania, USA, 25 Aug 1888
Died: New Castle, Pennsylvania, 8 Nov 1960
World title fights: 4 (all middleweight) won 2, lost 1, ND 1

DATE	WEIGHT	OPPONENT	VENUE	RESULT
11 Oct 1913	M	Frankie Klaus	Pittsburgh	Won KO–6
23 Dec 1913	M	Frankie Klaus	Pittsburgh	Won KO–5
7 Apr 1914	M	Al McCoy	Brooklyn, New York	Lost KO–1
17 Jan 1921	M	Johnny Wilson	Pittsburgh	ND–12

Sot CHITALADA

Born: Bangkok, Thailand, 24 May 1962
World title fights: 14 (1 junior-fly, 13 flyweight) won 11, lost 2, drew 1

DATE	WEIGHT	OPPONENT	VENUE	RESULT
31 Mar 1984	JFl (WBC)	Jung-Koo Chang	Pusan, S Korea	Lost PTS–12
8 Oct 1984	Fl (WBC)	Gabriel Bernal	Bangkok	Won PTS–12
20 Feb 1985	Fl (WBC)	Charlie Magri	London	Won RSF–4
22 Jun 1985	Fl (WBC)	Gabriel Bernal	Bangkok	Drew 12
22 Feb 1986	Fl (WBC)	Freddie Castillo	Kuwait	Won PTS–12
10 Dec 1986	Fl (WBC)	Gabriel Bernal	Bangkok	Won PTS–12
6 Sep 1987	Fl (WBC)	Rae-Ki Ahn	Bangkok	Won KO–4
31 Jan 1988	Fl (WBC)	Hideaki Kamishiro	Osaka, Japan	Won RSF–7
23 Jul 1988	Fl (WBC)	Yung-Kang Kim	Pohang, S Korea	Lost PTS–12
3 Jun 1989	Fl (WBC)	Yung-Kang Kim	Trang, Thailand	Won PTS–12
30 Jan 1990	Fl (WBC)	Ric Siodoro	Bangkok	Won PTS–12
1 May 1990	Fl (WBC)	Carlos Salazar	Bangkok	Won PTS–12
9 Sep 1990	Fl (WBC)	Richard Clarke	Kingston, Jamaica	Won KO–11
24 Nov 1990	Fl (WBC)	Jung-Koo Chang	Seoul	Won PTS–12

Kid CHOCOLATE

Born: Cerro, Cuba, 6 Jan 1910
World title fights: 9 (5 featherweight, 3 junior-light,
1 junior-welter/lightweight) won 6, lost 3

DATE	WEIGHT	OPPONENT	VENUE	RESULT	
12 Dec 1930	Fe	Battling Battalino	New York	Lost	PTS–15
15 Jul 1931	JL	Benny Bass	Philadelphia	Won	RSF–7
20 Nov 1931	JW/L	Tony Canzoneri	New York	Lost	PTS–15
4 Aug 1932	Fe (NY)	Eddie Shea	Chicago	Won	PTS–10
13 Oct 1932	Fe (NY)	Lew Feldman	New York	Won	KO–12
9 Dec 1932	Fe (NY)	Fidel La Barba	New York	Won	PTS–15
1 May 1933	JL	Johnny Farr	Philadelphia	Won	PTS–10
19 May 1933	Fe (NY)	Seaman Tommy Watson	New York	Won	PTS–15
26 Dec 1933	JL	Frankie Klick	Philadelphia	Lost	KO–7

Chang-Ho CHOI

Born: Seoul, South Korea, 10 Feb 1964
World title fights: 3 (2 flyweight, 1 junior-bantam) won 1, lost 2

DATE	WEIGHT	OPPONENT	VENUE	RESULT	
5 Sep 1987	Fl (IBF)	Dodie Penalosa	Manila	Won	KO–11
16 Jan 1988	Fl (IBF)	Rolando Bohol	Manila	Lost	PTS–15
9 Oct 1988	JB (WBA)	Kaosai Galaxy	Seoul	Lost	KO–8

Jum-Hwan CHOI

Born: Pusan, South Korea, 9 Jun 1963
World title fights: 8 (6 junior-fly, 2 strawweight) won 5, lost 3

DATE	WEIGHT	OPPONENT	VENUE	RESULT	
16 Nov 1984	JFl (IBF)	Dodie Penalosa	Manila	Lost	PTS–15
7 Dec 1986	JFl (IBF)	Cho-Woon Park	Pusan, S Korea	Won	PTS–15
29 Mar 1987	JFl (IBF)	Tacy Macalos	Seoul	Won	PTS–15

4 Jul 1987	JFl (IBF)	Toshihiko Matsuda	Seoul	Won KO-4
9 Aug 1987	JFl (IBF)	Azadin Anhar	Jakarta	Won KO-3
5 Nov 1988	JFl (IBF)	Tacy Macalos	Manila	Lost PTS-12
12 Nov 1989	S (WBC)	Napa Kiatwanchai	Seoul	Won RSF-12
7 Feb 1990	S (WBC)	Hideyuki Ohashi	Tokyo	Lost KO-9

Anton CHRISTOFORIDIS

Born: Messina, Greece, 26 May 1917
Died: Athens, Nov 1986
World title fights: 2 (both light-heavy) won 1, lost 1

13 Jan 1941	LH (NBA)	Melio Bettina	Cleveland	Won PTS-15
22 May 1941	LH (NBA)	Gus Lesnevich	New York	Lost PTS-15

Joo-Do CHUN

Born: South Korea, 25 Jan 1964
World title fights: 7 (all junior-bantam) won 6, lost 1

10 Dec 1983	JB (IBF)	Ken Kasugai	Osaka, Japan	Won RSF-5
28 Jan 1984	JB (IBF)	Prayurasak Muangsurin	Seoul	Won KO-12
17 Mar 1984	JB (IBF)	Diego de Villa	Kwangju, S Korea	Won KO-1
26 May 1984	JB (IBF)	Felix Marquez	Chonju, S Korea	Won KO-6
20 Jul 1984	JB (IBF)	William Develos	Pusan, S Korea	Won KO-7
3 Jan 1985	JB (IBF)	Kwang-Gu Park	Ulsan, S Korea	Won KO-15
3 May 1985	JB (IBF)	Ellyas Pical	Jakarta	Lost KO-8

Bi-Won CHUNG

Born: Seoul, South Korea, 15 Jan 1960
World title fights: 2 (both flyweight) won 1, lost 1

DATE	WEIGHT	OPPONENT	VENUE	RESULT
27 Apr 1986	Fl (IBF)	Chong-Kwan Chung	Pusan, S Korea	Won PTS–15
2 Aug 1986	Fl (IBF)	Hi-Sup Shin	Inchon, S Korea	Lost KO–15

Chong-Kwan CHUNG

Born: South Korea, 30 Nov 1961
World title fights: 4 (all flyweight) won 1, lost 1, drew 2

DATE	WEIGHT	OPPONENT	VENUE	RESULT
25 Jan 1985	Fl (IBF)	Soo-Chun Kwon	Taejon, S Korea	Drew 15
17 Jul 1985	Fl (IBF)	Soo-Chun Kwon	Masan, S Korea	Drew 15
20 Dec 1985	Fl (IBF)	Soo-Chun Kwon	Pusan, S Korea	Won RSF–4
27 Apr 1986	Fl (IBF)	Bi-Won Chung	Pusan	Lost PTS–15

Ki-Yung CHUNG

Born: South Korea, 23 Nov 1959
World title fights: 4 (all featherweight) won 3, lost 1

DATE	WEIGHT	OPPONENT	VENUE	RESULT
29 Nov 1985	Fe (IBF)	Min-Keum Oh	Seoul	Won KO–15
16 Feb 1986	Fe (IBF)	Tyrone Jackson	Ulsan, S Korea	Won KO–6
18 May 1986	Fe (IBF)	Richard Savage	Seoul	Won PTS–15
30 Aug 1986	Fe (IBF)	Antonio Rivera	Seoul	Lost RTD–10

Cassius CLAY
see Muhammad ALI

Freddie 'Red' COCHRANE

Born: Elizabeth, New Jersey, USA, 6 May 1915
World title fights: 2 (both welterweight) won 1, lost 1

29 Jul 1941	W	Fritzie Zivic	Newark, New Jersey	Won	PTS–15
1 Feb 1946	W	Marty Servo	New York	Lost	KO–4

Gerrie COETZEE

Born: Boksburg, Transvaal, South Africa, 4 Aug 1955
World title fights: 4 (all heavyweight) won 1, lost 3

20 Oct 1979	H (WBA)	John Tate	Johannesburg	Lost	PTS–15
25 Oct 1980	H (WBA)	Mike Weaver	Sun City, S Africa	Lost	KO–13
23 Sep 1983	H (WBA)	Michael Dokes	Cleveland	Won	KO–10
1 Dec 1984	H (WBA)	Greg Page	Sun City	Lost	KO–8

Juan Martin COGGI

Born: Figuera, Santa Fe, Argentina, 19 Dec 1961
World title fights: 6 (all junior-welter) won 5, lost 1

4 Jul 1987	JW (WBA)	Patrizio Oliva	Ribera, Italy	Won	KO–3
7 May 1988	JW (WBA)	Sang-Ho Lee	Abruzzi, Italy	Won	KO–2
21 Jan 1989	JW (WBA)	Harold Brazier	Vasto, Italy	Won	PTS–12
29 Apr 1989	JW (WBA)	Akinobu Hiranaka	Vasto	Won	PTS–12
24 Mar 1990	JW (WBA)	Jose Luis Ramirez	Ajaccio, Corsica	Won	PTS–12
17 Aug 1990	JW (WBA)	Loreto Garza	Nice	Lost	PTS–12

Robert COHEN

Born: Bone, Algeria, 15 Nov 1930
World title fights: 3 (all bantamweight) won 1, lost 1, drew 1

DATE	WEIGHT	OPPONENT	VENUE	RESULT	
19 Sep 1954	B	Chamrern Songkitrat	Bangkok	Won	PTS–15
3 Sep 1955	B (NY)	Willie Toweel	Johannesburg	Drew	15
29 Jun 1956	B (NY)	Mario D'Agata	Rome	Lost	RTD–6

Curtis COKES

Born: Dallas, USA, 15 Jun 1937
World title fights: 8 (all welterweight) won 6, lost 2

DATE	WEIGHT	OPPONENT	VENUE	RESULT	
24 Aug 1966	W (WBA)	Manuel Gonzalez	New Orleans	Won	PTS–15
28 Nov 1966	W	Jean Josselin	Dallas	Won	PTS–15
19 May 1967	W	Francois Pavilla	Dallas	Won	RSF–10
2 Oct 1967	W	Charlie Shipes	Oakland, California	Won	RSF–8
16 Apr 1968	W	Willie Ludick	Dallas	Won	RSF–5
21 Oct 1968	W	Ramon LaCruz	New Orleans	Won	PTS–15
18 Apr 1969	W	Jose Napoles	Los Angeles	Lost	RSF–13
29 Jun 1969	W	Jose Napoles	Mexico City	Lost	RSF–10

Billy CONN

Born: East Liberty, Pittsburgh, USA, 8 Oct 1917
World title fights: 6 (4 light-heavy, 2 heavyweight) won 4, lost 2

DATE	WEIGHT	OPPONENT	VENUE	RESULT	
13 Jul 1939	LH	Melio Bettina	New York	Won	PTS–15
25 Sep 1939	LH	Melio Bettina	Pittsburgh	Won	PTS–15
17 Nov 1939	LH	Gus Lesnevich	New York	Won	PTS–15
5 Jun 1940	LH	Gus Lesnevich	Detroit	Won	PTS–15
18 Jun 1941	H	Joe Louis	New York	Lost	KO–13
19 Jun 1946	H	Joe Louis	New York	Lost	KO–8

John CONTEH

Born: Liverpool, England, 27 May 1951
World title fights: 7 (all light-heavy) won 4, lost 3

DATE	WEIGHT	OPPONENT	VENUE	RESULT
1 Oct 1974	LH (WBC)	Jorge Ahumada	London	Won PTS–15
11 Mar 1975	LH (WBC)	Lonnie Bennett	London	Won RSF–5
9 Oct 1976	LH (WBC)	Alvaro Lopez	Copenhagen	Won PTS–15
5 Mar 1977	LH (WBC)	Len Hutchins	Liverpool	Won RSF–3
17 Jun 1978	LH (WBC)	Mate Parlov	Belgrade	Lost PTS–15
18 Aug 1979	LH (WBC)	Matt Franklin	Atlantic City	Lost PTS–15
29 Mar 1980	LH (WBC)	Matt Saad Muhammad (formerly Matt Franklin)	Atlantic City	Lost RSF–4

Israel CONTRERAS

Born: Guiria, Venezuela, 27 Dec 1960
World title fights: 3 (2 bantamweight, 1 junior-bantam) won 2, lost 1

DATE	WEIGHT	OPPONENT	VENUE	RESULT
1 Nov 1986	JB (WBA)	Kaosai Galaxy	Willemstad, Dutch Antilles	Lost KO–5
4 Feb 1989	B (WBO)	Maurizio Lupino	Caracas	Won KO–1
2 Sep 1990	B (WBO)	Ray Minus	Nassau, Bahamas	Won RSF–9

James J CORBETT

Born: San Francisco, USA, 1 Jan 1866
Died: Bayside, New York, 18 Feb 1933
World title fights: 5 (all heavyweight) won 2, lost 3

DATE	WEIGHT	OPPONENT	VENUE	RESULT
7 Sep 1892	H	John L Sullivan	New Orleans	Won KO–21
25 Jan 1894	H	Charlie Mitchell	Jacksonville, Florida	Won KO–3
17 Mar 1897	H	Bob Fitzsimmons	Carson City, Nevada	Lost KO–14
11 May 1900	H	James J Jeffries	Coney Island, New York	Lost KO–23
14 Aug 1903	H	James J Jeffries	San Francisco	Lost KO–10

DATE	WEIGHT	OPPONENT	VENUE	RESULT

Young CORBETT

Born: Denver, USA, 4 Oct 1880
Died: Denver, 10 Apr 1927
World title fights: 1 (featherweight) won 1, lost 0

DATE	WEIGHT	OPPONENT	VENUE	RESULT
28 Nov 1901	Fe	Terry McGovern	Hartford, Connecticut	Won KO-2

Young CORBETT III

Born: Protenza, Campania, Italy, 27 May 1905
World title fights: 3 (2 welterweight, 1 middleweight) won 1, lost 2

DATE	WEIGHT	OPPONENT	VENUE	RESULT
22 Feb 1933	W	Jackie Fields	San Francisco	Won PTS-10
29 May 1933	W	Jimmy McLarnin	Los Angeles	Lost KO-1
18 Nov 1938	M (NY)	Fred Apostoli	New York	Lost KO-8

Hugo CORRO

Born: San Carlos, Mendoza, Argentina, 5 Nov 1953
World title fights: 4 (all middleweight) won 3, lost 1

DATE	WEIGHT	OPPONENT	VENUE	RESULT
22 Apr 1978	M	Rodrigo Valdez	San Remo, Italy	Won PTS-15
5 Aug 1978	M	Ronnie Harris	Buenos Aires	Won PTS-15
11 Nov 1978	M	Rodrigo Valdez	Buenos Aires	Won PTS-15
30 Jun 1979	M	Vito Antuofermo	Monte Carlo	Lost PTS-15

Billy COSTELLO

Born: Kingston, New York, USA, 10 Apr 1956
World title fights: 5 (all junior-welter) won 4, lost 1

DATE	WEIGHT	OPPONENT	VENUE	RESULT
29 Jan 1984	JW (WBC)	Bruce Curry	Beaumont, Texas	Won RSF-10
16 Jul 1984	JW (WBC)	Ronnie Shields	New York	Won PTS-12
3 Nov 1984	JW (WBC)	Saoul Mamby	New York	Won PTS-12

DATE	WEIGHT	OPPONENT	VENUE	RESULT

DATE	WEIGHT	OPPONENT	VENUE	RESULT
16 Feb 1985	JW (WBC)	Leroy Haley	New York	Won PTS–12
22 Aug 1985	JW (WBC)	Lonnie Smith	New York	Lost RSF–8

Johnny COULON

Born: Toronto, Canada, 12 Feb 1889
Died: Chicago, 29 Oct 1973
World title fights: 6 (all bantamweight) won 4, lost 1, ND 1

DATE	WEIGHT	OPPONENT	VENUE	RESULT
6 Mar 1910	B	Jim Kendrick	New Orleans	Won KO–19
19 Dec 1910	B	Earl Denning	Memphis	Won PTS–15
3 Feb 1912	B	Frankie Conley	Vernon, California	Won PTS–20
18 Feb 1912	B	Frankie Burns	New Orleans	Won PTS–20
18 Oct 1912	B	Kid Williams	New York	ND–10
3 Jun 1914	B	Kid Williams	Los Angeles	Lost KO–3

Eugene CRIQUI

Born: Belleville, France, 15 Aug 1893
Died: Villepinte, France, 7 Mar 1977
World title fights: 2 (both featherweight) won 1, lost 1

DATE	WEIGHT	OPPONENT	VENUE	RESULT
2 Jun 1923	Fe	Johnny Kilbane	New York	Won KO–6
26 Jul 1923	Fe	Johnny Dundee	New York	Lost PTS–15

Piet CROUS

Born: Johannesburg, South Africa, 2 Jul 1955
World title fights: 3 (all cruiserweight) won 2, lost 1

DATE	WEIGHT	OPPONENT	VENUE	RESULT
1 Dec 1984	C (WBA)	Ossie Ocasio	Sun City, S Africa	Won PTS–15
30 Mar 1985	C (WBA)	Randy Stephens	Sun City	Won TKO–3
28 Jul 1985	C (WBA)	Dwight Muhammad Qawi	Sun City	Lost KO–11

DATE	WEIGHT	OPPONENT	VENUE	RESULT

Carlos Teo CRUZ

Born: Santiago de los Caballeros, Dominican Republic, 4 Nov 1937
Died: Dominican Republic, 15 Feb 1970
World title fights: 3 (all lightweight) won 2, lost 1

DATE	WEIGHT	OPPONENT	VENUE	RESULT	
29 Jun 1968	L	Carlos Ortiz	Santo Domingo	Won	PTS-15
27 Sep 1968	L	Mando Ramos	Los Angeles	Won	PTS-15
18 Feb 1969	L	Mando Ramos	Los Angeles	Lost	RSF-11

Leonardo CRUZ

Born: Santiago, Dominican Republic, 17 Jan 1953
World title fights: 7 (all junior-feather) won 4, lost 3

DATE	WEIGHT	OPPONENT	VENUE	RESULT	
9 Sep 1978	JFe (WBC)	Wilfredo Gomez	San Juan	Lost	RSF-13
4 Apr 1981	JFe (WBA)	Sergio Palma	Buenos Aires	Lost	PTS-15
12 Jun 1982	JFe (WBA)	Sergio Palma	Miami	Won	PTS-15
13 Nov 1982	JFe (WBA)	Benito Badilla	San Juan	Won	KO-8
16 Mar 1983	JFe (WBA)	Soo-Hyun Chung	San Juan	Won	PTS-15
26 Aug 1983	JFe (WBA)	Cleo Garcia	Santo Domingo	Won	PTS-15
22 Feb 1984	JFe (WBA)	Loris Stecca	Milan	Lost	RSF-12

Roberto CRUZ

Born: Baguilo, Philippines, 2 Nov 1941
World title fights: 2 (both junior-welter) won 1, lost 1

DATE	WEIGHT	OPPONENT	VENUE	RESULT	
21 Mar 1963	JW (WBA)	Battling Torres	Los Angeles	Won	KO-1
15 Jun 1963	JW	Eddie Perkins	Manila	Lost	PTS-15

Steve CRUZ

Born: Fort Worth, Texas, USA, 2 Nov 1963
World title fights: 3 (all featherweight) won 1, lost 2

DATE	WEIGHT	OPPONENT	VENUE	RESULT	
23 Jun 1986	Fe (WBA)	Barry McGuigan	Las Vegas	Won	PTS–15
6 Mar 1987	Fe (WBA)	Antonio Esparragoza	Fort Worth, Texas	Lost	RSF–12
6 Aug 1989	Fe (IBF)	Jorge Paez	El Paso, Texas	Lost	PTS–12

Miguel Angel CUELLO

Born: Elortondo, Santa Fe, Argentina, 27 Feb 1946
World title fights: 2 (both light-heavy) won 1, lost 1

DATE	WEIGHT	OPPONENT	VENUE	RESULT	
21 May 1977	LH (WBC)	Jesse Burnett	Monte Carlo	Won	KO–9
7 Jan 1978	LH (WBC)	Mate Parlov	Milan	Lost	KO–9

Pipino CUEVAS

Born: Mexico City, Mexico, 27 Dec 1957
World title fights: 13 (all welterweight) won 12, lost 1

DATE	WEIGHT	OPPONENT	VENUE	RESULT	
17 Jul 1976	W (WBA)	Angel Espada	Mexicali, Mexico	Won	RSF–2
27 Oct 1976	W (WBA)	Shoji Tsujimoto	Kanazawa, Japan	Won	KO–6
12 Mar 1977	W (WBA)	Miguel Campanino	Mexico City	Won	RSF–2
6 Aug 1977	W (WBA)	Clyde Gray	Los Angeles	Won	KO–2
19 Nov 1977	W (WBA)	Angel Espada	San Juan	Won	RSF–11
4 Mar 1978	W (WBA)	Harold Weston	Los Angeles	Won	RSF–9
20 May 1978	W (WBA)	Billy Backus	Los Angeles	Won	RSF–2
9 Sep 1978	W (WBA)	Pete Ranzany	Sacramento, California	Won	RSF–2
29 Jan 1979	W (WBA)	Scott Clark	Los Angeles	Won	RSF–2
30 Jul 1979	W (WBA)	Randy Shields	Chicago	Won	PTS–15
8 Dec 1979	W (WBA)	Angel Espada	Los Angeles	Won	RSF–10

DATE	WEIGHT	OPPONENT	VENUE	RESULT
6 Apr 1980	W (WBA)	Harold Volbrecht	Houston	Won KO–5
2 Aug 1980	W (WBA)	Thomas Hearns	Detroit	Lost RSF–2

Bruce CURRY

Born: Marlin, Texas, USA, 29 Mar 1956
World title fights: 4 (all junior-welter) won 3, lost 1

DATE	WEIGHT	OPPONENT	VENUE	RESULT
18 May 1983	JW (WBC)	Leroy Haley	Las Vegas	Won PTS–12
7 Jul 1983	JW (WBC)	Hidekazu Akai	Osaka, Japan	Won KO–7
20 Oct 1983	JW (WBC)	Leroy Haley	Las Vegas	Won PTS–12
29 Jan 1984	JW (WBC)	Billy Costello	Beaumont, Texas	Lost RSF–10

Donald CURRY

Born: Fort Worth, Texas, USA, 7 Sep 1961
World title fights: 13 (9 welterweight, 3 junior-middle, 1 middleweight)
won 9, lost 4

DATE	WEIGHT	OPPONENT	VENUE	RESULT
13 Feb 1983	W (WBA)	Jun-Sok Hwang	Fort Worth, Texas	Won PTS–15
2 Sep 1983	W (WBA)	Roger Stafford	Marsala, Sicily	Won KO–1
4 Feb 1984	W (WBA)	Marlon Starling	Atlantic City	Won PTS–15
21 Apr 1984	W (WBA)	Elio Diaz	Fort Worth	Won RTD–7
22 Sep 1984	W (WBA)	Nino La Rocca	Monte Carlo	Won KO–6
19 Jan 1985	W (WBA)	Colin Jones	Birmingham	Won RSF–4
6 Dec 1985	W	Milton McCrory	Las Vegas	Won KO–2
9 Mar 1986	W	Eduardo Rodriguez	Fort Worth	Won KO–2
27 Sep 1986	W	Lloyd Honeyghan	Atlantic City	Lost RTD–6
18 Jul 1987	JM (WBA)	Mike McCallum	Las Vegas	Lost KO–5
8 Jul 1988	JM (WBC)	Gianfranco Rosi	San Remo, Italy	Won RTD–9
11 Feb 1989	JM (WBC)	Rene Jacquot	Grenoble, France	Lost PTS–12
18 Oct 1990	M (IBF)	Michael Nunn	Paris	Lost RSF–10

DATE	WEIGHT	OPPONENT	VENUE	RESULT

Bobby CZYZ

Born: Wanaque, New Jersey, USA, 10 Feb 1962
World title fights: 7 (all light-heavy) won 4, lost 3

DATE	WEIGHT	OPPONENT	VENUE	RESULT	
6 Sep 1986	LH (IBF)	Slobodan Kacar	Las Vegas	Won	RSF–5
26 Dec 1986	LH (IBF)	David Sears	West Orange, New Jersey	Won	KO–1
21 Feb 1987	LH (IBF)	Willie Edwards	Atlantic City	Won	KO–2
4 May 1987	LH (IBF)	Jim McDonald	Atlantic City	Won	RSF–6
29 Oct 1987	LH (IBF)	Prince Charles Williams	Las Vegas	Lost	TKO–9
4 Mar 1989	LH (WBA)	Virgil Hill	Bismarck, North Dakota	Lost	PTS–12
25 Jun 1989	LH (IBF)	Prince Charles Williams	Atlantic City	Lost	TKO–10

Harold DADE

Born: Chicago, USA, 24 Mar 1923
Died: Los Angeles, 17 Jul 1962
World title fights: 2 (both bantamweight) won 1, lost 1

DATE	WEIGHT	OPPONENT	VENUE	RESULT	
6 Jan 1947	B	Manuel Ortiz	San Francisco	Won	PTS–15
11 Mar 1947	B	Manuel Ortiz	Los Angeles	Lost	PTS–15

Mario D'AGATA

Born: Arezzo, Tuscany, Italy, 29 May 1926
World title fights: 2 (both bantamweight) won 1, lost 1

DATE	WEIGHT	OPPONENT	VENUE	RESULT	
29 Jun 1956	B (NY)	Robert Cohen	Rome	Won	RTD–6
1 Apr 1957	B (NY)	Alphonse Halimi	Paris	Lost	PTS–15

Eckhard DAGGE

Born: Berlin, Germany, 27 Feb 1948
World title fights: 4 (all junior-middle) won 2, lost 1, drew 1

18 Jun 1976	JM (WBC)	Elisha Obed	Berlin	Won	RTD–10
18 Sep 1976	JM (WBC)	Emile Griffith	Berlin	Won	PTS–15
15 Mar 1977	JM (WBC)	Maurice Hope	Berlin	Drew	15
6 Aug 1977	JM (WBC)	Rocky Mattioli	Berlin	Lost	KO–5

Francesco DAMIANI

Born: Bagnocavallo, Italy, 4 Oct 1958
World title fights: 2 (both heavyweight) won 2, lost 0

6 May 1989	H (WBO)	Johnny Du Ploy	Syracuse, Italy	Won	KO–3
16 Dec 1989	H (WBO)	Daniel Netto	Cesena, Italy	Won	RSF–2

Robert DANIELS

Born: Miami, USA, 30 Aug 1966
World title fights: 3 (all cruiserweight) won 2, drew 1

28 Nov 1989	C (WBA)	Dwight Muhammad Qawi	Paris	Won	PTS–12
19 Jul 1990	C (WBA)	Craig Bodzianowski	Seattle	Won	PTS–12
23 Nov 1990	C (WBA)	Toufik Belbouli	Madrid	Drew	12

Alberto DAVILA

Born: Olion, Texas, USA, 10 Aug 1954
World title fights: 7 (all bantamweight) won 2, lost 5

25 Feb 1978	B (WBC)	Carlos Zarate	Los Angeles	Lost	RSF–8
15 Sep 1978	B (WBA)	Jorge Lujan	New Orleans	Lost	PTS–15
19 Dec 1980	B (WBC)	Lupe Pintor	Las Vegas	Lost	PTS–15

DATE	WEIGHT	OPPONENT	VENUE	RESULT
1 Sep 1983	B (WBC)	Kiko Bejines	Los Angeles	Won KO–12
26 May 1984	B (WBC)	Enrique Sanchez	Miami	Won RSF–11
15 Nov 1986	B (WBC)	Miguel 'Happy' Lora	Barranquilla, Colombia	Lost PTS–12
1 Aug 1988	B (WBC)	Miguel 'Happy' Lora	Los Angeles	Lost PTS–12

Aaron DAVIS

Born: Bronx, New York, USA, 7 Apr 1967
World title fights: 1 (welterweight) won 1, lost 0

9 Jul 1990	W (WBA)	Mark Breland	Reno, Nevada	Won KO–9

Pedro DECIMA

Born: Tucuman, Argentina, 10 Mar 1964
World title fights: 1 (junior-feather) won 1, lost 0

5 Nov 1990	JFe (WBC)	Paul Banke	Inglewood, California	Won RSF–4

Esteban De JESUS

Born: Carolina, Puerto Rico, 2 Aug 1951
Died: San Juan, 11 May 1989
World title fights: 8 (6 lightweight, 2 junior-welter) won 4, lost 4

16 Mar 1974	L (WBA)	Roberto Duran	Panama City	Lost KO–11
17 May 1975	JW (WBA)	Antonio Cervantes	Panama City	Lost PTS–15
8 May 1976	L (WBC)	Guts Ishimatsu	San Juan	Won PTS–15
11 Sep 1976	L (WBC)	Hector Medina	Bayamon, Puerto Rico	Won KO–7
12 Feb 1977	L (WBC)	Buzzsaw Yamabe	Bayamon	Won RSF–4
25 Jun 1977	L (WBC)	Vicente Saldivar Majores	Bayamon	Won KO–11
21 Jan 1978	L	Roberto Duran	Las Vegas	Lost KO–12
7 Jul 1980	JW (WBC)	Saoul Mamby	Minneapolis	Lost TKO–13

Jose De JESUS

Born: Maunabo, Puerto Rico, 12 Aug 1963
World title fights: 5 (all junior-fly) won 3, lost 2

9 Mar 1986	JFl (WBA)	Myung-Woo Yuh	Suwon, S Korea	Lost	PTS–15
12 Jun 1988	JFl (WBA)	Myung-Woo Yuh	Seoul	Lost	PTS–12
19 May 1989	JFl (WBO)	Fernando Martinez	San Juan	Won	RSF–12
21 Oct 1989	JFl (WBO)	Isidro Perez	San Juan	Won	PTS–12
5 May 1990	JFl (WBO)	Ali Galvez	Talcahuano, Chile	Won	KO–5

Jack DELANEY

Born: St Francis du Lac, Quebec, Canada, 18 Mar 1900
Died: Katonah, New York, 27 Nov 1948
World title fights: 2 (both light-heavy) won 1, lost 1

11 Dec 1925	LH	Paul Berlenbach	New York	Lost	PTS–15
16 Jul 1926	LH	Paul Berlenbach	New York	Won	PTS–15

Carlos De LEON

Born: Rio Piedras, Puerto Rico, 3 May 1959
World title fights: 16 (all cruiserweight) won 11, lost 4, drew 1

25 Nov 1980	C (WBC)	Marvin Camel	New Orleans	Won	PTS–15
24 Feb 1982	C (WBC)	Marvin Camel	Atlantic City	Won	RSF–7
27 Jun 1982	C (WBC)	S T Gordon	Highland Heights, Ohio	Lost	RSF–2
17 Jul 1983	C (WBC)	S T Gordon	Las Vegas	Won	PTS–12
21 Sep 1983	C (WBC)	Alvaro Lopez	San Jose, California	Won	RSF–4
9 Mar 1984	C (WBC)	Anthony Davis	Las Vegas	Won	PTS–12
3 Jun 1984	C (WBC)	Bashiru Ali	Oakland, California	Won	PTS–12
6 Jun 1985	C (WBC)	Alfonzo Ratliff	Las Vegas	Lost	PTS–12

DATE	WEIGHT	OPPONENT	VENUE	RESULT
22 Mar 1986	C (WBC)	Bernard Benton	Las Vegas	Won PTS–12
10 Aug 1986	C (WBC)	Michael Greer	Giardini Naxos, Italy	Won RSF–8
21 Feb 1987	C (WBC)	Angelo Rottoli	Bergamo, Italy	Won RSF–4
22 Jan 1988	C (WBC)	Jose Maria Flores	Atlantic City	Won PTS–12
9 Apr 1988	C	Evander Holyfield	Las Vegas	Lost RSF–8
17 May 1989	C (WBC)	Sammy Reeson	London	Won RSF–9
27 Jan 1990	C (WBC)	Johnny Nelson	Sheffield	Drew 12
27 Jul 1990	C (WBC)	Massimiliano Duran	Capo D'Orlando, Italy	Lost DIS–11

Paddy De MARCO

Born: Brooklyn, New York, USA, 10 Feb 1928
World title fights: 2 (both lightweight) won 1, lost 1

5 Mar 1954	L	Jimmy Carter	New York	Won PTS–15
17 Nov 1954	L	Jimmy Carter	San Francisco	Lost RSF–15

Tony De MARCO

Born: Boston, USA, 14 Jan 1932
World title fights: 3 (all welterweight) won 1, lost 2

1 Apr 1955	W	Johnny Saxton	Boston	Won RSF–14
10 Jun 1955	W	Carmen Basilio	Syracuse, New York	Lost RSF–12
30 Nov 1955	W	Carmen Basilio	Boston	Lost KO–12

Jack DEMPSEY

Born: Manassa, Colorado, USA, 24 Jun 1895
Died: New York, 31 May 1983
World title fights: 8 (all heavyweight) won 6, lost 2

4 Jul 1919	H	Jess Willard	Toledo, Ohio	Won RTD–3
6 Sep 1920	H	Billy Miske	Benton Harbour, Michigan	Won KO–3

DATE	WEIGHT	OPPONENT	VENUE	RESULT

14 Dec 1920	H	Bill Brennan	New York	Won KO–12
2 Jul 1921	H	Georges Carpentier	New Jersey	Won KO–4
4 Jul 1923	H	Tommy Gibbons	Shelby, Montana	Won PTS–15
14 Sep 1923	H	Luis Angel Firpo	New York	Won KO–2
23 Sep 1926	H	Gene Tunney	Philadelphia	Lost PTS–10
22 Sep 1927	H	Gene Tunney	Chicago	Lost PTS–10

Jack DEMPSEY (Nonpareil)

Born: County Kildare, Ireland, 15 Dec 1862
Died: Portland, Oregon, 2 Nov 1895
World title fights: 8 (7 middleweight, 1 welterweight) won 5, lost 3

30 Jul 1884	M	George Fulljames	New York	Won KO–22
3 Feb 1886	M	Jack Fogerty	New York	Won KO–27
4 Mar 1886	M	George LaBlanche	New York	Won KO–13
13 Dec 1887	M	Johnny Reagan	Long Island, New York	Won KO–45
27 Aug 1889	M	George La Blanche	San Francisco	*Lost KO–32
18 Feb 1890	M	Billy McCarthy	San Francisco	Won KO–28
14 Jan 1891	M	Bob Fitzsimmons	New Orleans	Lost TKO–13
18 Jan 1895	W	Tommy Ryan	New York	Lost KO–3

* La Blanche won with an illegal pivot blow and was also over the weight limit. Dempsey therefore retained his title despite losing

Miguel De OLIVEIRA

Born: Sao Paulo, Brazil, 30 Sep 1947
World title fights: 4 (all junior-middle) won 1, lost 2, drew 1

9 Jan 1973	JM	Koichi Wajima	Tokyo	Drew 15
5 Feb 1974	JM	Koichi Wajima	Tokyo	Lost PTS–15
7 May 1975	JM (WBC)	Jose Duran	Monte Carlo	Won PTS–15
13 Nov 1975	JM (WBC)	Elisha Obed	Paris	Lost RTD–10

DATE	WEIGHT	OPPONENT	VENUE	RESULT

Doug De WITT

Born: Youngstown, Ohio, USA, 13 Aug 1961
World title fights: 4 (all middleweight) won 2, lost 2

DATE	WEIGHT	OPPONENT	VENUE	RESULT	
8 Nov 1988	M (WBA)	Sumbu Kalambay	Monte Carlo	Lost	KO–7
18 Apr 1989	M (WBO)	Robbie Sims	Atlantic City	Won	PTS–12
15 Jan 1990	M (WBO)	Matthew Hilton	Atlantic City	Won	RTD–11
29 Apr 1990	M (WBO)	Nigel Benn	Atlantic City	Lost	RSF–8

Jack DILLON

Born: Frankfort, Indiana, USA, 2 Feb 1891
Died: Chattahoochee, Florida, 7 Aug 1942
World title fights: 4 (all light-heavy) won 3, lost 1

DATE	WEIGHT	OPPONENT	VENUE	RESULT	
28 Apr 1914	LH	Al Norton	Kansas City	Won	PTS–10
25 Apr 1916	LH	Battling Levinsky	Kansas City	Won	PTS–15
17 Oct 1916	LH	Tom O'Neill	New York	Won	PTS–10
24 Oct 1916	LH	Battling Levinsky	Boston	Lost	PTS–12

George DIXON

Born: Halifax, Nova Scotia, Canada, 29 Jul 1870
Died: New York City, 6 Jan 1909
World title fights: 22 (3 bantamweight, 19 featherweight) won 18, lost 2, drew 2

DATE	WEIGHT	OPPONENT	VENUE	RESULT	
27 Jun 1890	B	Nunc Wallace	London	Won	KO–18
23 Oct 1890	B	Johnny Murphy	Providence, Rhode Island	Won	PTS–40
31 Mar 1891	B	Cal McCarthy	Troy, New York	Won	RSF–22
28 Jul 1891	Fe	Abe Willis	San Francisco	Won	KO–5
27 Jun 1892	Fe	Fred Johnson	Coney Island, New York	Won	KO–14
6 Sep 1892	Fe	Jack Skelly	New Orleans	Won	KO–8
8 Aug 1893	Fe	Eddie Pierce	Coney Island	Won	KO–3

DATE	WEIGHT	OPPONENT	VENUE	RESULT
25 Sep 1893	Fe	Solly Smith	Coney Island	Won KO–7
26 Sep 1894	Fe	Young Griffo	Boston	Drew 20
27 Aug 1895	Fe	Johnny Griffin	Boston	Won PTS–25
7 Aug 1897	Fe	Frank Erne	New York	Won PTS–25
4 Oct 1897	Fe	Solly Smith	San Francisco	Lost PTS–20
11 Nov 1898	Fe	Dave Sullivan	New York	Won DIS–10
29 Nov 1898	Fe	Oscar Gardner	New York	Won PTS–25
17 Jan 1899	Fe	Young Pluto	New York	Won KO–10
15 May 1899	Fe	Kid Broad	Buffalo	Won PTS–20
2 Jun 1899	Fe	Joe Bernstein	New York	Won PTS–25
1 Jul 1899	Fe	Tommy White	Denver	Won PTS–20
11 Aug 1899	Fe	Eddie Santry	New York	Drew 20
2 Nov 1899	Fe	Will Curley	New York	Won PTS–25
21 Nov 1899	Fe	Eddie Lenny	New York	Won PTS–25
9 Jan 1900	Fe	Terry McGovern	New York	Lost KO–8

Michael DOKES

Born: Akron, Ohio, USA, 10 Aug 1958
World title fights: 3 (all heavyweight) won 1, lost 1, drew 1

DATE	WEIGHT	OPPONENT	VENUE	RESULT
10 Dec 1982	H (WBA)	Mike Weaver	Las Vegas	Won RSF–1
20 May 1983	H (WBA)	Mike Weaver	Las Vegas	Drew 15
23 Sep 1983	H (WBA)	Gerrie Coetzee	Cleveland	Lost KO–10

DATE	WEIGHT	OPPONENT	VENUE	RESULT

James 'Buster' DOUGLAS

Born: Columbus, Ohio, USA, 7 Jul 1960
World title fights: 3 (all heavyweight) won 1, lost 2

DATE	WEIGHT	OPPONENT	VENUE	RESULT	
30 May 1987	H (IBF)	Tony Tucker	Las Vegas	Lost	KO–10
11 Feb 1990	H (WBC/WBA/ IBF)	Mike Tyson	Tokyo	Won	KO–10
25 Oct 1990	H (WBC/WBA/ IBF)	Evander Holyfield	Las Vegas	Lost	KO–3

Terry DOWNES

Born: Paddington, London, England, 9 May 1936
World title fights: 4 (3 middleweight, 1 light-heavy) won 1, lost 3

DATE	WEIGHT	OPPONENT	VENUE	RESULT	
14 Jan 1961	M	Paul Pender	Boston	Lost	RSF–7
11 Jul 1961	M	Paul Pender	London	Won	RTD–9
7 Apr 1962	M	Paul Pender	Boston	Lost	PTS–15
30 Nov 1964	LH	Willie Pastrano	Manchester	Lost	RSF–11

Buster DRAYTON

Born: Philadelphia, USA, 2 Mar 1953
World title fights: 4 (all junior-middle) won 2, lost 2

DATE	WEIGHT	OPPONENT	VENUE	RESULT	
4 Jun 1986	JM (IBF)	Carlos Santos	East Rutherford, New Jersey	Won	PTS–15
24 Aug 1986	JM (IBF)	Davey Moore	Juan-les-Pins, France	Won	RSF–10
27 Jun 1987	JM (IBF)	Matthew Hilton	Montreal	Lost	PTS–15
30 Jul 1988	JM (WBA)	Julian Jackson	Atlantic City	Lost	KO–3

Paddy DUFFY

Born: Boston, USA, 12 Nov 1864
Died: Boston, 19 Jul 1890
World title fights: 2 (both welterweight) won 2, lost 0

DATE	WEIGHT	OPPONENT	VENUE	RESULT
30 Oct 1888	W	William McMillan	Fort Foote, Virginia	Won KO–17
29 Mar 1889	W	Tom Meadows	San Francisco	Won DIS–45

Joe DUNDEE

Born: Rome, Italy, 16 Aug 1903
Died: Baltimore, 31 Mar 1982
World title fights: 3 (all welterweight) won 2, lost 1

DATE	WEIGHT	OPPONENT	VENUE	RESULT
3 Jun 1927	W	Pete Latzo	New York	Won PTS–15
7 Jul 1928	W	Hilario Martinez	Philadelphia	Won KO–8
25 Jul 1929	W	Jackie Fields	Detroit	Lost DIS–2

Johnny DUNDEE

Born: Sciacca, Sicily, 22 Nov 1893
Died: East Orange, New Jersey, 22 Apr 1965
World title fights: 10 (4 featherweight, 6 junior-light) won 6, lost 3, drew 1

DATE	WEIGHT	OPPONENT	VENUE	RESULT
29 Apr 1913	Fe	Johnny Kilbane	Vernon, California	Drew 20
18 Nov 1921	JL	George Chaney	New York	Won DIS–5
8 Jul 1922	JL	Little Jack Sharkey	New York	Won PTS–15
15 Aug 1922	Fe (NY)	Danny Frush	Brooklyn, New York	Won KO–9
2 Feb 1923	JL	Elino Flores	New York	Won PTS–15
30 May 1923	JL	Jack Bernstein	New York	Lost PTS–15
26 Jul 1923	Fe	Eugene Criqui	New York	Won PTS–15
17 Dec 1923	JL	Jack Bernstein	New York	Won PTS–15

DATE	WEIGHT	OPPONENT	VENUE	RESULT	
20 Jun 1924	JL	Steve 'Kid' Sullivan	New York	Lost	PTS–10
24 Oct 1927	Fe (NY)	Tony Canzoneri	New York	Lost	PTS–15

Vince DUNDEE

Born: Baltimore, USA, 22 Oct 1907
Died: Glendale, California, 27 Jul 1949
World title fights: 5 (all middleweight) won 3, lost 1, drew 1

DATE	WEIGHT	OPPONENT	VENUE	RESULT	
17 Mar 1933	M (NY)	Ben Jeby	New York	Drew 15	
30 Oct 1933	M (NY)	Lou Brouillard	Boston	Won	PTS–15
8 Dec 1933	M (NY)	Andy Callahan	Boston	Won	PTS–15
1 May 1934	M (NY)	Al Diamond	Paterson, New Jersey	Won	PTS–15
11 Sep 1934	M (NY)	Teddy Yarosz	Pittsburgh	Lost	PTS–15

Ralph DUPAS

Born: New Orleans, USA, 14 Oct 1935
World title fights: 6 (1 lightweight, 1 welterweight, 4 junior-middle) won 2, lost 4

DATE	WEIGHT	OPPONENT	VENUE	RESULT	
7 May 1958	L	Joe Brown	Houston	Lost	RSF–8
13 Jul 1962	W	Emile Griffith	Las Vegas	Lost	PTS–15
29 Apr 1963	JM	Denny Moyer	New Orleans	Won	PTS–15
17 Jun 1963	JM	Denny Moyer	Baltimore	Won	PTS–15
7 Sep 1963	JM	Sandro Mazzinghi	Milan	Lost	KO–9
2 Dec 1963	JM	Sandro Mazzinghi	Sydney	Lost	KO–13

Jose DURAN

Born: Madrid, Spain, 9 Oct 1945
World title fights: 4 (all junior-middle) won 1, lost 3

DATE	WEIGHT	OPPONENT	VENUE	RESULT	
7 May 1975	JM (WBC)	Miguel De Oliveira	Monte Carlo	Lost	PTS–15

DATE	WEIGHT	OPPONENT	VENUE	RESULT

DATE	WEIGHT	OPPONENT	VENUE	RESULT
18 May 1976	JM (WBA)	Koichi Wajima	Tokyo	Won KO–14
8 Oct 1976	JM (WBA)	Miguel Angel Castellini	Madrid	Lost PTS–15
14 May 1978	JM (WBC)	Rocky Mattioli	Pescara, Italy	Lost RSF–5

Massimiliano DURAN

Born: Ferrara, Italy, 3 Nov 1963
World title fights: 2 (both cruiserweight) won 2, lost 0

DATE	WEIGHT	OPPONENT	VENUE	RESULT
27 Jul 1990	C (WBC)	Carlos De Leon	Capo D'Orlando, Italy	Won DIS–11
8 Dec 1990	C (WBC)	Anaclet Wamba	Ferrara, Italy	Won DIS–12

Roberto DURAN

Born: Guarare, Panama, 16 Jun 1951
World title fights: 21 (13 lightweight, 2 welterweight, 3 junior-middle, 2 middleweight, 1 super-middle) won 16, lost 5

DATE	WEIGHT	OPPONENT	VENUE	RESULT
26 Jun 1972	L (WBA)	Ken Buchanan	New York	Won RSF–13
20 Jan 1973	L (WBA)	Jimmy Robertson	Panama City	Won KO–5
2 Jun 1973	L (WBA)	Hector Thompson	Panama City	Won RSF–8
8 Sep 1973	L (WBA)	Ishimatsu Suzuki	Panama City	Won RSF–10
16 Mar 1974	L (WBA)	Esteban De Jesus	Panama City	Won KO–11
21 Dec 1974	L (WBA)	Mastaka Takayama	San Jose, Costa Rica	Won RSF–1
2 Mar 1975	L (WBA)	Ray Lampkin	Panama City	Won KO–14
19 Dec 1975	L (WBA)	Leoncio Ortiz	San Juan	Won KO–15
23 May 1976	L (WBA)	Lou Bizzaro	Erie, Pennsylvania	Won KO–14
15 Oct 1976	L (WBA)	Alvaro Rojas	Hollywood	Won KO–1
29 Jan 1977	L (WBA)	Vilomar Fernandez	Miami	Won KO–13
15 Sep 1977	L (WBA)	Edwin Viruet	Philadelphia	Won PTS–15
21 Jan 1978	L	Esteban De Jesus	Las Vegas	Won KO–12
20 Jun 1980	W	Sugar Ray Leonard	Montreal	Won PTS–15
25 Nov 1980	W	Sugar Ray Leonard	New Orleans	Lost RTD–8

DATE	WEIGHT	OPPONENT	VENUE	RESULT

DATE	WEIGHT	OPPONENT	VENUE	RESULT
30 Jan 1982	JM (WBC)	Wilfred Benitez	Las Vegas	Lost PTS–15
16 Jun 1983	JM (WBA)	Davey Moore	New York	Won RSF–8
10 Nov 1983	M	Marvin Hagler	Las Vegas	Lost PTS–15
16 Jun 1984	JM (WBC)	Thomas Hearns	Las Vegas	Lost RSF–2
24 Feb 1989	M (WBC)	Iran Barkley	Atlantic City	Won PTS–12
7 Dec 1989	SM (WBC)	Sugar Ray Leonard	Las Vegas	Lost PTS–12

Hiroyuki EBIHARA

Born: Tokyo, Japan, 26 Mar 1940
World title fights: 6 (all flyweight) won 2, lost 4

DATE	WEIGHT	OPPONENT	VENUE	RESULT
18 Sep 1963	Fl	Pone Kingpetch	Tokyo	Won KO–1
23 Jan 1964	Fl	Pone Kingpetch	Bangkok	Lost PTS–15
15 Jul 1966	Fl (WBA)	Horacio Accavallo	Buenos Aires	Lost PTS–15
13 Aug 1967	Fl (WBA)	Horacio Accavallo	Buenos Aires	Lost PTS–15
30 Mar 1969	Fl (WBA)	Jose Severino	Sapporo, Japan	Won PTS–15
19 Oct 1969	Fl (WBA)	Bernabe Villacampo	Osaka, Japan	Lost PTS–15

Jimmy ELLIS

Born: Louisville, Kentucky, USA, 24 Feb 1940
World title fights: 3 (all heavyweight) won 2, lost 1

DATE	WEIGHT	OPPONENT	VENUE	RESULT
27 Apr 1968	H (WBA)	Jerry Quarry	Oakland, California	Won PTS–15
14 Sep 1968	H (WBA)	Floyd Patterson	Stockholm	Won PTS–15
16 Feb 1970	H	Joe Frazier	New York	Lost · RTD–4

Lester ELLIS

Born: Blackpool, England, 15 Mar 1965
World title fights: 3 (all junior-light) won 2, lost 1

DATE	WEIGHT	OPPONENT	VENUE	RESULT
15 Feb 1985	JL (IBF)	Hwan-Kil Yuh	Melbourne	Won PTS–15
26 Apr 1985	JL (IBF)	Rod Sequenan	Melbourne	Won RSF–13
12 Jul 1985	JL (IBF)	Barry Michael	Melbourne	Lost PTS–15

Gabriel 'Flash' ELORDE

Born: Bogo, Cebu, Philippines, 22 Mar 1935
Died: Manila, 2 Jan 1985
World title fights: 15 (1 featherweight, 12 junior-light, 2 lightweight)
won 11, lost 4

DATE	WEIGHT	OPPONENT	VENUE	RESULT
18 Jan 1956	Fe	Sandy Saddler	San Francisco	Lost RSF–13
16 Mar 1960	JL	Harold Gomes	Manila	Won RSF–7
17 Aug 1960	JL	Harold Gomes	San Francisco	Won KO–1
19 Mar 1961	JL	Joey Lopez	Manila	Won PTS–15
16 Dec 1961	JL	Sergio Caprari	Manila	Won KO–1
23 Jun 1962	JL	Auburn Copeland	Manila	Won PTS–15
16 Feb 1963	JL	Johnny Bizzaro	Manila	Won PTS–15
16 Nov 1963	JL	Love Allotey	Manila	Won DIS–11
15 Feb 1964	L	Carlos Ortiz	Manila	Lost RSF–14
27 Jul 1964	JL	Teruo Kosaka	Tokyo	Won RSF–12
5 Jun 1965	JL	Teruo Kosaka	Manila	Won KO–15
4 Dec 1965	JL	Kang-Il Suh	Manila	Won PTS–15
22 Oct 1966	JL	Vicente Derado	Manila	Won PTS–15
28 Nov 1966	L (WBA)	Carlos Ortiz	New York	Lost KO–14
15 Jun 1967	JL	Yoshiaki Numata	Tokyo	Lost PTS–15

Frank ERNE

Born: Zurich, Switzerland, 8 Jan 1875
Died: New York City, 17 Sep 1954
World title fights: 7 (1 featherweight, 5 lightweight, 1 welterweight)
won 2, lost 3, drew 2

DATE	WEIGHT	OPPONENT	VENUE	RESULT	
7 Apr 1897	Fe	George Dixon	New York	Lost	PTS-25
28 Sep 1898	L	George 'Kid' Lavigne	Coney Island, New York	Drew	20
3 Jul 1899	L	George 'Kid' Lavigne	Buffalo	Won	PTS-20
4 Dec 1899	L	Jack O'Brien	Coney Island	Drew	25
23 Mar 1900	L	Joe Gans	New York	Won	KO-12
23 Sep 1901	W	Rube Ferns	Fort Erie, Canada	Lost	KO-9
12 May 1902	L	Joe Gans	Fort Erie, Canada	Lost	KO-1

Alfredo ESCALERA

Born: Carolina, Puerto Rico, 21 Mar 1952
World title fights: 13 (all junior-light) won 10, lost 2, drew 1

DATE	WEIGHT	OPPONENT	VENUE	RESULT	
5 Jul 1975	JL (WBC)	Kuniaki Shibata	Mito, Japan	Won	KO-2
20 Sep 1975	JL (WBC)	Leonel Hernandez	Caracas	Drew	15
12 Dec 1975	JL (WBC)	Svein-Erik Paulsen	Oslo	Won	RSF-9
20 Feb 1976	JL (WBC)	Jose Fernandez	San Juan	Won	KO-13
1 Apr 1976	JL (WBC)	Buzzsaw Yamabe	Nara, Japan	Won	RSF-6
1 Jul 1976	JL (WBC)	Buzzsaw Yamabe	Nara	Won	PTS-15
18 Sep 1976	JL (WBC)	Ray Lunny III	San Juan	Won	RTD-12
30 Nov 1976	JL (WBC)	Tyrone Everett	Philadelphia	Won	PTS-15
17 Mar 1977	JL (WBC)	Ron McGarvey	San Juan	Won	RSF-6
16 May 1977	JL (WBC)	Carlos Becceril	Landover, Maryland	Won	KO-8
10 Sep 1977	JL (WBC)	Sigfredo Rodriguez	San Juan	Won	PTS-15
28 Jan 1978	JL (WBC)	Alexis Arguello	San Juan	Lost	RSF-13
4 Feb 1979	JL (WBC)	Alexis Arguello	Rimini, Italy	Lost	KO-13

Sixto ESCOBAR

Born: Barcelona, Puerto Rico, 23 Mar 1913
Died: Puerto Rico, 17 Nov 1979
World title fights: 10 (all bantamweight) won 8, lost 2

DATE	WEIGHT	OPPONENT	VENUE	RESULT
2 Jun 1934	B (NBA)	Baby Casanova	Montreal	Won KO–9
8 Aug 1934	B (NBA)	Eugene Huat	Montreal	Won PTS–15
26 Aug 1935	B (NBA)	Lou Salica	New York	Lost PTS–15
15 Nov 1935	B (NBA)	Lou Salica	New York	Won PTS–15
31 Aug 1936	B	Tony Marino	New York	Won RSF–13
13 Oct 1936	B	Indian Quintana	New York	Won KO–1
21 Feb 1937	B	Lou Salica	San Juan	Won PTS–15
23 Sep 1937	B	Harry Jeffra	New York	Lost PTS–15
20 Feb 1938	B	Harry Jeffra	San Juan	Won PTS–15
2 Apr 1939	B	Johnny 'KO' Morgan	San Juan	Won PTS–15

Angel ESPADA

Born: Salinas, Puerto Rico, 2 Feb 1948
World title fights: 6 (all welterweight) won 3, lost 3

DATE	WEIGHT	OPPONENT	VENUE	RESULT
28 Jun 1975	W (WBA)	Clyde Gray	San Juan	Won PTS–15
11 Oct 1975	W (WBA)	Johnny Gant	San Juan	Won PTS–15
27 Apr 1976	W (WBA)	Alfonso Hayman	San Juan	Won RSF–8
17 Jul 1976	W (WBA)	Pipino Cuevas	Mexicali, Mexico	Lost RSF–2
19 Nov 1977	W (WBA)	Pipino Cuevas	San Juan	Lost RSF–11
8 Dec 1979	W (WBA)	Pipino Cuevas	Los Angeles	Lost RSF–10

Gustavo 'Guty' ESPADAS

Born: Yucatan, Mexico, 20 Dec 1954
World title fights: 8 (7 flyweight, 1 junior-bantam) won 5, lost 3

DATE	WEIGHT	OPPONENT	VENUE	RESULT	
2 Oct 1976	Fl (WBA)	Alfonso Lopez	Los Angeles	Won	RSF–13
1 Jan 1977	Fl (WBA)	Jiro Takada	Tokyo	Won	RTD–7
30 Apr 1977	Fl (WBA)	Alfonso Lopez	Merida, Mexico	Won	RSF–13
19 Nov 1977	Fl (WBA)	Alex Santana	Los Angeles	Won	KO–8
2 Jan 1978	Fl (WBA)	Kimio Furesawa	Tokyo	Won	RSF–7
13 Aug 1978	Fl (WBA)	Betulio Gonzalez	Maracay, Venezuela	Lost	PTS–15
16 Dec 1979	Fl (WBC)	Chan-Hee Park	Pusan, S Korea	Lost	KO–2
28 Mar 1984	JB (WBC)	Payao Poontarat	Bangkok	Lost	TKO–10

Ernesto ESPANA

Born: LaFlor, Venezuela, 7 Nov 1954
World title fights: 6 (all lightweight) won 2, lost 4

DATE	WEIGHT	OPPONENT	VENUE	RESULT	
16 Jun 1979	L (WBA)	Claude Noel	San Juan	Won	KO–13
4 Aug 1979	L (WBA)	Johnny Lira	Chicago	Won	RSF–10
2 Mar 1980	L (WBA)	Hilmer Kenty	Detroit	Lost	RSF–9
20 Sep 1980	L (WBA)	Hilmer Kenty	San Juan	Lost	KO–4
30 Jan 1982	L (WBA)	Arturo Frias	Los Angeles	Lost	TKO–9
24 Jul 1982	L (WBA)	Ray Mancini	Warren, Michigan	Lost	RSF–6

Antonio ESPARRAGOZA

Born: Cumana, Venezuela, 2 Sep 1959
World title fights: 8 (all featherweight) won 7, drew 1

DATE	WEIGHT	OPPONENT	VENUE	RESULT	
6 Mar 1987	Fe (WBA)	Steve Cruz	Fort Worth, Texas	Won	RSF–12
26 Jul 1987	Fe (WBA)	Pascual Aranda	Houston	Won	KO–10

DATE	WEIGHT	OPPONENT	VENUE	RESULT

23 Jun 1988	Fe (WBA)	Marcos Villasana	Los Angeles	Drew 12
5 Nov 1988	Fe (WBA)	Jose Marmolejo	Marsala, Italy	Won KO–8
25 Mar 1989	Fe (WBA)	Mitsuru Sugiya	Kawasaki, Japan	Won KO–10
3 Jun 1989	Fe (WBA)	Jean-Marc Renard	Manur, Belgium	Won KO–6
22 Sep 1989	Fe (WBA)	Eduardo Monotoyo	Mexicali, Mexico	Won KO–5
13 May 1990	Fe (WBA)	Chan-Mok Park	Seoul	Won PTS–12

Luisito ESPINOSA

Born: Manila, Philippines, 26 Jun 1967
World title fights: 3 (all bantamweight) won 3, lost 0

17 Oct 1989	B (WBA)	Kaokor Galaxy	Bangkok	Won RSF–1
30 May 1990	B (WBA)	Hurley Snead	Bangkok	Won RTD–9
29 Nov 1990	B (WBA)	Thalerngsak Sitbohbeh	Bangkok	Won PTS–12

Louie ESPINOZA

Born: Phoenix, Arizona, USA, 12 May 1962
World title fights: 7 (4 junior-feather, 3 featherweight) won 4, lost 2, drew 1

16 Jan 1987	JFe (WBA)	Tommy Valoy	Phoenix	Won RSF–4
15 Jul 1987	JFe (WBA)	Manuel Vilchez	Phoenix	Won RSF–15
15 Aug 1987	JFe (WBA)	Mike Ayala	San Antonio, Texas	Won KO–9
28 Nov 1987	JFe (WBA)	Julio Gervacio	San Juan	Lost PTS–12
22 May 1989	Fe (IBF)	Jorge Paez	Phoenix	Drew 12
11 Nov 1989	Fe (WBO)	Maurizio Stecca	Rimini, Italy	Won RSF–7
7 Apr 1990	Fe (IBF/WBO)	Jorge Paez	Las Vegas	Lost PTS–12

Luis ESTABA

Born: Sucre, Venezuela, 13 Aug 1941
World title fights: 14 (all junior-fly) won 12, lost 2

DATE	WEIGHT	OPPONENT	VENUE	RESULT	
13 Sep 1975	JFl (WBC)	Rafael Lovera	Caracas	Won	RSF–4
17 Dec 1975	JFl (WBC)	Takenobu Shimabukuro	Ikinawa, Japan	Won	TKO–10
14 Feb 1976	JFl (WBC)	Leo Palacios	Caracas	Won	PTS–15
1 May 1976	JFl (WBC)	Juan Alvarez	Caracas	Won	PTS–15
18 Jul 1976	JFl (WBC)	Franco Udella	Caracas	Won	KO–3
26 Sep 1976	JFl (WBC)	Rodolfo Rodriguez	Caracas	Won	RTD–10
21 Nov 1976	JFl (WBC)	Valentin Martinez	Caracas	Won	RSF–11
15 May 1977	JFl (WBC)	Rafael Pedroza	Caracas	Won	PTS–15
17 Jul 1977	JFl (WBC)	Ricardo Estupinan	Puerto de la Cruz, Venezuela	Won	PTS–15
21 Aug 1977	JFl (WBC)	Juan Alvarez	Puerto de la Cruz	Won	RSF–11
18 Sep 1977	JFl (WBC)	Orlando Hernandez	Caracas	Won	KO–15
29 Oct 1977	JFl (WBC)	Netrnoi Vorasingh	Caracas	Won	PTS–15
19 Feb 1978	JFl (WBC)	Freddie Castillo	Caracas	Lost	RSF–14
29 Jul 1978	JFl (WBC)	Netrnoi Vorasingh	Caracas	Lost	KO–5

Juan Jose ESTRADA

Born: Tijuana, Mexico, 28 Nov 1963
World title fights: 5 (all junior-feather) won 4, lost 1

DATE	WEIGHT	OPPONENT	VENUE	RESULT	
28 May 1988	JFe (WBA)	Bernardo Pinango	Tijuana, Mexico	Won	PTS–12
15 Oct 1988	JFe (WBA)	Takuya Muguruma	Moriguchi, Japan	Won	RSF–11
5 Apr 1989	JFe (WBA)	Jesus Poll	Los Angeles	Won	RSF–10
12 Jul 1989	JFe (WBA)	Luis Mendoza	Tijuana	Won	PTS–12
11 Dec 1989	JFe (WBA)	Jesus Salud	Los Angeles	Lost	DIS–9

DATE	WEIGHT	OPPONENT	VENUE	RESULT

Chris EUBANK

Born: Dulwich, London, England, 8 Aug 1966
World title fights: 1 (middleweight) won 1, lost 0

DATE	WEIGHT	OPPONENT	VENUE	RESULT
5 Nov 1990	M (WBO)	Nigel Benn	Birmingham	Won RSF-9

Johnny FAMECHON

Born: Paris, France, 28 Mar 1945
World title fights: 4 (all featherweight) won 3, lost 1

DATE	WEIGHT	OPPONENT	VENUE	RESULT
21 Jan 1969	Fe (WBC)	Jose Legra	London	Won PTS-15
28 Jul 1969	Fe (WBC)	Fighting Harada	Sydney	Won PTS-15
6 Jan 1970	Fe (WBC)	Fighting Harada	Tokyo	Won KO-14
9 May 1970	Fe (WBC)	Vicente Saldivar	Rome	Lost PTS-15

Jeff FENECH

Born: Sydney, Australia, 28 May 1964
World title fights: 11 (4 bantamweight, 3 junior-feather, 4 featherweight) won 11, lost 0

DATE	WEIGHT	OPPONENT	VENUE	RESULT
26 Apr 1985	B (IBF)	Satoshi Shingaki	Sydney	Won RSF-9
23 Aug 1985	B (IBF)	Satoshi Shingaki	Sydney	Won RSF-3
1 Dec 1985	B (IBF)	Jerome Coffee	Sydney	Won PTS-15
18 Jul 1986	B (IBF)	Steve McCrory	Sydney	Won RSF-14
8 May 1987	JFe (WBC)	Samart Payakaroon	Sydney	Won RSF-4
10 Jul 1987	JFe (WBC)	Greg Richardson	Sydney	Won RSF-5
16 Oct 1987	JFe (WBC)	Carlos Zarate	Sydney	Won TKO-4
7 Mar 1988	Fe (WBC)	Victor Callejas	Sydney	Won RSF-10
8 Aug 1988	Fe (WBC)	Tyrone Downes	Melbourne	Won RSF-5
30 Nov 1988	Fe (WBC)	George Navarro	Melbourne	Won RSF-5
8 Apr 1989	Fe (WBC)	Marcos Villasana	Melbourne	Won PTS-12

DATE	WEIGHT	OPPONENT	VENUE	RESULT

Orlando FERNANDEZ

Born: Puerto Rico, 18 Jan 1963
World title fights: 1 (junior-feather) won 1, lost 0

DATE	WEIGHT	OPPONENT	VENUE	RESULT
12 May 1990	JFe (WBO)	Valerio Nati	Sassari, Italy	Won RSF–10

Perico FERNANDEZ

Born: Zaragoza, Spain, 19 Nov 1952
World title fights: 4 (all junior-welter) won 2, lost 2

DATE	WEIGHT	OPPONENT	VENUE	RESULT
24 Sep 1974	JW (WBC)	Tetsuo Lion Furuyama	Rome	Won PTS–15
19 Apr 1975	JW (WBC)	Joao Henrique	Barcelona	Won KO–9
15 Jul 1975	JW (WBC)	Saensak Muangsurin	Bangkok	Lost RTD–8
17 Jun 1977	JW (WBC)	Saensak Muangsurin	Madrid	Lost PTS–15

Rube FERNS

Born: Pittsburg, Kansas, USA, 20 Jan 1874
Died: Pittsburg, 11 Jun 1952
World title fights: 5 (all welterweight) won 3, lost 2

DATE	WEIGHT	OPPONENT	VENUE	RESULT
15 Jan 1900	W	Mysterious Billy Smith	Buffalo	Won DIS–21
16 Oct 1900	W	Matty Matthews	Detroit	Lost PTS–15
24 May 1901	W	Matty Matthews	Toronto	Won KO–10
23 Sep 1901	W	Frank Erne	Fort Erie, Canada	Won KO–9
18 Dec 1901	W	Joe Walcott	Fort Erie, Canada	Lost KO–5

Jackie FIELDS

Born: Chicago, USA, 9 Feb 1908
World title fights: 5 (all welterweight) won 3, lost 2

DATE	WEIGHT	OPPONENT	VENUE	RESULT
25 Mar 1929	W	Young Jack Thompson	Chicago	Won PTS–10
25 Jul 1929	W	Joe Dundee	Detroit	Won DIS–2

DATE	WEIGHT	OPPONENT	VENUE	RESULT
9 May 1930	W	Young Jack Thompson	Detroit	Lost PTS–15
28 Jan 1932	W	Lou Brouillard	Chicago	Won PTS–10
22 Feb 1933	W	Young Corbett III	San Francisco	Lost PTS–10

Bob FITZSIMMONS

Born: Helston, Cornwall, England, 26 May 1863
Died: Chicago, 22 Oct 1917
World title fights: 7 (3 heavyweight, 2 middleweight, 2 light-heavy) won 4, lost 3

DATE	WEIGHT	OPPONENT	VENUE	RESULT
14 Jan 1891	M	Jack Dempsey	New Orleans	Won TKO–13
26 Sep 1894	M	Dan Creedon	New Orleans	Won KO–2
17 Mar 1897	H	James J Corbett	Carson City, Nevada	Won KO–14
9 Jun 1899	H	James J Jeffries	Coney Island, New York	Lost KO–11
25 Jul 1902	H	James J Jeffries	San Francisco	Lost KO–8
25 Nov 1903	LH	George Gardner	San Francisco	Won PTS–20
20 Dec 1905	LH	Philadelphia Jack O'Brien	San Francisco	Lost KO–13

Pedro FLORES

Born: Jalisco, Mexico, 14 Jan 1951
World title fights: 3 (all junior-fly) won 1, lost 2

DATE	WEIGHT	OPPONENT	VENUE	RESULT
12 Oct 1980	JFl (WBA)	Yoko Gushiken	Kanazawa, Japan	Lost PTS–15
8 Mar 1981	JFl (WBA)	Yoko Gushiken	Nama, Japan	Won TKO–12
19 Jul 1981	JFl (WBA)	Hwan-Jin Kim	Seoul	Lost RSF–13

Tiger FLOWERS

Born: Camille, Georgia, USA, 5 Aug 1895
Died: New York City, 16 Nov 1927
World title fights: 3 (all middleweight) won 2, lost 1

DATE	WEIGHT	OPPONENT	VENUE	RESULT
26 Feb 1926	M	Harry Greb	New York	Won PTS–15

DATE	WEIGHT	OPPONENT	VENUE	RESULT

19 Aug 1926	M	Harry Greb	New York	Won PTS–15
3 Dec 1926	M	Mickey Walker	Chicago	Lost PTS–10

Harry FORBES

Born: Rockford, Illinois, USA, 13 May 1879
Died: Chicago, 19 Dec 1946
World title fights: 11 (9 bantamweight, 2 featherweight) won 5, lost 5, drew 1

22 Dec 1899	B	Terry McGovern	New York	Lost KO–2
6 Sep 1900	B	Casper Leon	St Joseph, Missouri	Drew 20
2 Apr 1901	B	Casper Leon	Memphis	Won PTS–15
23 Jan 1902	B	Dan Dougherty	St Louis	Won KO–4
27 Feb 1902	B	Tommy Feltz	St Louis	Won PTS–15
23 Dec 1902	B	Frankie Neil	Oakland, California	Won RSF–7
27 Feb 1903	B	Andy Tokell	Detroit	Won PTS–10
13 Aug 1903	B	Frankie Neil	San Francisco	Lost KO–2
1 Feb 1904	Fe	Abe Attell	St Louis	Lost KO–5
17 Jun 1904	B	Frankie Neil	Chicago	Lost KO–3
28 Feb 1910	Fe	Abe Attell	New York	Lost KO–6

George FOREMAN

Born: Marshall, Texas, USA, 22 Jan 1948
World title fights: 4 (all heavyweight) won 3, lost 1

22 Jan 1973	H	Joe Frazier	Kingston, Jamaica	Won RSF–2
1 Sep 1973	H	Joe Roman	Tokyo	Won KO–1
26 Mar 1974	H	Ken Norton	Caracas	Won RSF–2
30 Oct 1974	H	Muhammad Ali	Kinshasa, Zaire	Lost KO–8

DATE	WEIGHT	OPPONENT	VENUE	RESULT

DATE	WEIGHT	OPPONENT	VENUE	RESULT

Bob FOSTER

Born: Albuquerque, New Mexico, USA, 15 Dec 1938
World title fights: 16 (15 light-heavy, 1 heavyweight) won 14, lost 1, drew 1

DATE	WEIGHT	OPPONENT	VENUE	RESULT
24 May 1968	LH	Dick Tiger	New York	Won KO-4
22 Jan 1969	LH	Frank de Paula	New York	Won KO-1
24 May 1969	LH	Andy Kendall	West Springfield, Massachusetts	Won KO-4
4 Apr 1970	LH	Roger Rouse	Missoula, Montana	Won RSF-4
27 Jun 1970	LH	Mark Tessman	Baltimore	Won KO-10
18 Nov 1970	H	Joe Frazier	Detroit	Lost KO-2
2 Mar 1971	LH (WBC)	Hal Carroll	Scranton, Pennsylvania	Won KO-4
24 Apr 1971	LH (WBC)	Ray Anderson	Tampa, Florida	Won PTS-15
30 Oct 1971	LH (WBC)	Tommy Hicks	Scranton	Won RSF-8
16 Dec 1971	LH (WBC)	Brian Kelly	Oklahoma City	Won RSF-3
7 Apr 1972	LH	Vicente Paul Rondon	Miami	Won KO-2
27 Jun 1972	LH	Mike Quarry	Las Vegas	Won KO-4
26 Sep 1972	LH	Chris Finnegan	London	Won KO-14
21 Aug 1973	LH	Pierre Fourie	Albuquerque, New Mexico	Won PTS-15
1 Dec 1973	LH	Pierre Fourie	Johannesburg	Won PTS-15
17 Jun 1974	LH	Jorge Ahumada	Albuquerque	Drew 15

Matt FRANKLIN
see Matthew Saad MUHAMMAD

Alfonso FRAZER

Born: Panama City, Panama, 17 Jan 1948
World title fights: 4 (all junior-welter) won 2, lost 2

DATE	WEIGHT	OPPONENT	VENUE	RESULT
10 Mar 1972	JW (WBA)	Nicolino Loche	Panama City	Won PTS-15

DATE	WEIGHT	OPPONENT	VENUE	RESULT

DATE	WEIGHT	OPPONENT	VENUE	RESULT
17 Jun 1972	JW (WBA)	Al Ford	Panama City	Won KO–5
29 Oct 1972	JW (WBA)	Antonio Cervantes	Panama City	Lost KO–10
19 May 1973	JW (WBA)	Antonio Cervantes	Panama City	Lost RSF–5

Joe FRAZIER

Born: Beaufort, South Carolina, USA, 12 Jan 1944
World title fights: 12 (all heavyweight) won 10, lost 2

DATE	WEIGHT	OPPONENT	VENUE	RESULT
4 Mar 1968	H (NY)	Buster Matthis	New York	Won RSF–11
24 Jun 1968	H (NY)	Manuel Ramos	New York	Won RTD–2
6 Dec 1968	H (NY)	Oscar Bonavena	Philadelphia	Won PTS–15
22 Apr 1969	H (NY)	Dave Zyglewicz	Houston	Won KO–1
23 Jun 1969	H (NY)	Jerry Quarry	New York	Won RSF–7
16 Feb 1970	H	Jimmy Ellis	New York	Won RTD–4
18 Nov 1970	H	Bob Foster	Detroit	Won KO–2
8 Mar 1971	H	Muhammad Ali	New York	Won PTS–15
15 Jan 1972	H	Terry Daniels	New Orleans	Won RSF–4
25 May 1972	H	Ron Stander	Omaha, Nebraska	Won RSF–5
22 Jan 1973	H	George Foreman	Kingston, Jamaica	Lost RSF–2
1 Oct 1975	H	Muhammad Ali	Manila	Lost RTD–14

Tommy FREEMAN

Born: Hot Springs, Arkansas, USA, 22 Jan 1904
Died: Little Rock, Arkansas, 25 Feb 1986
World title fights: 7 (all welterweight) won 6, lost 1

DATE	WEIGHT	OPPONENT	VENUE	RESULT
5 Sep 1930	W	Young Jack Thompson	Cleveland	Won PTS–15
9 Jan 1931	W	Pete August	Hot Springs, Arkansas	Won PTS–10
26 Jan 1931	W	Eddie Murdock	Oklahoma City	Won PTS–10
5 Feb 1931	W	Duke Trammel	Memphis	Won KO–5

DATE	WEIGHT	OPPONENT	VENUE	RESULT

DATE	WEIGHT	OPPONENT	VENUE	RESULT
9 Feb 1931	W	Al 'Kid' Kober	New Orleans	Won KO–5
1 Mar 1931	W	Alfredo Gaona	Mexico City	Won KO–12
14 Apr 1931	W	Young Jack Thompson	Cleveland	Lost KO–12

Arturio FRIAS

Born: Montebello, California, USA, 27 Oct 1956
World title fights: 3 (all lightweight) won 2, lost 1

DATE	WEIGHT	OPPONENT	VENUE	RESULT
5 Dec 1981	L (WBA)	Claude Noel	Las Vegas	Won KO–8
30 Jan 1982	L (WBA)	Ernesto Espana	Los Angeles	Won TKO–9
8 May 1982	L (WBA)	Ray Mancini	Las Vegas	Lost RSF–1

Paul FUJII

Born: Honolulu, Hawaii, USA, 6 Jul 1940
World title fights: 3 (all junior-welter) won 2, lost 1

DATE	WEIGHT	OPPONENT	VENUE	RESULT
30 Apr 1967	JW	Sandro Lopopolo	Tokyo	Won RTD–2
16 Nov 1967	JW	Willi Quatour	Tokyo	Won KO–4
12 Dec 1968	JW (WBA)	Nicolino Loche	Tokyo	Lost RTD–9

Gene FULLMER

Born: West Jordan, Utah, USA, 21 Jul 1931
World title fights: 13 (all middleweight) won 7, lost 3, drew 3

DATE	WEIGHT	OPPONENT	VENUE	RESULT
2 Jan 1957	M	Sugar Ray Robinson	New York	Won PTS–15
1 May 1957	M	Sugar Ray Robinson	Chicago	Lost KO–5
28 Aug 1959	M (NBA)	Carmen Basilio	San Francisco	Won KO–14
4 Dec 1959	M (NBA)	Spider Webb	Logan, Utah	Won PTS–15
20 Apr 1960	M (NBA)	Joey Giardello	Bozeman, Montana	Drew 15
29 Jun 1960	M (NBA)	Carmen Basilio	Salt Lake City	Won KO–12

DATE	WEIGHT	OPPONENT	VENUE	RESULT

DATE	WEIGHT	OPPONENT	VENUE	RESULT
3 Dec 1960	M (NBA)	Sugar Ray Robinson	Los Angeles	Drew 15
4 Mar 1961	M (NBA)	Sugar Ray Robinson	Las Vegas	Won PTS–15
5 Aug 1961	M (NBA)	Florentino Fernandez	Ogden, Utah	Won PTS–15
9 Dec 1961	M (NBA)	Benny Paret	Las Vegas	Won KO–10
23 Oct 1962	M (NBA)	Dick Tiger	San Francisco	Lost PTS–15
23 Feb 1963	M	Dick Tiger	Las Vegas	Drew 15
10 Aug 1963	M	Dick Tiger	Ibadan, Nigeria	Lost KO–7

Kaokor GALAXY

Born: Petchaboon, Thailand, 15 May 1959
World title fights: 4 (all bantamweight) won 2, lost 2

DATE	WEIGHT	OPPONENT	VENUE	RESULT
9 May 1988	B (WBA)	Wilfredo Vasquez	Bangkok	Won PTS–12
14 Aug 1988	B (WBA)	Sung-Kil Moon	Pusan, S Korea	Lost TD–6
7 Jul 1989	B (WBA)	Sung-Kil Moon	Bangkok	Won PTS–12
17 Oct 1989	B (WBA)	Luisito Espinosa	Bangkok	Lost RSF–1

Kaosai GALAXY

Born: Petchaboon, Thailand, 15 May 1959
World title fights: 17 (all junior-bantam) won 17, lost 0

DATE	WEIGHT	OPPONENT	VENUE	RESULT
21 Nov 1984	JB (WBA)	Eusebio Espinal	Bangkok	Won KO–6
6 Mar 1985	JB (WBA)	Dong-Chun Lee	Bangkok	Won KO–7
17 Jul 1985	JB (WBA)	Rafael Orono	Bangkok	Won RSF–5
23 Dec 1985	JB (WBA)	Edgar Monserrat	Bangkok	Won TKO–2
1 Nov 1986	JB (WBA)	Israel Contreras	Willemstad, Netherlands Antilles	Won KO–5
28 Feb 1987	JB (WBA)	Ellyas Pical	Jakarta	Won KO–14
12 Oct 1987	JB (WBA)	Byong-Kwan Chung	Bangkok	Won KO–3
26 Jan 1988	JB (WBA)	Kongtoranee Payakaroon	Bangkok	Won PTS–12

DATE	WEIGHT	OPPONENT	VENUE	RESULT

DATE	WEIGHT	OPPONENT	VENUE	RESULT
9 Oct 1988	JB (WBA)	Chang-Ho Choi	Seoul	Won KO–8
15 Jan 1989	JB (WBA)	Tae-Il Chang	Bangkok	Won KO–2
8 Apr 1989	JB (WBA)	Kenji Matsumura	Yokohama, Japan	Won PTS–12
29 Jul 1989	JB (WBA)	Alberto Castro	Surin, Thailand	Won RTD–10
31 Oct 1989	JB (WBA)	Kenji Matsumura	Kobe, Japan	Won KO–12
29 Mar 1990	JB (WBA)	Ari Blanca	Bangkok	Won KO–5
30 Jun 1990	JB (WBA)	Shunichi Nakajima	Chiangmai, Thailand	Won RSF–8
29 Sep 1990	JB (WBA)	Yong-Kang Kim	Suphan Buri, Thailand	Won KO–6
9 Dec 1990	JB (WBA)	Ernesto Ford	Petchabun, Thailand	Won KO–6

Victor GALINDEZ

Born: Vedia, Buenos Aires, Argentina, 2 Nov 1948
Died: De Mayo, Argentina, 26 Oct 1980
World title fights: 14 (all light-heavy) won 12, lost 2

DATE	WEIGHT	OPPONENT	VENUE	RESULT
7 Dec 1974	LH (WBA)	Len Hutchins	Buenos Aires	Won RTD–13
7 Apr 1975	LH (WBA)	Pierre Fourie	Johannesburg	Won PTS–15
30 Jun 1975	LH (WBA)	Jorge Ahumada	New York	Won PTS–15
13 Sep 1975	LH (WBA)	Pierre Fourie	Johannesburg	Won PTS–15
28 Mar 1976	LH (WBA)	Harald Skog	Oslo	Won RTD–3
22 May 1976	LH (WBA)	Richie Kates	Johannesburg	Won KO–15
5 Oct 1976	LH (WBA)	Kosie Smith	Johannesburg	Won PTS–15
18 Jun 1977	LH (WBA)	Richie Kates	Rome	Won PTS–15
17 Sep 1977	LH (WBA)	Alvaro Lopez	Rome	Won PTS–15
19 Nov 1977	LH (WBA)	Eddie Gregory	Turin	Won PTS–15
6 May 1978	LH (WBA)	Alvaro Lopez	Via Reggio, Italy	Won PTS–15
15 Sep 1978	LH (WBA)	Mike Rossman	New Orleans	Lost RSF–13
14 Apr 1979	LH (WBA)	Mike Rossman	New Orleans	Won RTD–10
30 Nov 1979	LH (WBA)	Marvin Johnson	New Orleans	Lost KO–11

DATE	WEIGHT	OPPONENT	VENUE	RESULT

Manning GALLOWAY

Born: Columbus, Ohio, USA, 27 Apr 1960
World title fights: 2 (both welterweight) won 2, lost 0

DATE	WEIGHT	OPPONENT	VENUE	RESULT	
15 Dec 1989	W (WBO)	Ali Hamza	Yabucua, Puerto Rico	Won	PTS–12
25 Aug 1990	W (WBO)	Nika Khumalo	Lewiston, Maine	Won	PTS–12

Leo GAMEZ

Born: Panama, 8 Aug 1963
World title fights: 4 (2 strawweight, 2 junior-fly) won 2, lost 2

DATE	WEIGHT	OPPONENT	VENUE	RESULT	
10 Jan 1988	S (WBA)	Kim-Bong Jun	Pusan, S Korea	Won	PTS–12
24 Apr 1988	S (WBA)	Kenji Yokozawa	Tokyo	Won	RSF–3
29 Apr 1990	JFl (WBA)	Myung-Woo Yuh	Seoul	Lost	PTS–12
10 Nov 1990	JFl (WBA)	Myung-Woo Yuh	Seoul	Lost	PTS–12

Joe GANS

Born: Baltimore, USA, 25 Nov 1874
Died: Baltimore, 10 Aug 1910
World title fights: 13 (all lightweight) won 10, lost 3

DATE	WEIGHT	OPPONENT	VENUE	RESULT	
23 Mar 1900	L	Frank Erne	New York	Lost	KO–12
12 May 1902	L	Frank Erne	Fort Erie, Canada	Won	KO–1
17 Sep 1902	L	Gus Gardner	Baltimore	Won	KO–5
11 Mar 1903	L	Steve Crosby	Hot Springs, Arkansas	Won	KO–11
28 Mar 1904	L	Gus Gardner	Saginaw, Michigan	Won	PTS–10
31 Oct 1904	L	Jimmy Britt	San Francisco	Won	DIS–5
3 Sep 1906	L	Battling Nelson	Goldfield, Nevada	Won	DIS–42
9 Sep 1907	L	Jimmy Britt	San Francisco	Won	KO–6
27 Sep 1907	L	George Memsic	Los Angeles	Won	PTS–20
1 Apr 1908	L	Spike Robson	Philadelphia	Won	KO–3

DATE	WEIGHT	OPPONENT	VENUE	RESULT

DATE	WEIGHT	OPPONENT	VENUE	RESULT
14 May 1908	L	Rudy Unholz	San Francisco	Won KO–11
4 Jul 1908	L	Battling Nelson	San Francisco	Lost KO–17
9 Sep 1908	L	Battling Nelson	Colma	Lost KO–21

Ceferino GARCIA

Born: Manila, Philippines, 26 Aug 1910
Died: San Diego, 1 Jan 1981
World title fights: 6 (2 welterweight, 4 middleweight) won 2, lost 3, drew 1

DATE	WEIGHT	OPPONENT	VENUE	RESULT
23 Sep 1937	W	Barney Ross	New York	Lost PTS–15
25 Nov 1938	W	Henry Armstrong	New York	Lost PTS–15
2 Oct 1939	M (NY)	Fred Apostoli	New York	Won KO–7
23 Dec 1939	M (NY)	Glen Lee	Manila	Won KO–13
1 Mar 1940	M (NY)	Henry Armstrong	Los Angeles	Drew 10
23 May 1940	M (NY)	Ken Overlin	New York	Lost PTS–15

George GARDNER

Born: Lindoonvarna, County Clare, Ireland, 17 Mar 1877
Died: Chicago, 8 Jul 1954
World title fights: 2 (both light-heavy) won 1, lost 1

DATE	WEIGHT	OPPONENT	VENUE	RESULT
4 Jul 1903	LH	Jack Root	Fort Erie, Canada	Won KO–12
25 Nov 1903	LH	Bob Fitzsimmons	San Francisco	Lost PTS–20

Jaime GARZA

Born: Santa Cruz, California, USA, 10 Sep 1959
World title fights: 3 (all junior-feather) won 2, lost 1

DATE	WEIGHT	OPPONENT	VENUE	RESULT
15 Jun 1983	JFe (WBC)	Bobby Berna	Los Angeles	Won RSF–2
26 May 1984	JFe (WBC)	Felipe Orozco	Miami	Won KO–3
3 Nov 1984	JFe (WBC)	Juan 'Kid' Meza	New York	Lost KO–1

DATE	WEIGHT	OPPONENT	VENUE	RESULT

Loreto GARZA

Born: Sacramento, California, USA, 23 May 1962
World title fights: 2 (both junior-welter) won 2, lost 0

DATE	WEIGHT	OPPONENT	VENUE	RESULT
17 Aug 1990	JW (WBA)	Juan Martin Coggi	Nice	Won PTS–12
1 Dec 1990	JW (WBA)	Vinny Pazienza	Sacramento, California	Won DIS–11

Kid GAVILAN

Born: Camaguey, Cuba, 6 Jan 1926
World title fights: 11 (10 welterweight, 1 middleweight) won 8, lost 3

DATE	WEIGHT	OPPONENT	VENUE	RESULT
11 Jul 1949	W	Sugar Ray Robinson	Philadelphia	Lost PTS–15
18 May 1951	W	Johnny Bratton	New York	Won PTS–15
29 Aug 1951	W	Billy Graham	New York	Won PTS–15
4 Feb 1952	W	Bobby Dykes	Miami	Won PTS–15
7 Jul 1952	W	Gil Turner	Philadelphia	Won KO–11
5 Oct 1952	W	Billy Graham	Havana	Won PTS–15
11 Feb 1953	W	Chuck Davey	Chicago	Won KO–10
18 Sep 1953	W	Carmen Basilio	Syracuse, New York	Won PTS–15
13 Nov 1953	W	Johnny Bratton	Chicago	Won PTS–15
2 Apr 1954	M	Carl 'Bobo' Olson	Chicago	Lost PTS–15
20 Oct 1954	W	Johnny Saxton	Philadelphia	Lost PTS–15

Eddie GAZO

Born: San Lorenzo, Managua, Nicaragua, 12 Sep 1950
World title fights: 5 (all junior-middle) won 4, lost 1

DATE	WEIGHT	OPPONENT	VENUE	RESULT
6 Mar 1977	JM (WBA)	Miguel Angel Castellini	Managua	Won PTS–15
7 Jun 1977	JM (WBA)	Koichi Wajima	Tokyo	Won RSF–11
13 Sep 1977	JM (WBA)	Kenji Shibata	Tokyo	Won PTS–15

18 Dec 1977	JM (WBA)	Lim-Jao Keun	Inchon, S Korea	Won PTS–15
9 Aug 1978	JM (WBA)	Masashi Kudo	Akita, Japan	Lost PTS–15

Frankie GENARO

Born: New York City, USA, 26 Aug 1901
Died: New York City, 27 Dec 1966
World title fights: 13 (all flyweight) won 8, lost 3, drew 2

28 Nov 1927	Fl (NBA)	Albert 'Frenchy' Belanger	Toronto	Lost PTS–10
6 Feb 1928	Fl (NBA)	Albert 'Frenchy' Belanger	Toronto	Won PTS–10
2 Mar 1929	Fl (NBA)	Emile Pladner	Paris	Lost KO–1
18 Apr 1929	Fl (NBA)	Emile Pladner	Paris	Won DIS–5
17 Oct 1929	Fl (NBA)	Ernie Jarvis	London	Won PTS–15
18 Jan 1930	Fl (NBA)	Yvon Trevidic	Paris	Won TKO–12
10 Jun 1930	Fl (NBA)	Albert 'Frenchy' Belanger	Toronto	Won PTS–10
6 Aug 1930	Fl (NBA)	Willie La Morte	Newark, New Jersey	Won PTS–10
26 Dec 1930	Fl (NBA)	Midget Wolgast	New York	Drew 15
25 Mar 1931	Fl (NBA)	Victor Ferrand	Barcelona	Drew 15
30 Jul 1931	Fl (NBA)	Jackie Harmon	Waterbury, Connecticut	Won KO–6
3 Oct 1931	Fl (NBA)	Valentin Angelmann	Paris	Won PTS–15
27 Oct 1931	Fl (NBA)	Young Perez	Paris	Lost KO–2

Julio GERVACIO

Born: La Romana, Dominican Republic, 17 Oct 1967
World title fights: 3 (all junior-feather) won 1, lost 2

28 Nov 1987	JFe (WBA)	Louie Espinoza	San Juan	Won PTS–12
27 Feb 1988	JFe (WBA)	Bernardo Pinango	San Juan	Lost PTS–12
29 Apr 1989	JFe (WBO)	Kenny Mitchell	San Juan	Lost PTS–12

Joey GIARDELLO

Born: Brooklyn, New York, USA, 16 Jul 1930
World title fights: 4 (all middleweight) won 2, lost 1, drew 1

DATE	WEIGHT	OPPONENT	VENUE	RESULT	
20 Apr 1960	M (NBA)	Gene Fullmer	Bozeman, Montana	Drew	15
7 Dec 1963	M	Dick Tiger	New York	Won	PTS–15
14 Dec 1964	M	Rubin Carter	Philadelphia	Won	PTS–15
21 Oct 1965	M	Dick Tiger	New York	Lost	PTS–15

Bob GODWIN

Born: Moultrie, Georgia, USA, 5 May 1911
World title fights: 2 (both light-heavy) won 1, lost 1

DATE	WEIGHT	OPPONENT	VENUE	RESULT	
1 Mar 1933	LH (NBA)	Joe Knight	West Palm Beach, Florida	Won	PTS–10
24 Mar 1933	LH	Maxie Rosenbloom	New York	Lost	KO–4

Abe GOLDSTEIN

Born: New York City, USA, 10 Sep 1898
Died: St Petersburg, Florida, 12 Feb 1977
World title fights: 5 (all bantamweight) won 4, lost 1

DATE	WEIGHT	OPPONENT	VENUE	RESULT	
19 Oct 1923	B (NY)	Joe Burman	New York	Won	PTS–12
21 Mar 1924	B	Joe Lynch	New York	Won	PTS–15
16 Jul 1924	B	Charles Ledoux	New York	Won	PTS–15
8 Sep 1924	B	Tommy Ryan	New York	Won	PTS–15
19 Dec 1924	B	Eddie 'Cannonball' Martin	New York	Lost	PTS–15

DATE	WEIGHT	OPPONENT	VENUE	RESULT

Harold GOMES

Born: Providence, Rhode Island, 22 Aug 1933
World title fights: 3 (all junior-light) won 1, lost 2

DATE	WEIGHT	OPPONENT	VENUE	RESULT	
20 Jul 1959	JL	Paul Jorgensen	Providence, Rhode Island	Won	PTS–15
16 Mar 1960	JL	Flash Elorde	Manila	Lost	RSF–7
17 Aug 1960	JL	Flash Elorde	San Francisco	Lost	KO–1

Antonio GOMEZ

Born: Cumana, Venezuela, 30 Sep 1945
World title fights: 4 (all featherweight) won 2, lost 2

DATE	WEIGHT	OPPONENT	VENUE	RESULT	
2 Sep 1971	Fe (WBA)	Sho Saijyo	Tokyo	Won	RSF–5
5 Feb 1972	Fe (WBA)	Raul Martinez	Maracay, Venezuela	Won	KO–7
19 Aug 1972	Fe (WBA)	Ernesto Marcel	Maracay	Lost	PTS–15
14 Jul 1973	Fe (WBA)	Ernesto Marcel	Panama City	Lost	RTD–11

Wilfredo GOMEZ

Born: Las Monjas, Puerto Rico, 29 Oct 1956
World title fights: 23 (18 junior-feather, 3 featherweight, 2 junior-light)
won 20, lost 3

DATE	WEIGHT	OPPONENT	VENUE	RESULT	
21 May 1977	JFe (WBC)	Dong-Kyun Yum	San Juan	Won	KO–12
11 Jul 1977	JFe (WBC)	Raul Tirado	San Juan	Won	KO–5
19 Jan 1978	JFe (WBC)	Royal Kobayashi	Kitakyushu, Japan	Won	KO–3
8 Apr 1978	JFe (WBC)	Juan Antonio Lopez	Bayamon, Puerto Rico	Won	RSF–7
2 Jun 1978	JFe (WBC)	Sakad Porntavee	Korat, Thailand	Won	RSF–3
9 Sep 1978	JFe (WBC)	Leonardo Cruz	San Juan	Won	RSF–13
28 Oct 1978	JFe (WBC)	Carlos Zarate	San Juan	Won	RSF–5
9 Mar 1979	JFe (WBC)	Nestor Jiminez	New York	Won	RSF–5
16 Jun 1979	JFe (WBC)	Julio Hernandez	San Juan	Won	KO–5

DATE	WEIGHT	OPPONENT	VENUE	RESULT

DATE	WEIGHT	OPPONENT	VENUE	RESULT
28 Sep 1979	JFe (WBC)	Carlos Mendoza	Las Vegas	Won KO–10
26 Oct 1979	JFe (WBC)	Nicky Perez	New York	Won KO–5
3 Feb 1980	JFe (WBC)	Ruben Valdez	Las Vegas	Won KO–6
22 Aug 1980	JFe (WBC)	Derrick Holmes	Las Vegas	Won RSF–5
13 Dec 1980	JFe (WBC)	Jose Cervantes	Miami	Won KO–3
21 Aug 1981	Fe (WBC)	Salvador Sanchez	Las Vegas	Lost RSF–8
27 Mar 1982	JFe (WBC)	Juan 'Kid' Meza	Atlantic City	Won RSF–6
11 Jun 1982	JFe (WBC)	Juan Antonio Lopez	Las Vegas	Won KO–10
18 Aug 1982	JFe (WBC)	Roberto Rubaldino	San Juan	Won RTD–7
3 Dec 1982	JFe (WBC)	Lupe Pintor	New Orleans	Won RSF–14
31 Mar 1984	Fe (WBC)	Juan Laporte	San Juan	Won PTS–12
8 Dec 1984	Fe (WBC)	Azumah Nelson	San Juan	Lost RSF–11
19 May 1985	JL (WBA)	Rocky Lockridge	San Juan	Won PTS–15
24 May 1986	JL (WBA)	Alfredo Layne	San Juan	Lost RSF–9

Betulio GONZALEZ

Born: Maracaibo, Venezuela, 24 Oct 1949
World title fights: 17 (all flyweight) won 7, lost 8, drew 2

DATE	WEIGHT	OPPONENT	VENUE	RESULT
1 Apr 1971	Fl (WBA)	Masao Ohba	Tokyo	Lost PTS–15
20 Nov 1971	Fl (WBC)	Erbito Salavarria	Maracaibo, Venezuela	Drew 15
3 Jun 1972	Fl (WBC)	Socrates Batoto	Caracas	Won KO–4
29 Sep 1972	Fl (WBC)	Venice Borkorsor	Bangkok	Lost RTD–10
4 Aug 1973	Fl (WBC)	Miguel Canto	Maracaibo	Won PTS–15
17 Nov 1973	Fl (WBC)	Alberto Morales	Caracas	Won RSF–11
20 Jul 1974	Fl (WBC)	Franco Udella	Sabbiadoro, Italy	Won RSF–10
1 Oct 1974	Fl (WBC)	Shoji Oguma	Tokyo	Lost PTS–15
24 May 1975	Fl (WBC)	Miguel Canto	Monterrey, Mexico	Lost PTS–15
3 Oct 1976	Fl (WBC)	Miguel Canto	Caracas	Lost PTS–15
13 Aug 1978	Fl (WBA)	Guty Espadas	Maracay, Venezuela	Won PTS–15

DATE	WEIGHT	OPPONENT	VENUE	RESULT

DATE	WEIGHT	OPPONENT	VENUE	RESULT
4 Nov 1978	Fl (WBA)	Martin Vargas	Maracay	Won RSF–12
29 Jan 1979	Fl (WBA)	Shoji Oguma	Hamamatsu, Japan	Drew 15
6 Jul 1979	Fl (WBA)	Shoji Oguma	Utsunomiya, Japan	Won KO–12
17 Nov 1979	Fl (WBA)	Luis Ibarra	Maracay	Lost PTS–15
20 Dec 1981	Fl (WBA)	Juan Herrera	Mexico City	Lost RSF–7
14 Aug 1982	Fl (WBA)	Santos Laciar	Maracaibo	Lost PTS–15

Humberto GONZALEZ

Born: Nezahualcoyotl, Mexico, 25 Mar 1966
World title fights: 5 (all junior-fly) won 5, lost 0

DATE	WEIGHT	OPPONENT	VENUE	RESULT
25 Jun 1989	JFl (WBC)	Yul-Woo Lee	Chongju, S Korea	Won PTS–12
9 Dec 1989	JFl (WBC)	Jung-Koo Chang	Seoul	Won PTS–12
24 Mar 1990	JFl (WBC)	Francisco Tejedor	Mexico City	Won KO–3
4 Jun 1990	JFl (WBC)	Luis Monzote	Inglewood, California	Won RSF–3
23 Jul 1990	JFl (WBC)	Jeung-Keun Lim	Inglewood	Won RSF–5

Rodolfo GONZALEZ

Born: Zapopan, Jalisco, Mexico, 16 Dec 1945
World title fights: 5 (all lightweight) won 3, lost 2

DATE	WEIGHT	OPPONENT	VENUE	RESULT
10 Nov 1972	L (WBC)	Chango Carmona	Los Angeles	Won RTD–12
17 Mar 1973	L (WBC)	Ruben Navarro	Los Angeles	Won RSF–9
27 Oct 1973	L (WBC)	Antonio Puddu	Los Angeles	Won RTD–10
11 Apr 1974	L (WBC)	Guts Ishimatsu	Tokyo	Lost KO–8
28 Nov 1974	L (WBC)	Guts Ishimatsu	Osaka, Japan	Lost KO–12

DATE	WEIGHT	OPPONENT	VENUE	RESULT

DATE	WEIGHT	OPPONENT	VENUE	RESULT

Jimmy GOODRICH

Born: Scranton, Pennsylvania, USA, 30 Jul 1900
Died: Fort Myers, Florida, 25 Dec 1982
World title fights: 2 (both lightweight) won 1, lost 1

DATE	WEIGHT	OPPONENT	VENUE	RESULT	
13 Jul 1925	L	Stanislaus Loayza	Long Island, New York	Won	RTD–2
8 Dec 1925	L	Rocky Kansas	Buffalo	Lost	PTS–15

S T GORDON

Born: Pascoe, Washington, USA, 18 Apr 1959
World title fights: 3 (all cruiserweight) won 2, lost 1

DATE	WEIGHT	OPPONENT	VENUE	RESULT	
27 Jun 1982	C (WBC)	Carlos DeLeon	Highland Heights, Ohio	Won	RSF–2
17 Feb 1983	C (WBC)	Jesse Burnett	East Rutherford, New Jersey	Won	RSF–8
17 Jul 1983	C (WBC)	Carlos DeLeon	Las Vegas	Lost	PTS–12

Bushy GRAHAM

Born: Italy, 18 Jun 1903
Died: Utica, New York, 5 Aug 1982
World title fights: 2 (both bantamweight) won 1, lost 1

DATE	WEIGHT	OPPONENT	VENUE	RESULT	
4 Feb 1927	B	Charley Phil Rosenberg	New York	Lost	PTS–15
23 May 1928	B (NY)	Izzy Schwartz	Brooklyn, New York	Won	PTS–15

Rocky GRAZIANO

Born: New York City, USA, 7 Jun 1922
Died: New York City, 23 May 1990
World title fights: 4 (all middleweight) won 1, lost 3

DATE	WEIGHT	OPPONENT	VENUE	RESULT	
27 Sep 1946	M	Tony Zale	New York	Lost	KO–6
16 Jul 1947	M	Tony Zale	Chicago	Won	KO–6

DATE	WEIGHT	OPPONENT	VENUE	RESULT

DATE	WEIGHT	OPPONENT	VENUE	RESULT
10 Jun 1948	M	Tony Zale	Newark, New Jersey	Lost KO–3
16 Apr 1952	M	Sugar Ray Robinson	Chicago	Lost KO–3

Harry GREB

Born: Pittsburgh, USA, 6 Jun 1894
Died: Atlantic City, 22 Oct 1926
World title fights: 9 (all middleweight) won 7, lost 2

DATE	WEIGHT	OPPONENT	VENUE	RESULT
31 Aug 1923	M	Johnny Wilson	New York	Won PTS–15
3 Dec 1923	M	Bryan Downey	Pittsburgh	Won PTS–10
18 Jan 1924	M	Johnny Wilson	New York	Won PTS–15
24 Mar 1924	M	Fay Keiser	Baltimore	Won KO–12
26 Jun 1924	M	Ted Moore	New York	Won PTS–15
2 Jul 1925	M	Mickey Walker	New York	Won PTS–15
13 Nov 1925	M	Tony Marullo	New Orleans	Won PTS–15
26 Feb 1926	M	Tiger Flowers	New York	Lost PTS–15
19 Aug 1926	M	Tiger Flowers	New York	Lost PTS–15

Eddie GREGORY
see Eddie Mustafa MUHAMMAD

Emile GRIFFITH

Born: St Thomas, Virgin Islands, 3 Feb 1938
World title fights: 22 (13 welterweight, 8 middleweight, 1 junior-middle)
won 14, lost 8

DATE	WEIGHT	OPPONENT	VENUE	RESULT
1 Apr 1961	W	Benny Paret	Miami	Won KO–13
3 Jun 1961	W	Gaspar Ortega	Los Angeles	Won RSF–12
30 Sep 1961	W	Benny Paret	New York	Lost PTS–15

DATE	WEIGHT	OPPONENT	VENUE	RESULT

DATE	WEIGHT	OPPONENT	VENUE	RESULT
24 Mar 1962	W	Benny Paret	New York	Won RSF–12
13 Jul 1962	W	Ralph Dupas	Las Vegas	Won PTS–15
8 Dec 1962	W	Jorge Fernandez	Las Vegas	Won RSF–9
21 Mar 1963	W	Luis Rodriguez	Los Angeles	Lost PTS–15
8 Jun 1963	W	Luis Rodriguez	New York	Won PTS–15
12 Jun 1964	W	Luis Rodriguez	Las Vegas	Won PTS–15
22 Sep 1964	W	Brian Curvis	London	Won PTS–15
30 Mar 1965	W	Jose Stable	New York	Won PTS–15
10 Dec 1965	W	Manuel Gonzalez	New York	Won PTS–15
25 Apr 1966	M	Dick Tiger	New York	Won PTS–15
13 Jul 1966	M	Joey Archer	New York	Won PTS–15
23 Jan 1967	M	Joey Archer	New York	Won PTS–15
17 Apr 1967	M	Nino Benvenuti	New York	Lost PTS–15
29 Sep 1967	M	Nino Benvenuti	New York	Won PTS–15
4 Mar 1968	M	Nino Benvenuti	New York	Lost PTS–15
17 Oct 1969	W	Jose Napoles	Los Angeles	Lost PTS–15
25 Sep 1971	M	Carlos Monzon	Buenos Aires	Lost RSF–14
2 Jun 1973	M	Carlos Monzon	Monte Carlo	Lost PTS–15
18 Sep 1976	JM (WBC)	Eckhard Dagge	Berlin	Lost PTS–15

Calvin GROVE

Born: Pottstown, Philadelphia, USA, 5 Aug 1962
World title fights: 4 (all featherweight) won 2, lost 2

DATE	WEIGHT	OPPONENT	VENUE	RESULT
23 Jan 1988	Fe (IBF)	Antonio Rivera	Gamaches, France	Won RSF–4
17 Apr 1988	Fe (IBF)	Myron Taylor	Atlantic City	Won PTS–15
4 Aug 1988	Fe (IBF)	Jorge Paez	Mexicali, Mexico	Lost PTS–15
30 Mar 1989	Fe (IBF)	Jorge Paez	Mexicali	Lost KO–11

DATE	WEIGHT	OPPONENT	VENUE	RESULT

Yoko GUSHIKEN

Born: Okinawa, Japan, 28 Jun 1955
World title fights: 15 (all junior-fly) won 14, lost 1

DATE	WEIGHT	OPPONENT	VENUE	RESULT
10 Oct 1976	JFl (WBA)	Juan Guzman	Kofu, Japan	Won KO–7
30 Jan 1977	JFl (WBA)	Jaime Rios	Tokyo	Won PTS–15
22 May 1977	JFl (WBA)	Rigoberto Marcano	Sapporo, Japan	Won PTS–15
9 Oct 1977	JFl (WBA)	Montsayarm Mahachai	Oita, Japan	Won KO–4
29 Jan 1978	JFl (WBA)	Anaceto Vargas	Nagoya, Japan	Won KO–14
7 May 1978	JFl (WBA)	Jaime Rios	Tokyo	Won RSF–13
15 Oct 1978	JFl (WBA)	Sang-Il Chung	Tokyo	Won KO–5
7 Jan 1979	JFl (WBA)	Rigoberto Marcano	Kawasaki, Japan	Won KO–7
8 Apr 1979	JFl (WBA)	Alfonso Lopez	Tokyo	Won KO–7
29 Jul 1979	JFl (WBA)	Rafael Pedroza	Kitakyashu, Japan	Won PTS–15
28 Oct 1979	JFl (WBA)	Tito Abella	Tokyo	Won RSF–7
27 Jan 1980	JFl (WBA)	Young-Hyun Kim	Osaka, Japan	Won PTS–15
1 Jun 1980	JFl (WBA)	Martin Vargas	Kochi, Japan	Won RSF–8
12 Oct 1980	JFl (WBA)	Pedro Flores	Kanazawa, Japan	Won PTS–15
8 Mar 1981	JFl (WBA)	Pedro Flores	Nama, Japan	Lost TKO–12

Juan GUZMAN

Born: Santiago, Dominican Republic, 21 Aug 1951
World title fights: 2 (both junior-fly) won 1, lost 1

DATE	WEIGHT	OPPONENT	VENUE	RESULT
1 Jul 1976	JFl (WBA)	Jaime Rios	Santo Domingo	Won PTS–15
10 Oct 1976	JFl (WBA)	Yoko Gushiken	Kofu, Japan	Lost KO–7

Marvin HAGLER

Born: Newark, New Jersey, USA, 23 May 1954
World title fights: 15 (all middleweight) won 13, lost 1, drew 1

DATE	WEIGHT	OPPONENT	VENUE	RESULT
30 Nov 1979	M	Vito Antuofermo	Las Vegas	Drew 15
27 Sep 1980	M	Alan Minter	London	Won RSF–3
17 Jan 1981	M	Fulgencio Obelmejias	Boston	Won RSF–8
13 Jun 1981	M	Vito Antuofermo	Boston	Won RTD–4
3 Oct 1981	M	Mustafa Hamsho	Rosemont, Illinois	Won RSF–11
7 Mar 1982	M	William Lee	Atlantic City	Won RSF–1
31 Oct 1982	M	Fulgencio Obelmejias	San Remo, Italy	Won KO–5
11 Feb 1983	M	Tony Sibson	Worcester, Massachusetts	Won RSF–6
27 May 1983	M	Wilford Scypion	Providence, Rhode Island	Won KO–4
10 Nov 1983	M	Roberto Duran	Las Vegas	Won PTS–15
30 Mar 1984	M	Juan Roldan	Las Vegas	Won RSF–10
20 Oct 1984	M	Mustafa Hamsho	New York	Won RSF–3
15 Apr 1985	M	Thomas Hearns	Las Vegas	Won RSF–3
10 Mar 1986	M	John Mugabi	Las Vegas	Won KO–11
6 Apr 1987	M (WBC)	Sugar Ray Leonard	Las Vegas	Lost PTS–12

Leroy HALEY

Born: Garland County, Arkansas, USA, 27 Dec 1954
World title fights: 6 (all junior-welter) won 3, lost 3

DATE	WEIGHT	OPPONENT	VENUE	RESULT
26 Jun 1982	JW (WBC)	Saoul Mamby	Highland Heights, Ohio	Won PTS–15
20 Oct 1982	JW (WBC)	Juan Jose Gimenez	Cleveland	Won PTS–15
13 Feb 1983	JW (WBC)	Saoul Mamby	Cleveland	Won PTS–12
18 May 1983	JW (WBC)	Bruce Curry	Las Vegas	Lost PTS–12
20 Oct 1983	JW (WBC)	Bruce Curry	Las Vegas	Lost PTS–12
16 Feb 1985	JW (WBC)	Billy Costello	New York	Lost PTS–12

Alphonse HALIMI

Born: Constantine, Algeria, 18 Jun 1932
World title fights: 7 (all bantamweight) won 3, lost 4

DATE	WEIGHT	OPPONENT	VENUE	RESULT	
1 Apr 1957	B (NY)	Mario D'Agata	Paris	Won	PTS–15
6 Nov 1957	B	Raton Macias	Los Angeles	Won	PTS–15
8 Jul 1959	B	Joe Becerra	Los Angeles	Lost	KO–8
4 Feb 1960	B	Joe Becerra	Los Angeles	Lost	KO–9
25 Oct 1960	B (EBU)	Freddie Gilroy	London	Won	PTS–15
27 May 1961	B (EBU)	Johnny Caldwell	London	Lost	PTS–15
31 Oct 1961	B (EBU)	Johnny Caldwell	London	Lost	PTS–15

Tsuyoshi HAMADA

Born: Nakagusuku, Okinawa, Japan, 29 Nov 1960
World title fights: 3 (all junior-welter) won 2, lost 1

DATE	WEIGHT	OPPONENT	VENUE	RESULT	
24 Jul 1986	JW (WBC)	Rene Arredondo	Tokyo	Won	KO–1
2 Dec 1986	JW (WBC)	Ronnie Shields	Tokyo	Won	PTS–12
22 Jul 1987	JW (WBC)	Rene Arredondo	Tokyo	Lost	RSF–6

Susumu HANAGATA

Born: Yokohama, Japan, 21 Jan 1946
World title fights: 8 (all flyweight) won 1, lost 7

DATE	WEIGHT	OPPONENT	VENUE	RESULT	
28 Nov 1969	Fl (WBC)	Efren Torres	Guadalajara, Mexico	Lost	PTS–15
30 Apr 1971	Fl (WBC)	Erbito Salavarria	Manila	Lost	PTS–15
4 Mar 1972	Fl (WBA)	Masao Ohba	Tokyo	Lost	PTS–15
27 Oct 1973	Fl (WBA)	Chartchai Chionoi	Bangkok	Lost	PTS–15
18 Oct 1974	Fl (WBA)	Chartchai Chionoi	Yokohama, Japan	Won	RSF–6
1 Apr 1975	Fl (WBA)	Erbito Salavarria	Toyama, Japan	Lost	PTS–15

17 Oct 1975	Fl (WBA)	Erbito Salavarria	Yokohama	Lost	PTS–15
15 May 1976	Fl (WBC)	Miguel Canto	Merida, Mexico	Lost	PTS–15

Masahiko 'Fighting' HARADA

Born: Tokyo, Japan, 5 Apr 1943
World title fights: 10 (2 flyweight, 6 bantamweight, 2 featherweight) won 6, lost 4

10 Oct 1962	Fl	Pone Kingpetch	Tokyo	Won	KO–11
12 Jan 1963	Fl	Pone Kingpetch	Bangkok	Lost	PTS–15
17 May 1965	B	Eder Jofre	Nagoya, Japan	Won	PTS–15
30 Nov 1965	B	Alan Rudkin	Tokyo	Won	PTS–15
1 Jun 1966	B	Eder Jofre	Tokyo	Won	PTS–15
3 Jan 1967	B	Joe Medel	Nagoya	Won	PTS–15
4 Jul 1967	B	Bernardo Caraballo	Tokyo	Won	PTS–15
26 Feb 1968	B	Lionel Rose	Tokyo	Lost	PTS–15
28 Jul 1969	Fe (WBC)	Johnny Famechon	Sydney	Lost	PTS–15
6 Jan 1970	Fe (WBC)	Johnny Famechon	Tokyo	Lost	KO–14

Jeff HARDING

Born: Australia, 5 Feb 1965
World title fights: 4 (all light-heavy) won 3, lost 1

24 Jun 1989	LH (WBC)	Dennis Andries	Atlantic City	Won	RSF–12
24 Oct 1989	LH (WBC)	Tom Collins	Brisbane	Won	TKO–2
18 Mar 1990	LH (WBC)	Nestor Giovanni	Atlantic City	Won	RSF–11
28 Jul 1990	LH (WBC)	Dennis Andries	Melbourne	Lost	KO–7

Marvin HART

Born: Jefferson County, Kentucky, USA, 16 Sep 1876
Died: Fern Creek, Kentucky, 17 Sep 1931
World title fights: 2 (both heavyweight) won 1, lost 1

DATE	WEIGHT	OPPONENT	VENUE	RESULT	
3 Jul 1905	H	Jack Root	Reno, Nevada	Won	RSF-12
23 Feb 1906	H	Tommy Burns	Los Angeles	Lost	PTS-20

Gene HATCHER

Born: Fort Worth, Texas, USA, 28 Jun 1959
World title fights: 4 (3 junior-welter, 1 welterweight) won 2, lost 2

DATE	WEIGHT	OPPONENT	VENUE	RESULT	
1 Jun 1984	JW (WBA)	Johnny Bumphus	Buffalo	Won	RSF-11
15 Dec 1984	JW (WBA)	Ubaldo Sacco	Fort Worth, Texas	Won	PTS-15
21 Jul 1985	JW (WBA)	Ubaldo Sacco	Campione d'Italia, Italy	Lost	RSF-9
30 Aug 1987	W (WBC/IBF)	Lloyd Honeyghan	Marbella, Spain	Lost	KO-1

Greg HAUGEN

Born: Auburn, Washington, USA, 31 Aug 1960
World title fights: 6 (all lightweight) won 4, lost 2

DATE	WEIGHT	OPPONENT	VENUE	RESULT	
6 Dec 1986	L (IBF)	Jimmy Paul	Las Vegas	Won	PTS-15
7 Jun 1987	L (IBF)	Vinny Pazienza	Providence, Rhode Island	Lost	PTS-15
6 Feb 1988	L (IBF)	Vinny Pazienza	Atlantic City	Won	PTS-15
11 Apr 1988	L (IBF)	Miguel Santana	Tacoma, Washington	Won	TD-11
28 Oct 1988	L (IBF)	Gert Bo Jacobsen	Copenhagen	Won	RSF-10
20 Feb 1989	L (IBF)	Pernell Whitaker	Hampton, Virginia	Lost	PTS-12

Magne HAVNAA

Born: Oslo, Norway, 16 Sep 1963
World title fights: 3 (all cruiserweight) won 2, lost 1

DATE	WEIGHT	OPPONENT	VENUE	RESULT
3 Dec 1989	C (WBO)	Richard Pultz	Copenhagen	Lost PTS–12
13 May 1990	C (WBO)	Richard Pultz	Aars, Denmark	Won RSF–5
8 Dec 1990	C (WBO)	Daniel Netto	Aalborg, Denmark	Won PTS–12

Thomas HEARNS

Born: Memphis, Tennessee, USA, 18 Oct 1958
World title fights: 17 (5 welterweight, 5 junior-middle, 3 middleweight,
1 light-heavy, 3 super-middle) won 13, lost 3, drew 1

DATE	WEIGHT	OPPONENT	VENUE	RESULT
2 Aug 1980	W (WBA)	Pipino Cuevas	Detroit	Won RSF–2
6 Dec 1980	W (WBA)	Luis Primera	Detroit	Won KO–6
25 Apr 1981	W (WBA)	Randy Shields	Phoenix	Won RSF–12
25 Jun 1981	W (WBA)	Juan Pablo Baez	Houston	Won KO–4
16 Sep 1981	W	Sugar Ray Leonard	Las Vegas	Lost RSF–14
3 Dec 1982	JM (WBC)	Wilfred Benitez	New Orleans	Won PTS–15
11 Feb 1984	JM (WBC)	Luigi Minchillo	Detroit	Won PTS–12
16 Jun 1984	JM (WBC)	Roberto Duran	Las Vegas	Won RSF–2
15 Sep 1984	JM (WBC)	Fred Hutchings	Saginaw, Michigan	Won RSF–3
15 Apr 1985	M	Marvin Hagler	Las Vegas	Lost RSF–3
23 Jun 1986	JM (WBC)	Mark Medal	Las Vegas	Won RSF–8
7 Mar 1987	LH (WBC)	Dennis Andries	Detroit	Won RSF–10
29 Oct 1987	M (WBC)	Juan Roldan	Las Vegas	Won KO–4
6 Jun 1988	M (WBC)	Iran Barkley	Las Vegas	Lost RSF–3
4 Nov 1988	SM (WBO)	James Kinchen	Atlantic City	Won PTS–12
12 Jun 1989	SM (WBC)	Sugar Ray Leonard	Las Vegas	Drew 12
28 Apr 1990	SM (WBO)	Michael Olijade	Atlantic City	Won PTS–12

DATE	WEIGHT	OPPONENT	VENUE	RESULT

Pete 'Kid' HERMAN

Born: New Orleans, USA, 12 Feb 1896
Died: New Orleans, 13 Apr 1973
World title fights: 6 (all bantamweight) won 3, lost 2, drew 1

DATE	WEIGHT	OPPONENT	VENUE	RESULT
7 Feb 1916	B	Kid Williams	New Orleans	Drew 20
9 Jan 1917	B	Kid Williams	New Orleans	Won PTS–20
5 Nov 1917	B	Frankie Burns	New Orleans	Won PTS–20
22 Dec 1920	B	Joe Lynch	New York	Lost PTS–15
25 Jul 1921	B	Joe Lynch	Brooklyn, New York	Won PTS–15
23 Sep 1921	B	Johnny Buff	New York	Lost PTS–15

Carlos HERNANDEZ

Born: Caracas, Venezuela, 22 Apr 1940
World title fights: 5 (all junior-welter) won 3, lost 2

DATE	WEIGHT	OPPONENT	VENUE	RESULT
18 Jan 1965	JW	Eddie Perkins	Caracas	Won PTS–15
16 May 1965	JW	Mario Rossito	Maracaibo, Venezuela	Won RSF–4
10 Jul 1965	JW	Percy Hayles	Kingston, Jamaica	Won KO–3
29 Apr 1966	JW	Sandro Lopopolo	Rome	Lost PTS–15
3 May 1969	JW (WBA)	Nicolino Loche	Buenos Aires	Lost PTS–15

Juan HERRERA

Born: Yucatan, Mexico, 12 Jan 1958
World title fights: 4 (all flyweight) won 2, lost 2

DATE	WEIGHT	OPPONENT	VENUE	RESULT
26 Sep 1981	Fl (WBA)	Luis Ibarra	Mexico City	Won KO–11
20 Dec 1981	Fl (WBA)	Betulio Gonzalez	Mexico City	Won RSF–7
1 May 1982	Fl (WBA)	Santos Laciar	Merida, Mexico	Lost RSF–13
28 Jan 1984	Fl (WBA)	Santos Laciar	Marsala, Italy	Lost PTS–15

Rafael HERRERA

Born: Michoacan, Mexico, 7 Jan 1945
World title fights: 6 (all bantamweight) won 4, lost 2

DATE	WEIGHT	OPPONENT	VENUE	RESULT
19 Mar 1972	B	Ruben Olivares	Mexico City	Won KO–8
29 Jul 1972	B	Enrique Pinder	Panama City	Lost PTS–15
14 Apr 1973	B (WBC)	Rodolfo Martinez	Monterrey, Mexico	Won RSF–12
13 Oct 1973	B (WBC)	Venice Borkorsor	Los Angeles	Won PTS–15
25 May 1974	B (WBC)	Romeo Anaya	Mexico City	Won KO–6
7 Dec 1974	B (WBC)	Rodolfo Martinez	Merida, Mexico	Lost RSF–4

Virgil HILL

Born: Clinton, Missouri, USA, 18 Jan 1964
World title fights: 10 (all light-heavy) won 10, lost 0

DATE	WEIGHT	OPPONENT	VENUE	RESULT
5 Sep 1987	LH (WBA)	Leslie Stewart	Atlantic City	Won RSF–4
22 Nov 1987	LH (WBA)	Rufino Angulo	Paris	Won PTS–12
3 Apr 1988	LH (WBA)	Jean-Marie Emebe	Bismarck, North Dakota	Won RTD–11
6 Jun 1988	LH (WBA)	Ramzi Hassan	Las Vegas	Won PTS–12
11 Nov 1988	LH (WBA)	Willy Featherstone	Bismarck	Won RSF–10
4 Mar 1989	LH (WBA)	Bobby Czyz	Bismarck	Won PTS–12
27 May 1989	LH (WBA)	Joe Lasisi	Bismarck	Won RSF–7
24 Oct 1989	LH (WBA)	James Kinchen	Bismarck	Won RSF–1
26 Feb 1990	LH (WBA)	David Vedder	Bismarck	Won PTS–12
7 Jul 1990	LH (WBA)	Tyrone Frazier	Bismarck	Won PTS–12

Matthew HILTON

Born: Port Credit, Ontario, Canada, 27 Dec 1965
World title fights: 4 (1 middleweight, 3 junior-middle) won 2, lost 2

DATE	WEIGHT	OPPONENT	VENUE	RESULT
27 Jun 1987	JM (IBF)	Buster Drayton	Montreal	Won PTS–15
16 Oct 1987	JM (IBF)	Jack Callahan	Atlantic City	Won RSF–2
4 Nov 1988	JM (IBF)	Robert Hines	Las Vegas	Lost PTS–12
15 Jan 1990	M (WBO)	Doug De Witt	Atlantic City	Lost RTD–11

Robert HINES

Born: Philadelphia, USA, 20 Mar 1962
World title fights: 2 (both junior-middle) won 1, lost 1

DATE	WEIGHT	OPPONENT	VENUE	RESULT
4 Nov 1988	JM (IBF)	Matthew Hilton	Las Vegas	Won PTS–12
4 Feb 1989	JM (IBF)	Darrin Van Horn	Atlantic City	Lost PTS–12

Gary HINTON

Born: Philadelphia, USA, 29 Aug 1956
World title fights: 3 (all junior-welter) won 1, lost 2

DATE	WEIGHT	OPPONENT	VENUE	RESULT
2 Mar 1985	JW (IBF)	Aaron Pryor	Atlantic City	Lost PTS–15
26 Apr 1986	JW (IBF)	Antonio Reyes	Lucca, Italy	Won PTS–15
30 Oct 1986	JW (IBF)	Joe Louis Manley	Hartford, Connecticut	Lost KO–10

Larry HOLMES

Born: Cuthbert, Georgia, USA, 3 Nov 1949
World title fights: 24 (all heavyweight) won 21, lost 3

DATE	WEIGHT	OPPONENT	VENUE	RESULT
10 Jun 1978	H (WBC)	Ken Norton	Las Vegas	Won PTS–15
10 Nov 1978	H (WBC)	Alfredo Evangelista	Las Vegas	Won KO–7
29 Mar 1979	H (WBC)	Osvaldo Ocasio	Las Vegas	Won RSF–7

DATE	WEIGHT	OPPONENT	VENUE	RESULT
22 Jun 1979	H (WBC)	Mike Weaver	New York	Won RSF–12
28 Sep 1979	H (WBC)	Earnie Shavers	Las Vegas	Won RSF–11
3 Feb 1980	H (WBC)	Lorenzo Zanon	Las Vegas	Won KO–6
31 Mar 1980	H (WBC)	Leroy Jones	Las Vegas	Won RSF–8
7 Jul 1980	H (WBC)	Scott LeDoux	Minneapolis	Won RSF–7
2 Oct 1980	H (WBC)	Muhammad Ali	Las Vegas	Won RTD–10
11 Apr 1981	H (WBC)	Trevor Berbick	Las Vegas	Won PTS–15
12 Jun 1981	H (WBC)	Leon Spinks	Detroit	Won RSF–3
6 Nov 1981	H (WBC)	Renaldo Snipes	Pittsburgh	Won RSF–11
11 Jun 1982	H (WBC)	Gerry Cooney	Las Vegas	Won RTD–13
25 Nov 1982	H (WBC)	Randall Cobb	Houston	Won PTS–15
26 Mar 1983	H (WBC)	Lucien Rodriquez	Scranton, Pennsylvania	Won PTS–12
20 May 1983	H (WBC)	Tim Witherspoon	Las Vegas	Won PTS–12
10 Sep 1983	H (WBC)	Scott Frank	Atlantic City	Won RSF–5
25 Nov 1983	H (WBC)	Marvis Frazier	Las Vegas	Won TKO–1
9 Nov 1984	H (IBF)	James Smith	Las Vegas	Won RSF–12
15 Mar 1985	H (IBF)	David Bey	Las Vegas	Won RSF–10
20 May 1985	H (IBF)	Carl Williams	Reno, Nevada	Won PTS–15
21 Sep 1985	H (IBF)	Michael Spinks	Las Vegas	Lost PTS–15
19 Apr 1986	H (IBF)	Michael Spinks	Las Vegas	Lost PTS–15
22 Jan 1988	H	Mike Tyson	Atlantic City	Lost RSF–4

Lindell HOLMES

Born: Detroit, USA, 15 Oct 1958
World title fights: 4 (all super-middle) won 2, lost 1, NC 1

6 Jul 1986	SM (IBF)	Chong-Pal Park	Seoul	NC–2*
2 May 1987	SM (IBF)	Chong-Pal Park	Inchon, S Korea	Lost PTS–15
27 Jan 1990	SM (IBF)	Frank Tate	New Orleans	Won PTS–12
20 Jul 1990	SM (IBF)	Carl Sullivan	Seattle	Won TKO–9

* Both fighters injured – result declared a 'No Contest'

DATE	WEIGHT	OPPONENT	VENUE	RESULT

Evander HOLYFIELD

Born: Atmore, Alabama, USA, 19 Oct 1962
World title fights: 7 (1 heavyweight, 6 cruiserweight) won 7, lost 0

DATE	WEIGHT	OPPONENT	VENUE	RESULT
12 Jul 1986	C (WBA)	Dwight Qawi	Atlanta	Won PTS–15
14 Feb 1987	C (WBA)	Henry Tillman	Reno, Nevada	Won RSF–7
16 May 1987	C (IBF)	Rickey Parkey	Las Vegas	Won RSF–3
15 Aug 1987	C (WBA/IBF)	Ossie Ocasio	St Tropez, France	Won RSF–11
5 Dec 1987	C (IBF)	Dwight Qawi	Atlantic City	Won KO–4
9 Apr 1988	C	Carlos DeLeon	Las Vegas	Won RSF–8
25 Oct 1990	H (WBC/WBA/ IBF)	James 'Buster' Douglas	Las Vegas	Won KO–3

Lloyd HONEYGHAN

Born: St Elizabeth, Jamaica, 22 Apr 1960
World title fights: 9 (all welterweight) won 6, lost 3

DATE	WEIGHT	OPPONENT	VENUE	RESULT
27 Sep 1986	W	Donald Curry	Atlantic City	Won RTD–6
22 Feb 1987	W (WBC/IBF)	Johnny Bumphus	London	Won RSF–2
18 Apr 1987	W (WBC/IBF)	Maurice Blocker	London	Won PTS–12
30 Aug 1987	W (WBC/IBF)	Gene Hatcher	Marbella, Spain	Won KO–1
28 Oct 1987	W (WBC)	Jorge Vaca	London	Lost TD–8
28 Mar 1988	W (WBC)	Jorge Vaca	London	Won KO–3
29 Jul 1988	W (WBC)	Yung-Kil Chung	Atlantic City	Won TKO–5
4 Feb 1989	W (WBC)	Marlon Starling	Las Vegas	Lost RSF–9
3 Mar 1990	W (WBA)	Mark Breland	London	Lost RSF–3

Soo-Hwan HONG

Born: Seoul, South Korea, 26 May 1950
World title fights: 7 (4 bantamweight, 3 junior-feather) won 4, lost 3

DATE	WEIGHT	OPPONENT	VENUE	RESULT	
3 Jul 1974	B (WBA)	Arnold Taylor	Durban	Won	PTS–15
28 Dec 1974	B (WBA)	Fernando Cabanela	Seoul	Won	PTS–15
14 Mar 1975	B (WBA)	Alfonso Zamora	Los Angeles	Lost	KO–4
16 Oct 1976	B (WBA)	Alfonso Zamora	Inchon, S Korea	Lost	RSF–12
26 Nov 1977	JFe (WBA)	Hector Carrasquilla	Panama City	Won	KO–3
1 Feb 1978	JFe (WBA)	Yu Kasahara	Tokyo	Won	PTS–15
6 May 1978	JFe (WBA)	Ricardo Cardona	Seoul	Lost	RSF–12

Maurice HOPE

Born: Antigua, West Indies, 6 Dec 1951
World title fights: 6 (all junior-middle) won 4, lost 1, drew 1

DATE	WEIGHT	OPPONENT	VENUE	RESULT	
15 Mar 1977	JM (WBC)	Eckhard Dagge	Berlin	Drew	15
4 Mar 1979	JM (WBC)	Rocky Mattioli	San Remo, Italy	Won	RTD–8
25 Sep 1979	JM (WBC)	Mike Baker	London	Won	RSF–7
12 Jul 1980	JM (WBC)	Rocky Mattioli	London	Won	RSF–11
26 Nov 1980	JM (WBC)	Carlos Herrera	London	Won	PTS–15
23 May 1981	JM (WBC)	Wilfred Benitez	Las Vegas	Lost	KO–12

Al HOSTAK

Born: Minneapolis, USA, 7 Jan 1916
World title fights: 6 (all middleweight) won 3, lost 3

DATE	WEIGHT	OPPONENT	VENUE	RESULT	
26 Jul 1938	M (NBA)	Freddie Steele	Seattle	Won	KO–1
1 Nov 1938	M (NBA)	Solly Kreiger	Seattle	Lost	PTS–15
27 Jun 1939	M (NBA)	Solly Kreiger	Seattle	Won	KO–4

DATE	WEIGHT	OPPONENT	VENUE	RESULT
11 Dec 1939	M (NBA)	Eric Seelig	Cleveland	Won KO–1
19 Jul 1940	M (NBA)	Tony Zale	Seattle	Lost KO–13
28 May 1941	M (NBA)	Tony Zale	Chicago	Lost KO–2

Luis IBARRA

Born: Colon, Panama, 23 Feb 1953
World title fights: 4 (all flyweight) won 2, lost 2

DATE	WEIGHT	OPPONENT	VENUE	RESULT
17 Nov 1979	Fl (WBA)	Betulio Gonzalez	Maracay, Venezuela	Won PTS–15
16 Feb 1980	Fl (WBA)	Tae-Shik Kim	Seoul	Lost KO–2
6 Jun 1981	Fl (WBA)	Santos Laciar	Buenos Aires	Won PTS–15
26 Sep 1981	Fl (WBA)	Juan Herrera	Mexico City	Lost KO–11

Hiroki IOKA

Born: Osaka, Japan, 8 Jan 1969
World title fights: 5 (all strawweight) won 2, lost 2, drew 1

DATE	WEIGHT	OPPONENT	VENUE	RESULT
18 Oct 1987	S (WBC)	Moi Thonburifarm	Osaka, Japan	Won PTS–12
31 Jan 1988	S (WBC)	Kyun-Yung Lee	Osaka	Won RSF–12
5 Jun 1988	S (WBC)	Napa Kiatwanchai	Osaka	Drew 12
13 Nov 1988	S (WBC)	Napa Kiatwanchai	Osaka	Lost PTS–12
10 Jun 1989	S (WBC)	Napa Kiatwanchai	Osaka	Lost RSF–11

Guts ISHIMATSU
(formerly Ishimatsu Suzuki)

Born: Tochigi Prefecture, Japan, 5 Jun 1949
World title fights: 10 (9 lightweight, 1 junior-welter) won 5, lost 4, drew 1

DATE	WEIGHT	OPPONENT	VENUE	RESULT
6 Jun 1970	L	Ismael Laguna	Panama City	Lost RSF–13
8 Sep 1973	L (WBA)	Roberto Duran	Panama City	Lost RSF–10

DATE	WEIGHT	OPPONENT	VENUE	RESULT

DATE	WEIGHT	OPPONENT	VENUE	RESULT
11 Apr 1974	L (WBC)	Rodolfo Gonzalez	Tokyo	Won KO–8
12 Sep 1974	L (WBC)	Arturo Pineda	Nagoya, Japan	Drew 15
28 Nov 1974	L (WBC)	Rodolfo Gonzalez	Osaka, Japan	Won KO–12
27 Feb 1975	L (WBC)	Ken Buchanan	Tokyo	Won PTS–15
5 Jun 1975	L (WBC)	Arturo Pineda	Osaka	Won PTS–15
4 Dec 1975	L (WBC)	Alvaro Rojas	Tokyo	Won KO–14
8 May 1976	L (WBC)	Esteban De Jesus	San Juan	Lost PTS–15
2 Apr 1977	JW (WBC)	Saensak Muangsurin	Tokyo	Lost KO–6

Beau JACK

Born: Augusta, Georgia, USA, 1 Apr 1921
World title fights: 5 (all lightweight) won 2, lost 3

DATE	WEIGHT	OPPONENT	VENUE	RESULT
18 Dec 1942	L (NY)	Tippy Larkin	New York	Won KO–3
21 May 1943	L (NY)	Bob Montgomery	New York	Lost PTS–15
19 Nov 1943	L (NY)	Bob Montgomery	New York	Won PTS–15
3 Mar 1944	L (NY)	Bob Montgomery	New York	Lost PTS–15
12 Jul 1948	L	Ike Williams	Philadelphia	Lost KO–6

John David JACKSON

Born: Denver, Colorado, USA, 17 May 1963
World title fights: 5 (all junior-middle) won 4, lost 0, NC 1

DATE	WEIGHT	OPPONENT	VENUE	RESULT
7 Dec 1988	JM (WBO)	Lupe Aquino	Detroit	Won RSF–8
22 Apr 1989	JM (WBO)	Steve Little	Auburn Hills, Michigan	Won RSF–8
1 Dec 1989	JM (WBO)	Ruben Villamen	Tucson, Arizona	Won KO–2
17 Feb 1990	JM (WBO)	Martin Camara	Deauville, France	NC
23 Oct 1990	JM (WBO)	Chris Pyatt	Leicester	Won PTS–12

DATE	WEIGHT	OPPONENT	VENUE	RESULT

Julian JACKSON

Born: St Thomas, Virgin Islands, USA, 12 Sep 1960
World title fights: 6 (5 junior-middle, 1 middleweight) won 5, lost 1

DATE	WEIGHT	OPPONENT	VENUE	RESULT	
23 Aug 1986	JM (WBA)	Mike McCallum	Miami	Lost	RSF-2
21 Nov 1987	JM (WBA)	In-Chul Baek	Las Vegas	Won	RSF-3
30 Jul 1988	JM (WBA)	Buster Drayton	Atlantic City	Won	KO-3
24 Feb 1989	JM (WBA)	Francisco De Jesus	Las Vegas	Won	KO-8
30 Jul 1989	JM (WBA)	Terry Norris	Atlantic City	Won	RSF-2
24 Nov 1990	M (WBC)	Herol Graham	Benalmadena, Spain	Won	KO-4

Rene JACQUOT

Born: Toulouse, France, 28 Jul 1961
World title fights: 4 (all junior-middle) won 1, lost 3

DATE	WEIGHT	OPPONENT	VENUE	RESULT	
11 Feb 1989	JM (WBC)	Don Curry	Grenoble, France	Won	PTS-12
8 Jul 1989	JM (WBC)	John Mugabi	Miraplis, France	Lost	KO-1
13 Jul 1990	JM (WBC)	Terry Norris	Annecy, France	Lost	PTS-12
30 Nov 1990	JM (IBF)	Gianfranco Rosi	Marsala, Italy	Lost	PTS-12

Johnny JADICK

Born: Philadelphia, USA, 16 Jun 1908
Died: Philadelphia, 3 Apr 1970
World title fights: 3 (all junior-welter) won 2, lost 1

DATE	WEIGHT	OPPONENT	VENUE	RESULT	
18 Jan 1932	JW	Tony Canzoneri	Philadelphia	Won	PTS-10
18 Jul 1932	JW	Tony Canzoneri	Philadelphia	Won	PTS-10
20 Feb 1933	JW	Battling Shaw	New Orleans	Lost	PTS-10

Ben JEBY

Born: New York City, USA, 27 Dec 1909
Died: Brooklyn, New York, 5 Oct 1985
World title fights: 5 (all middleweight) won 3, lost 1, drew 1

DATE	WEIGHT	OPPONENT	VENUE	RESULT	
21 Nov 1932	M (NY)	Chick Devlin	New York	Won	PTS–15
13 Jan 1933	M (NY)	Frank Battaglia	New York	Won	KO–12
17 Mar 1933	M (NY)	Vince Dundee	New York	Drew	15
10 Jul 1933	M (NY)	Young Terry	Newark, New Jersey	Won	PTS–15
9 Aug 1933	M (NY)	Lou Brouillard	New York	Lost	KO–7

Harry JEFFRA

Born: Baltimore, USA, 30 Nov 1914
World title fights: 7 (2 bantamweight, 5 featherweight) won 3, lost 4

DATE	WEIGHT	OPPONENT	VENUE	RESULT	
23 Sep 1937	B	Sixto Escobar	New York	Won	PTS–15
20 Feb 1938	B	Sixto Escobar	San Juan	Lost	PTS–15
28 Sep 1939	Fe	Joey Archibald	Washington DC	Lost	PTS–15
20 May 1940	Fe (NY)	Joey Archibald	Baltimore	Won	PTS–15
29 Jul 1940	Fe (NY)	Spider Armstrong	Baltimore	Won	PTS–15
12 May 1941	Fe (NY)	Joey Archibald	Washington DC	Lost	PTS–15
19 Jun 1942	Fe (NY)	Chalky Wright	Baltimore	Lost	KO–10

James J JEFFRIES

Born: Carroll, Ohio, USA, 15 Apr 1875
Died: Burbank, California, 3 Mar 1953
World title fights: 8 (all heavyweight) won 7, lost 1

DATE	WEIGHT	OPPONENT	VENUE	RESULT	
9 Jun 1899	H	Bob Fitzsimmons	Coney Island, New York	Won	KO–11
3 Nov 1899	H	Tom Sharkey	Coney Island	Won	PTS–25
11 May 1900	H	James J Corbett	Coney Island	Won	KO–23

Date	Weight	Opponent	Venue	Result
15 Nov 1901	H	Gus Ruthlin	San Francisco	Won RTD–5
25 Jul 1902	H	Bob Fitzsimmons	San Francisco	Won KO–8
14 Aug 1903	H	James J Corbett	San Francisco	Won KO–10
26 Aug 1904	H	Jack Munro	San Francisco	Won KO–2
4 Jul 1910	H	Jack Johnson	Reno, Nevada	Lost RSF–15

Lew JENKINS

Born: Milburn, Texas, USA, 4 Dec 1916
Died: Oakland, California, 30 Oct 1981
World title fights: 3 (all lighweight) won 2, lost 1

Date	Weight	Opponent	Venue	Result
10 May 1940	L (NY)	Lou Ambers	New York	Won RSF–3
22 Nov 1940	L (NY)	Pete Lello	New York	Won RSF–2
19 Dec 1941	L	Sammy Angott	New York	Lost PTS–15

Eder JOFRE

Born: Sao Paulo, Brazil, 26 Mar 1936
World title fights: 13 (11 bantamweight, 2 featherweight) won 11, lost 2

Date	Weight	Opponent	Venue	Result
18 Nov 1960	B (NBA)	Eloy Sanchez	Los Angeles	Won KO–6
25 Mar 1961	B (NBA)	Piero Rollo	Rio de Janeiro	Won RTD–9
19 Aug 1961	B (NBA)	Ramon Arias	Caracas	Won RTD–7
18 Jan 1962	B	Johnny Caldwell	Sao Paulo, Brazil	Won RTD–10
4 May 1962	B	Herman Marquez	San Francisco	Won RSF–10
11 Sep 1962	B	Joe Medel	Sao Paulo	Won KO–6
4 Apr 1963	B	Katsutoshi Aoki	Tokyo	Won KO–3
18 May 1963	B	Johnny Jamito	Manila	Won RTD–11
27 Nov 1964	B	Bernardo Caraballo	Bogota	Won KO–7
17 May 1965	B	Fighting Harada	Nagoya, Japan	Lost PTS–15
1 Jun 1966	B	Fighting Harada	Tokyo	Lost PTS–15

5 May 1973	Fe (WBC)	Jose Legra	Brasilia	Won	PTS–15
21 Oct 1973	Fe (WBC)	Vicente Saldivar	Salvador, Brazil	Won	KO–4

Ingemar JOHANSSON

Born: Gothenburg, Sweden, 22 Sep 1932
World title fights: 3 (all heavyweight) won 1, lost 2

26 Jun 1959	H	Floyd Patterson	New York	Won	RSF–3
20 Jun 1960	H	Floyd Patterson	New York	Lost	KO–5
13 Mar 1961	H	Floyd Patterson	Miami	Lost	KO–6

Harold JOHNSON

Born: Manayunk, Pennsylvania, USA, 9 Aug 1928
World title fights: 7 (all light-heavy) won 5, lost 2

11 Aug 1954	LH	Archie Moore	New York	Lost	KO–14
7 Feb 1961	LH (NBA)	Jesse Bowdry	Miami	Won	KO–9
24 Apr 1961	LH (NBA)	Von Clay	Philadelphia	Won	KO–2
29 Aug 1961	LH (NBA)	Eddie Cotton	Seattle	Won	PTS–15
12 May 1962	LH	Doug Jones	Philadelphia	Won	PTS–15
23 Jun 1962	LH	Gustav Scholz	Berlin	Won	PTS–15
1 Jun 1963	LH	Willie Pastrano	Las Vegas	Lost	PTS–15

Jack JOHNSON

Born: Galveston, Texas, USA, 31 Mar 1878
Died: Raleigh, North Carolina, 10 Jun 1946
World title fights: 8 (all heavyweight) won 6, lost 1, drew 1

26 Dec 1908	H	Tommy Burns	Sydney	Won	RSF–14
16 Oct 1909	H	Stanley Ketchel	Colma, California	Won	KO–12

4 Jul 1910	H	James J Jeffries	Reno, Nevada	Won	RSF–15
4 Jul 1912	H	Jim Flynn	Las Vegas	Won	RSF–9
28 Nov 1913	H	Andre Sproul	Paris	Won	KO–2
19 Dec 1913	H	Jim Johnson	Paris	Drew	10
27 Jun 1914	H	Frank Moran	Paris	Won	PTS–20
5 Apr 1915	H	Jess Willard	Havana	Lost	KO–26

Marvin JOHNSON

Born: Indianapolis, USA, 12 Apr 1954
World title fights: 7 (all light-heavy) won 4, lost 3

2 Dec 1978	LH (WBC)	Mate Parlov	Marsala, Italy	Won	RSF–10
22 Apr 1979	LH (WBC)	Matt Franklin	Indianapolis	Lost	RSF–8
30 Nov 1979	LH (WBA)	Victor Galindez	New Orleans	Won	KO–11
31 Mar 1980	LH (WBA)	Eddie Gregory	Knoxville, Tennessee	Lost	RSF–11
9 Feb 1986	LH (WBA)	Leslie Stewart	Indianpolis	Won	RSF–7
20 Sep 1986	LH (WBA)	Jean-Marie Emebe	Indianapolis	Won	RSF–13
23 May 1987	LH (WBA)	Leslie Stewart	Port of Spain, Trinidad	Lost	RSF–8

Gorilla JONES

Born: Memphis, Tennessee, USA, 4 May 1910
Died: Los Angeles, 4 Jan 1982
World title fights: 6 (all middleweight) won 4, lost 2

25 Aug 1931	M (NBA)	Tiger Thomas	Milwaukee	Won	PTS–10
25 Jan 1932	M (NBA)	Oddone Piazza	Milwaukee	Won	KO–6
26 Apr 1932	M (NBA)	Young Terry	Trenton, New Jersey	Won	PTS–12
11 Jun 1932	M (NBA)	Marcel Thil	Paris	Lost	DIS–11
30 Jan 1933	M (NBA)	Sammy Slaughter	Cleveland	Won	KO–7
1 Jan 1937	M (NY)	Freddie Steele	Milwaukee	Lost	PTS–10

DATE	WEIGHT	OPPONENT	VENUE	RESULT

Don JORDAN

Born: Los Angeles, USA, 22 Jun 1934
World title fights: 4 (all welterweight) won 3, lost 1

DATE	WEIGHT	OPPONENT	VENUE	RESULT	
5 Dec 1958	W	Virgil Akins	Los Angeles	Won	PTS–15
24 Apr 1959	W	Virgil Akins	St Louis	Won	PTS–15
10 Jul 1959	W	Denny Moyer	Portland, Oregon	Won	PTS–15
27 May 1960	W	Benny Paret	Las Vegas	Lost	PTS–15

Kim-Bong JUN

Born: Chon-Nam, South Korea, 13 May 1964
World title fights: 7 (all strawweight) won 6, lost 1

DATE	WEIGHT	OPPONENT	VENUE	RESULT	
10 Jan 1988	S (WBA)	Leo Gamez	Pusan, S Korea	Lost	PTS–12
16 Apr 1989	S (WBA)	Agustin Garcia	Pohang, S Korea	Won	RSF–7
6 Aug 1989	S (WBA)	Sam-Jung Lee	Seoul	Won	PTS–12
22 Oct 1989	S (WBA)	John Arief	Pohang	Won	RSF–9
10 Feb 1990	S (WBA)	Petthal Chuvatana	Seoul	Won	KO–4
13 May 1990	S (WBA)	Silverio Barcenas	Seoul	Won	PTS–12
3 Nov 1990	S (WBA)	Silverio Barceras	Taegu, S Korea	Won	PTS–12

Slobodan KACAR

Born: Belgrade, Yugoslavia, 15 Sep 1957
World title fights: 2 (both light-heavy) won 1, lost 1

DATE	WEIGHT	OPPONENT	VENUE	RESULT	
21 Dec 1985	LH (IBF)	Eddie Mustafa Muhammad	Pesaro, Italy	Won	PTS–15
6 Sep 1986	LH (IBF)	Bobby Czyz	Las Vegas	Lost	RSF–5

| DATE | WEIGHT | OPPONENT | VENUE | RESULT |

Sumbu KALAMBAY

Born: Lubunbashi, Zaire, 10 Apr 1956
World title fights: 5 (all middleweight) won 4, lost 1

DATE	WEIGHT	OPPONENT	VENUE	RESULT
23 Oct 1987	M (WBA)	Iran Barkley	Livorno, Italy	Won PTS–15
5 Mar 1988	M (WBA)	Mike McCallum	Pesaro, Italy	Won PTS–12
12 Jun 1988	M (WBA)	Robbie Sims	Ravenna, Italy	Won PTS–12
8 Nov 1988	M (WBA)	Doug De Witt	Monte Carlo	Won KO–7
25 Mar 1989	M (IBF)	Michael Nunn	Las Vegas	Lost KO–1

Ayub KALULE

Born: Kampala, Uganda, 6 Jan 1954
World title fights: 7 (all junior-middle) won 5, lost 2

DATE	WEIGHT	OPPONENT	VENUE	RESULT
24 Oct 1979	JM (WBA)	Masashi Kudo	Akita, Japan	Won PTS–15
6 Dec 1979	JM (WBA)	Steve Gregory	Copenhagen	Won PTS–15
18 Apr 1980	JM (WBA)	Emiliano Villa	Copenhagen	Won RSF–11
13 Jun 1980	JM (WBA)	Marijan Benes	Randers, Denmark	Won PTS–15
6 Sep 1980	JM (WBA)	Bushy Bester	Aarhus, Denmark	Won PTS–15
25 Jun 1981	JM (WBA)	Sugar Ray Leonard	Houston	Lost KO–9
17 Jul 1982	JM (WBA)	Davey Moore	Atlantic City	Lost RSF–10

Peter KANE

Born: Golborne, England, 28 Feb 1918
World title fights: 4 (all flyweight) won 1, lost 2, drew 1

DATE	WEIGHT	OPPONENT	VENUE	RESULT
13 Oct 1937	Fl	Benny Lynch	Glasgow	Lost KO–13
24 Mar 1938	Fl	Benny Lynch	Liverpool	Drew 15
22 Sep 1938	Fl	Jackie Jurich	Liverpool	Won PTS–15
19 Jun 1943	Fl	Jackie Paterson	Glasgow	Lost KO–1

DATE	WEIGHT	OPPONENT	VENUE	RESULT

Rocky KANSAS

Born: Buffalo, USA, 21 Apr 1895
Died: Buffalo, 10 Jan 1954
World title fights: 4 (all lightweight) won 1, lost 3

DATE	WEIGHT	OPPONENT	VENUE	RESULT	
10 Feb 1922	L	Benny Leonard	New York	Lost	PTS–15
4 Jul 1922	L	Benny Leonard	Michigan City, Indiana	Lost	RTD–8
8 Dec 1925	L	Jimmy Goodrich	Buffalo	Won	PTS–15
3 Jul 1926	L	Sammy Mandell	Chicago	Lost	PTS–10

Louis 'Kid' KAPLAN

Born: Kiev, Russia, 15 Oct 1901
Died: Norwich, Connecticut, 26 Oct 1970
World title fights: 3 (all featherweight) won 2, drew 1

DATE	WEIGHT	OPPONENT	VENUE	RESULT	
2 Jan 1925	Fe	Danny Kramer	New York	Won	RTD–9
27 Aug 1925	Fe	Babe Herman	Waterbury, Connecticut	Drew	15
18 Dec 1925	Fe	Babe Herman	New York	Won	PTS–15

Hilmer KENTY

Born: Austin, Texas, USA, 30 Jul 1955
World title fights: 5 (all lightweight) won 4, lost 1

DATE	WEIGHT	OPPONENT	VENUE	RESULT	
2 Mar 1980	L (WBA)	Ernesto Espana	Detroit	Won	RSF–9
2 Aug 1980	L (WBA)	Young-Ho Oh	Detroit	Won	RSF–9
20 Sep 1980	L (WBA)	Ernesto Espana	San Juan	Won	KO–4
9 Nov 1980	L (WBA)	Vilomar Fernandez	Detroit	Won	PTS–15
12 Apr 1981	L (WBA)	Sean O'Grady	Atlantic City	Lost	PTS–15

Stanley KETCHEL

Born: Grand Rapids, Michigan, USA, 14 Sep 1886
Died: Conway, Missouri, 15 Oct 1910
World title fights: 10 (9 middleweight, 1 heavyweight) won 8, lost 2

DATE	WEIGHT	OPPONENT	VENUE	RESULT
2 Sep 1907	M	Joey Thomas	Colma, California	Won KO–32
12 Dec 1907	M	Joey Thomas	San Francisco	Won PTS–20
22 Feb 1908	M	Mike 'Twin' Sullivan	Colma	Won KO–1
4 Jun 1908	M	Billy Papke	Milwaukee	Won PTS–10
31 Jul 1908	M	Hugo Kelly	San Francisco	Won KO–3
18 Aug 1908	M	Joey Thomas	San Francisco	Won KO–2
7 Sep 1908	M	Billy Papke	Vernon, California	Lost KO–12
26 Nov 1908	M	Billy Papke	Colma	Won KO–11
5 Jul 1909	M	Billy Papke	Colma	Won PTS–20
16 Oct 1909	H	Jack Johnson	Colma	Lost KO–12

Napa KIATWANCHAI

Born: Nakonratchasima, Thailand, 27 Jul 1967
World title fights: 6 (all strawweight) won 3, lost 2, drew 1

DATE	WEIGHT	OPPONENT	VENUE	RESULT
5 Jun 1988	S (WBC)	Hiroki Ioka	Osaka, Japan	Drew 12
13 Nov 1988	S (WBC)	Hiroki Ioka	Osaka	Won PTS–12
11 Feb 1989	S (WBC)	John Arief	Korat, Thailand	Won PTS–12
10 Jun 1989	S (WBC)	Hiroki Ioka	Osaka	Won RSF–11
12 Nov 1989	S (WBC)	Jum-Hwan Choi	Seoul	Lost RSF–12
8 Jun 1990	S (WBC)	Hideyuki Ohashi	Tokyo	Lost PTS–12

Dixie KID

Born: Fulton, Missouri, USA, 23 Dec 1883
Died: Los Angeles, 3 Oct 1935
World title fights: 2 (both welterweight) won 1, drew 1

DATE	WEIGHT	OPPONENT	VENUE	RESULT
30 Apr 1904	W	Joe Walcott	San Francisco	Won DIS–20
12 May 1904	W	Joe Walcott	San Francisco	Drew 20

Johnny KILBANE

Born: Cleveland, USA, 18 Apr 1889
Died: Cleveland, 31 May 1957
World title fights: 8 (7 featherweight, 1 lightweight) won 4, lost 2, drew 2

DATE	WEIGHT	OPPONENT	VENUE	RESULT
22 Feb 1912	Fe	Abe Attell	Vernon, California	Won PTS–20
21 May 1912	Fe	Jimmy Walsh	Boston	Drew 12
29 Apr 1913	Fe	Johnny Dundee	Vernon	Drew 20
4 Sep 1916	Fe	George 'KO' Chaney	Cedar Point, Ohio	Won KO–3
25 Jul 1917	L	Benny Leonard	Philadelphia	Lost RTD–3
21 Apr 1920	Fe	Alvie Miller	Lorain, Ohio	Won KO–7
17 Sep 1921	Fe	Danny Frush	Cleveland	Won KO–7
2 Jun 1923	Fe	Eugene Criqui	New York	Lost KO–6

Chi-Won KIM

Born: South Korea, 6 Aug 1959
World title fights: 5 (all junior-feather) won 5, lost 0

DATE	WEIGHT	OPPONENT	VENUE	RESULT
3 Jan 1985	JFe (IBF)	Seung-Il Suh	Seoul	Won KO–10
30 Mar 1985	JFe (IBF)	Dario Palacios	Suwon, S Korea	Won PTS–15
28 Jun 1985	JFe (IBF)	Bobby Berna	Pusan, S Korea	Won KO–4
9 Oct 1985	JFe (IBF)	Seung-Il Suh	Chunju, S Korea	Won KO–1
1 Jun 1986	JFe (IBF)	Rudy Casicas	Inchon, S Korea	Won RSF–2

DATE	WEIGHT	OPPONENT	VENUE	RESULT

Chul-Ho KIM

Born: Ohsan, South Korea, 3 Mar 1961
World title fights: 7 (all junior-bantam) won 5, drew 1, lost 1

DATE	WEIGHT	OPPONENT	VENUE	RESULT	
24 Jan 1981	JB (WBC)	Rafael Orono	San Cristobel, Venezuela	Won	KO–9
22 Apr 1981	JB (WBC)	Jiro Watanabe	Seoul	Won	PTS–15
29 Jul 1981	JB (WBC)	Willie Jensen	Pusan, S Korea	Won	KO–13
18 Nov 1981	JB (WBC)	Ryotsu Maruyama	Pusan	Won	RSF–9
10 Feb 1982	JB (WBC)	Koki Ishii	Taegu, S Korea	Won	KO–8
4 Jul 1982	JB (WBC)	Raul Valdez	Taejon, S Korea	Drew	15
28 Nov 1982	JB (WBC)	Rafael Orono	Seoul	Lost	RSF–6

Hwan-Jin KIM

Born: Kyungnam, South Korea, 25 Jun 1955
World title fights: 4 (all junior-fly) won 2, lost 2

DATE	WEIGHT	OPPONENT	VENUE	RESULT	
19 Jul 1981	JFl (WBA)	Pedro Flores	Seoul	Won	RSF–13
11 Oct 1981	JFl (WBA)	Alfonso Lopez	Seoul	Won	PTS–15
16 Dec 1981	JFl (WBA)	Katsuo Tokashiki	Sendai, Japan	Lost	PTS–15
9 Jan 1983	JFl (WBA)	Katsuo Tokashiki	Kyoto, Japan	Lost	PTS–15

Ki-Soo KIM

Born: Buk-Chong, Ham-kyongnamdo, South Korea, 17 Sep 1939
World title fights: 4 (all junior-middle) won 3, lost 1

DATE	WEIGHT	OPPONENT	VENUE	RESULT	
25 Jun 1966	JM	Nino Benvenuti	Seoul	Won	PTS–15
17 Dec 1966	JM	Stan Harrington	Seoul	Won	PTS–15
3 Oct 1967	JM	Freddie Little	Seoul	Won	PTS–15
26 May 1968	JM	Sandro Mazzinghi	Milan	Lost	PTS–15

Sang-Hyun KIM

Born: Pusan, South Korea, 18 Jan 1955
World title fights: 5 (all junior-welter) won 3, lost 2

DATE	WEIGHT	OPPONENT	VENUE	RESULT
30 Dec 1978	JW (WBC)	Saensak Muangsurin	Seoul	Won RSF–13
1 Jun 1979	JW (WBC)	Fitzroy Guisseppi	Seoul	Won PTS–15
3 Oct 1979	JW (WBC)	Masahiro Yokai	Tokyo	Won KO–11
23 Feb 1980	JW (WBC)	Saoul Mamby	Seoul	Lost RSF–14
2 Apr 1983	JW (WBA)	Aaron Pryor	Atlantic City	Lost RSF–3

Sung-Jun KIM

Born: Seoul, South Korea, 3 Jun 1953
World title fights: 6 (5 junior-fly, 1 flyweight) won 3, lost 2, drew 1

DATE	WEIGHT	OPPONENT	VENUE	RESULT
30 Sep 1978	JFl (WBC)	Netrnoi Vorasingh	Seoul	Won KO–3
31 Mar 1979	JFl (WBC)	Hector Melendez	Seoul	Drew 15
28 Jul 1979	JFl (WBC)	Siony Carupo	Seoul	Won PTS–15
21 Oct 1979	JFl (WBC)	Hector Melendez	Seoul	Won PTS–15
3 Jan 1980	JFl (WBC)	Shigeo Nakajima	Tokyo	Lost PTS–15
28 Jul 1980	Fl (WBC)	Shoji Oguma	Tokyo	Lost PTS–15

Tae-Shik KIM

Born: Kanwon-Do, South Korea, 4 Jul 1957
World title fights: 4 (all flyweight) won 2, lost 2

DATE	WEIGHT	OPPONENT	VENUE	RESULT
16 Feb 1980	Fl (WBA)	Luis Ibarra	Seoul	Won KO–2
29 Jun 1980	Fl (WBA)	Arnel Arrozal	Seoul	Won PTS–15
13 Dec 1980	Fl (WBA)	Peter Mathebula	Los Angeles	Lost PTS–15
30 Aug 1981	Fl (WBC)	Antonio Avelar	Seoul	Lost KO–2

Yung-Kang KIM

Born: Hwasoon Kun Chunnam, South Korea, 3 Jan 1965
World title fights: 5 (4 flyweight, 1 junior-bantam) won 3, lost 2

23 Jul 1988	Fl (WBC)	Sot Chitalada	Pohang, S Korea	Won	PTS–12
13 Nov 1988	Fl (WBC)	Emil Matsushima	Chongju, S Korea	Won	PTS–12
5 Mar 1989	Fl (WBC)	Yukhito Tamakuma	Aomori, Japan	Won	PTS–12
3 Jun 1989	Fl (WBC)	Sot Chitalada	Trang, Thailand	Lost	PTS–12
29 Sep 1990	JB (WBA)	Kaosai Galaxy	Suphan Buri, Thailand	Lost	KO–6

Pone KINGPETCH

Born: Hui Hui, Thailand, 12 Feb 1936
Died: Bangkok, 31 May 1982
World title fights: 9 (all flyweight) won 6, lost 3

16 Apr 1960	Fl	Pascual Perez	Bangkok	Won	PTS–15
22 Sep 1960	Fl	Pascual Perez	Los Angeles	Won	RSF–8
27 Jun 1961	Fl	Mitsunori Seki	Tokyo	Won	PTS–15
30 May 1962	Fl	Kyo Noguchi	Tokyo	Won	PTS–15
10 Oct 1962	Fl	Fighting Harada	Tokyo	Lost	KO–11
12 Jan 1963	Fl	Fighting Harada	Bangkok	Won	PTS–15
18 Sep 1963	Fl	Hiroyuki Ebihara	Tokyo	Lost	KO–1
23 Jan 1964	Fl	Hiroyuki Ebihara	Bangkok	Won	PTS–15
23 Apr 1965	Fl	Salvatore Burruni	Rome	Lost	PTS–15

Muangchai KITTIKASEM

Born: Chainat, Thailand, 6 May 1968
World title fights: 5 (all junior-fly) won 4, lost 1

2 May 1989	JFl (IBF)	Tacy Macalos	Bangkok	Won	PTS–12
6 Oct 1989	JFl (IBF)	Tacy Macalos	Bangkok	Won	RSF–7

DATE	WEIGHT	OPPONENT	VENUE	RESULT
19 Jan 1990	JFl (IBF)	Jeung-Jai Lee	Bangkok	Won KO–3
10 Apr 1990	JFl (IBF)	Abdy Pohan	Bangkok	Won PTS–12
29 Jul 1990	JFl (IBF)	Michael Carbajal	Phoenix	Lost RSF–7

Frankie KLAUS

Born: Pittsburgh, USA, 30 Dec 1887
Died: Pittsburgh, 8 Feb 1948
World title fights: 3 (all middleweight) won 1, lost 2

DATE	WEIGHT	OPPONENT	VENUE	RESULT
5 Mar 1913	M	Billy Papke	Paris	Won DIS–15
11 Oct 1913	M	George Chip	Pittsburgh	Lost KO–6
23 Dec 1913	M	George Chip	Pittsburgh	Lost KO–5

Frankie KLICK

Born: San Francisco, USA, 5 May 1907
Died: San Francisco, 18 May 1982
World title fights: 3 (1 junior-light, 2 junior-welter) won 1, lost 1, drew 1

DATE	WEIGHT	OPPONENT	VENUE	RESULT
26 Dec 1933	JL	Kid Chocolate	Philadelphia	Won KO–7
5 Mar 1934	JW	Barney Ross	San Francisco	Drew 10
28 Jan 1935	JW	Barney Ross	Miami	Lost PTS–10

Hiroshi KOBAYASHI

Born: Isesaki, Gumma, Japan, 23 Aug 1944
World title fights: 8 (all junior-light) won 6, lost 1, drew 1

DATE	WEIGHT	OPPONENT	VENUE	RESULT
14 Dec 1967	JL	Yoshiaki Numata	Tokyo	Won KO–12
30 Mar 1968	JL	Rene Barrientos	Tokyo	Drew 15
6 Oct 1968	JL	Jaime Valladares	Tokyo	Won PTS–15
6 Apr 1969	JL (WBA)	Antonio Amaya	Tokyo	Won PTS–15

DATE	WEIGHT	OPPONENT	VENUE	RESULT
9 Nov 1969	JL (WBA)	Carlos Canete	Tokyo	Won PTS–15
23 Aug 1970	JL (WBA)	Antonio Amaya	Tokyo	Won PTS–15
4 Mar 1971	JL (WBA)	Ricardo Arredondo	Utsunomija, Japan	Won PTS–15
29 Jul 1971	JL (WBA)	Alfredo Marcano	Aomori, Japan	Lost RTD–10

Koji KOBAYASHI

Born: Tokyo, Japan, 27 Aug 1957
World title fights: 2 (both flyweight) won 1, lost 1

18 Jan 1984	Fl (WBC)	Frank Cedeno	Tokyo	Won RSF–2
9 Apr 1984	Fl (WBC)	Gabriel Bernal	Tokyo	Lost RSF–2

Kazuo 'Royal' KOBAYASHI

Born: Fukuoka, Japan, 10 Oct 1949
World title fights: 5 (2 featherweight, 3 junior-feather) won 1, lost 4

12 Oct 1975	Fe (WBA)	Alexis Arguello	Tokyo	Lost KO–5
9 Oct 1976	JFe (WBC)	Rigoberto Riasco	Tokyo	Won RSF–8
24 Nov 1976	JFe (WBC)	Dong-Kyun Yum	Seoul	Lost PTS–15
19 Jan 1978	JFe (WBC)	Wilfredo Gomez	Kitakyushu, Japan	Lost KO–3
9 Jan 1979	Fe (WBA)	Eusebio Pedroza	Tokyo	Lost RTD–13

Nana Yaw KONADU

Born: Sonyani, Ghana, 14 Feb 1965
World title fights: 2 (both junior-bantam) won 1, lost 1

7 Nov 1989	JB (WBC)	Gilberto Roman	Mexico City	Won PTS–12
20 Jan 1990	JB (WBC)	Sung-Kil Moon	Seoul	Lost TD–9

DATE	WEIGHT	OPPONENT	VENUE	RESULT

David 'Poison' KOTEY

Born: Accra, Ghana, 7 Dec 1950
World title fights: 5 (all featherweight) won 3, lost 2

DATE	WEIGHT	OPPONENT	VENUE	RESULT
20 Sep 1975	Fe (WBC)	Ruben Olivares	Los Angeles	Won PTS–15
6 Mar 1976	Fe (WBC)	Yasutsune Uehara	Accra	Won RSF–12
16 Jul 1976	Fe (WBC)	Shig Fukuyama	Tokyo	Won RSF–3
5 Nov 1976	Fe (WBC)	Danny Lopez	Accra	Lost PTS–15
15 Feb 1978	Fe (WBC)	Danny Lopez	Las Vegas	Lost RSF–6

Solly KREIGER

Born: Brooklyn, New York, USA, 28 Mar 1909
Died: Las Vegas, 24 Sep 1964
World title fights: 2 (both middleweight) won 1, lost 1

DATE	WEIGHT	OPPONENT	VENUE	RESULT
1 Nov 1938	M (NBA)	Al Hostak	Seattle	Won PTS–15
27 Jun 1939	M (NBA)	Al Hostak	Seattle	Lost KO–4

Masashi KUDO

Born: Gojome-cho, Akita-Gun, Japan, 24 Aug 1951
World title fights: 5 (all junior-middle) won 4, lost 1

DATE	WEIGHT	OPPONENT	VENUE	RESULT
9 Aug 1978	JM (WBA)	Eddie Gazo	Akita, Japan	Won PTS–15
14 Dec 1978	JM (WBA)	Ho-In Joo	Osaka, Japan	Won PTS–15
14 Mar 1979	JM (WBA)	Manuel Gonzalez	Tokyo	Won PTS–15
20 Jun 1979	JM (WBA)	Manuel Gonzalez	Yokaichi, Japan	Won RTD–12
24 Oct 1979	JM (WBA)	Ayub Kalule	Akita	Lost PTS–15

Soo-Chun KWON

Born: Kyong-Ki Do, South Korea, 24 Apr 1959
World title fights: 9 (1 junior-bantam, 8 flyweight) won 5, lost 2, drew 2

DATE	WEIGHT	OPPONENT	VENUE	RESULT
5 Oct 1983	JB (WBA)	Jiro Watanabe	Osaka, Japan	Lost TD–11
24 Dec 1983	Fl (IBF)	Rene Busayong	Seoul	Won KO–5
25 Feb 1984	Fl (IBF)	Roger Castillo	Seoul	Won PTS–15
19 May 1984	Fl (IBF)	Ian Clyde	Taejon, S Korea	Won PTS–15
7 Sep 1984	Fl (IBF)	Joaquin Caraballo	Seoul	Won RSF–12
25 Jan 1985	Fl (IBF)	Chong-Kwan Chung	Taejon	Drew 15
14 Apr 1985	Fl (IBF)	Shinobu Kawashima	Seoul	Won KO–3
17 Jul 1985	Fl (IBF)	Chong-Kwan Chung	Masan, S Korea	Drew 15
20 Dec 1985	Fl (IBF)	Chong-Kwan Chung	Pusan, S Korea	Lost RSF–4

Fidel La BARBA

Born: New York City, USA, 29 Sep 1905
Died: Los Angeles, 3 Oct 1981
World title fights: 4 (2 flyweight, 2 featherweight) won 2, lost 2

DATE	WEIGHT	OPPONENT	VENUE	RESULT
22 Aug 1925	Fl	Frankie Genaro	Los Angeles	Won PTS–10
21 Jan 1927	Fl	Elky Clark	New York	Won PTS–12
22 May 1931	Fe	Battling Battalino	New York	Lost PTS–15
9 Dec 1932	Fe (NY)	Kid Chocolate	New York	Lost PTS–15

Santos LACIAR

Born: Cordoba, Argentina, 31 Jan 1959
World title fights: 16 (12 flyweight, 4 junior-bantam) won 12, lost 3, drew 1

DATE	WEIGHT	OPPONENT	VENUE	RESULT
28 Mar 1981	Fl (WBA)	Peter Mathebula	Johannesburg	Won KO–7
6 Jun 1981	Fl (WBA)	Luis Ibarra	Buenos Aires	Lost PTS–15
1 May 1982	Fl (WBA)	Juan Herrera	Merida, Mexico	Won RSF–13

DATE	WEIGHT	OPPONENT	VENUE	RESULT
14 Aug 1982	Fl (WBA)	Betulio Gonzalez	Maracaibo, Venezuela	Won PTS-15
5 Nov 1982	Fl (WBA)	Stephen Muchoki	Copenhagen	Won RSF-13
4 Mar 1983	Fl (WBA)	Raymond Neri	Cordoba, Argentina	Won KO-9
5 May 1983	Fl (WBA)	Shuichi Hozumi	Shizuoka, Japan	Won RSF-2
17 Jul 1983	Fl (WBA)	Hi-Sup Shin	Cheju, S Korea	Won RSF-1
28 Jan 1984	Fl (WBA)	Juan Herrera	Marsala, Italy	Won PTS-15
15 Sep 1984	Fl (WBA)	Prudencio Cardona	Cordoba, Argentina	Won KO-10
8 Dec 1984	Fl (WBA)	Hilario Zapata	Buenos Aires	Won PTS-15
6 May 1985	Fl (WBA)	Antoine Montero	Grenoble, France	Won PTS-15
30 Aug 1986	JB (WBC)	Gilberto Roman	Cordoba, Mexico	Drew 12
16 May 1987	JB (WBC)	Gilberto Roman	Reims, France	Won RSF-11
8 Aug 1987	JB (WBC)	Baby Rojas	Miami	Lost PTS-12
12 Sep 1989	JB (WBC)	Gilberto Roman	Los Angeles	Lost PTS-12

Ismael LAGUNA

Born: Colon, Panama, 28 Jun 1943
World title fights: 7 (all lightweight) won 3, lost 4

DATE	WEIGHT	OPPONENT	VENUE	RESULT
10 Apr 1965	L	Carlos Ortiz	Panama City	Won PTS-15
13 Nov 1965	L	Carlos Ortiz	San Juan	Lost PTS-15
16 Aug 1967	L	Carlos Ortiz	New York	Lost PTS-15
3 Mar 1970	L	Mando Ramos	Los Angeles	Won RTD-9
6 Jun 1970	L	Ishimatsu Suzuki	Panama City	Won RSF-13
26 Sep 1970	L	Ken Buchanan	San Juan	Lost PTS-15
13 Sep 1971	L	Ken Buchanan	New York	Lost PTS-15

DATE	WEIGHT	OPPONENT	VENUE	RESULT

Donny LALONDE

Born: Kitchener, Ontario, Canada, 12 Mar 1960
World title fights: 3 (2 light-heavy, 1 light-heavy/super-middle) won 2, lost 1

DATE	WEIGHT	OPPONENT	VENUE	RESULT	
27 Nov 1987	LH (WBC)	Eddie Davis	Port of Spain, Trinidad	Won	RSF-2
29 May 1988	LH (WBC)	Leslie Stewart	Port of Spain	Won	RSF-5
7 Nov 1988	LH (WBC)/ SM (WBC)	Sugar Ray Leonard	Las Vegas	Lost	RSF-9

Jake LA MOTTA

Born: Bronx, New York, USA, 10 Jul 1921
World title fights: 4 (all middleweight) won 3, lost 1

DATE	WEIGHT	OPPONENT	VENUE	RESULT	
16 Jun 1949	M	Marcel Cerdan	Detroit	Won	RTD-10
12 Jul 1950	M	Tiberio Mitri	New York	Won	PTS-15
13 Sep 1950	M	Laurent Dauthuille	Detroit	Won	KO-15
14 Feb 1951	M	Sugar Ray Robinson	Chicago	Lost	RSF-13

Jeff LAMPKIN

Born: Youngstown, Ohio, USA, 21 Sep 1959
World title fights: 2 (both cruiserweight) won 2, lost 0

DATE	WEIGHT	OPPONENT	VENUE	RESULT	
22 Mar 1990	C (IBF)	Glenn McCrory	Gateshead, England	Won	KO-3
29 Jul 1990	C (IBF)	Siza Makhathini	St Petersburg, Florida	Won	KO-8

Juan LAPORTE

Born: Guyama, Puerto Rico, 24 Nov 1959
World title fights: 9 (6 featherweight, 3 junior-light) won 3, lost 6

DATE	WEIGHT	OPPONENT	VENUE	RESULT	
13 Dec 1980	Fe (WBC)	Salvador Sanchez	El Paso, Texas	Lost	PTS-15
24 Jan 1982	Fe (WBA)	Eusebio Pedroza	Atlantic City	Lost	PTS-15

DATE	WEIGHT	OPPONENT	VENUE	RESULT
15 Sep 1982	Fe (WBC)	Mario Miranda	New York	Won RSF–10
20 Feb 1983	Fe (WBC)	Ruben Castillo	San Juan	Won PTS–12
25 Jun 1983	Fe (WBC)	Johnny de la Rosa	San Juan	Won PTS–12
31 Mar 1984	Fe (WBC)	Wilfredo Gomez	San Juan	Lost PTS–12
12 Dec 1986	JL (WBC)	Julio Cesar Chavez	New York	Lost PTS–12
29 Apr 1989	JL (WBO)	Juan Molina	San Juan	Lost PTS–12
13 Oct 1990	JL (WBC)	Azumah Nelson	Sydney	Lost PTS–12

Tippy LARKIN

Born: Garfield, New Jersey, USA, 11 Nov 1917
World title fights: 3 (1 lightweight, 2 junior-welter) won 2, lost 1

DATE	WEIGHT	OPPONENT	VENUE	RESULT
18 Dec 1942	L (NY)	Beau Jack	New York	Lost KO–3
29 Apr 1946	JW	Willie Joyce	Boston	Won PTS–12
13 Sep 1946	JW	Willie Joyce	New York	Won PTS–12

Cecilio LASTRA

Born: Monte, Santander, Spain, 12 Aug 1951
World title fights: 2 (both featherweight) won 1, lost 1

DATE	WEIGHT	OPPONENT	VENUE	RESULT
17 Dec 1977	Fe (WBA)	Rafael Ortega	Torrelavega, Spain	Won PTS–15
15 Apr 1978	Fe (WBA)	Eusebio Pedroza	Panama City	Lost KO–13

Pete LATZO

Born: Coloraine, Pennsylvania, USA, 1 Aug 1902
Died: Atlantic City, USA, 7 Jul 1968
World title fights: 7 (5 welterweight, 2 light-heavy) won 3, lost 3, ND 1

DATE	WEIGHT	OPPONENT	VENUE	RESULT
22 Mar 1923	W	Mickey Walker	Newark, New Jersey	ND–12
20 May 1926	W	Mickey Walker	Scranton, Pennsylvania	Won PTS–10

DATE	WEIGHT	OPPONENT	VENUE	RESULT

29 Jun 1926	W	Willie Harmon	Newark	Won KO–5
9 Jul 1926	W	George Levine	New York	Won DIS–4
3 Jun 1927	W	Joe Dundee	New York	Lost PTS–15
1 Jun 1928	LH	Tommy Loughran	Brooklyn, New York	Lost PTS–15
16 Jul 1928	LH	Tommy Loughran	Wilkes-Barre, Pennsylvania	Lost PTS–10

George 'Kid' LAVIGNE

Born: Bay City, Michigan, USA, 6 Dec 1869
Died: Detroit, 9 Mar 1928
World title fights: 10 (9 lightweight, 1 welterweight) won 6, lost 2, drew 2)

1 Jun 1896	L	Dick Burge	London	Won KO–17
27 Oct 1896	L	Jack Everhardt	New York	Won KO–24
8 Feb 1897	L	Kid McPartland	New York	Won PTS–25
28 Apr 1897	L	Eddie Connolly	New York	Won KO–11
29 Oct 1897	L	Joe Walcott	San Francisco	Won PTS–12
17 Mar 1898	L	Jack Daly	Cleveland	Drew 20
28 Sep 1898	L	Frank Erne	Coney Island, New York	Drew 20
25 Nov 1898	L	Tom Tracy	San Francisco	Won PTS–20
10 Mar 1899	W	Mysterious Billy Smith	San Francisco	Lost RSF–14
3 Jul 1899	L	Frank Erne	Buffalo	Lost PTS–20

Alfredo LAYNE

Born: Panama City, Panama, 9 Oct 1959
World title fights: 2 (both junior-light) won 1, lost 1

24 May 1986	JL (WBA)	Wilfredo Gomez	San Juan	Won RSF–9
27 Sep 1986	JL (WBA)	Brian Mitchell	Sun City, S Africa	Lost RSF–10

Kyung-Yun LEE

Born: Poongki-Kyungnam, South Korea, 4 Dec 1966
World title fights: 2 (both strawweight) won 1, lost 1

DATE	WEIGHT	OPPONENT	VENUE	RESULT
14 Jun 1987	S (IBF)	Masaharu Kawakami	Bukok, S Korea	Won RSF-2
31 Jan 1988	S (WBC)	Hiroki Ioka	Osaka, Japan	Lost RSF-12

Seung-Hoon LEE

Born: Chunbuk, South Korea, 26 Jul 1960
World title fights: 8 (1 junior-bantam, 1 bantamweight, 6 junior-feather) won 4, lost 3, drew 1

DATE	WEIGHT	OPPONENT	VENUE	RESULT
2 Feb 1980	JB (WBC)	Rafael Orono	Caracas	Lost PTS-15
3 Jun 1982	B (WBC)	Lupe Pintor	Los Angeles	Lost RSF-11
2 Feb 1985	JFe (WBA)	Victor Callejas	San Juan	Lost PTS-15
18 Jan 1987	JFe (IBF)	Prayurasak Muangsurin	Pohang, S Korea	Won KO-9
5 Apr 1987	JFe (IBF)	Jorge Urbina Diaz	Seoul	Won KO-10
18 Jul 1987	JFe (IBF)	Leo Collins	Pohang	Won KO-5
27 Dec 1987	JFe (IBF)	Jose Sanabria	Pohang	Won PTS-15
29 May 1988	JFe (WBC)	Daniel Zaragoza	Seoul	Drew 12

Yul-Woo LEE

Born: Chungcheong-nam, South Korea, 25 Jan 1967
World title fights: 4 (2 junior-fly, 2 flyweight) won 2, lost 2

DATE	WEIGHT	OPPONENT	VENUE	RESULT
19 Mar 1989	JFl (WBC)	German Torres	Seoul	Won RSF-9
25 Jun 1989	JFl (WBC)	Humberto Gonzalez	Chongju, S Korea	Lost PTS-12
10 Mar 1990	Fl (WBA)	Jesus Rojas	Taejon City, S Korea	Won PTS-12
28 Jul 1990	Fl (WBA)	Yukito Tamakuma	Mito, Japan	Lost RSF-10

DATE	WEIGHT	OPPONENT	VENUE	RESULT

Jose LEGRA

Born: Baracoa, Cuba, 19 Apr 1943
World title fights: 4 (all featherweight) won 2, lost 2

DATE	WEIGHT	OPPONENT	VENUE	RESULT	
24 Jul 1968	Fe (WBC)	Howard Winstone	Porthcawl, Wales	Won	RSF-5
21 Jan 1969	Fe (WBC)	Johnny Famechon	London	Lost	PTS-15
16 Dec 1972	Fe (WBC)	Clemente Sanchez	Monterrey, Mexico	Won	RSF-10
5 May 1973	Fe (WBC)	Eder Jofre	Brasília	Lost	PTS-15

Richie LEMOS

Born: Los Angeles, USA, 6 Feb 1920
World title fights: 3 (all featherweight) won 1, lost 2

DATE	WEIGHT	OPPONENT	VENUE	RESULT	
1 Jul 1941	Fe (NBA)	Petey Scalzo	Los Angeles	Won	KO-5
18 Nov 1941	Fe (NBA)	Jackie Wilson	Los Angeles	Lost	PTS-12
12 Dec 1941	Fe (NBA)	Jackie Wilson	Los Angeles	Lost	PTS-12

Genaro LEON

Born: Culiacan, Mexico, 10 Aug 1960
World title fights: 1 (welterweight) won 1, lost 0

DATE	WEIGHT	OPPONENT	VENUE	RESULT	
6 May 1989	W (WBO)	Danny Garcia	Santa Ana, California	Won	RSF-1

Benny LEONARD

Born: New York City, USA, 7 Apr 1896
Died: New York City, 18 Apr 1947
World title fights: 9 (8 lightweight, 1 welterweight) won 8, lost 1

DATE	WEIGHT	OPPONENT	VENUE	RESULT	
28 May 1917	L	Freddie Welsh	New York	Won	KO-9
25 Jul 1917	L	Johnny Kilbane	Philadelphia	Won	RTD-3
5 Jul 1920	L	Charlie White	Benton Harbour, Michigan	Won	KO-8

DATE	WEIGHT	OPPONENT	VENUE	RESULT

DATE	WEIGHT	OPPONENT	VENUE	RESULT
26 Nov 1920	L	Joe Welling	New York	Won RSF–14
14 Jan 1921	L	Ritchie Mitchell	New York	Won RSF–6
10 Feb 1922	L	Rocky Kansas	New York	Won PTS–15
26 Jun 1922	W	Jack Britton	New York	Lost DIS–13
4 Jul 1922	L	Rocky Kansas	Michigan City, Indiana	Won RTD–8
24 Jul 1923	L	Lew Tendler	New York	Won PTS–15

Sugar Ray LEONARD

Born: Wilmington, South Carolina, USA, 17 May 1956
World title fights: 12 (7 welterweight, 1 junior-middle, 1 middleweight,
1 light-heavy/super-middle, 2 super-middle) won 10, lost 1, drew 1

DATE	WEIGHT	OPPONENT	VENUE	RESULT
30 Nov 1979	W (WBC)	Wilfred Benitez	Las Vegas	Won RSF–15
31 Mar 1980	W (WBC)	Dave 'Boy' Green	Landover, Maryland	Won KO–4
20 Jun 1980	W (WBC)	Roberto Duran	Montreal	Lost PTS–15
25 Nov 1980	W (WBC)	Roberto Duran	New Orleans	Won RTD–8
28 Mar 1981	W (WBC)	Larry Bonds	Syracuse, New York	Won RSF–10
25 Jun 1981	JM (WBA)	Ayube Kalule	Houston	Won KO–9
16 Sep 1981	W	Thomas Hearns	Las Vegas	Won RSF–14
15 Feb 1982	W (WBC)	Bruce Finch	Reno, Nevada	Won RSF–3
6 Apr 1987	M (WBC)	Marvin Hagler	Las Vegas	Won PTS–12
7 Nov 1988	LH (WBC)/ SM (WBC)	Donny Lalonde	Las Vegas	Won RSF–9
12 Jun 1989	SM (WBC)	Thomas Hearns	Las Vegas	Drew 12
7 Dec 1989	SM (WBC)	Roberto Duran	Las Vegas	Won PTS–12

DATE	WEIGHT	OPPONENT	VENUE	RESULT

Gus LESNEVICH

Born: Cliffside Park, New Jersey, USA, 22 Feb 1915
Died: Cliffside Park, 28 Feb 1964
World title fights: 10 (9 light-heavy, 1 heavyweight) won 6, lost 4

DATE	WEIGHT	OPPONENT	VENUE	RESULT	
17 Nov 1939	LH	Billy Conn	New York	Lost	PTS-15
5 Jun 1940	LH	Billy Conn	Detroit	Lost	PTS-15
22 May 1941	LH	Anton Christoforidis	New York	Won	PTS-15
26 Aug 1941	LH	Tami Mauriello	New York	Won	PTS-15
14 Nov 1941	LH	Tami Mauriello	New York	Won	PTS-15
14 May 1946	LH	Freddie Mills	London	Won	RSF-10
28 Feb 1947	LH	Billy Fox	New York	Won	KO-10
5 Mar 1948	LH	Billy Fox	New York	Won	KO-1
26 Jul 1948	LH	Freddie Mills	London	Lost	PTS-15
10 Aug 1949	H (NBA)	Ezzard Charles	New York	Lost	RSF-7

Battling LEVINSKY

Born: Philadelphia, USA, 10 Jun 1891
Died: Philadelphia, 12 Feb 1949
World title fights: 3 (all light-heavy) won 1, lost 2

DATE	WEIGHT	OPPONENT	VENUE	RESULT	
25 Apr 1916	LH	Jack Dillon	Kansas City	Lost	PTS-15
24 Oct 1916	LH	Jack Dillon	Boston	Won	PTS-12
12 Oct 1920	LH	Georges Carpentier	Jersey City, New Jersey	Lost	KO-4

John Henry LEWIS

Born: Los Angeles, USA, 1 May 1914
Died: Berkeley, California, 18 Apr 1974
World title fights: 7 (6 light-heavy, 1 heavyweight) won 6, lost 1

DATE	WEIGHT	OPPONENT	VENUE	RESULT	
31 Oct 1935	LH	Bob Olin	St Louis	Won	PTS-15

DATE	WEIGHT	OPPONENT	VENUE	RESULT

DATE	WEIGHT	OPPONENT	VENUE	RESULT
13 Mar 1936	LH	Jock McAvoy	New York	Won PTS-15
9 Nov 1936	LH	Len Harvey	London	Won PTS-15
3 Jun 1937	LH	Bob Olin	St Louis	Won KO-8
25 Apr 1938	LH	Emilio Martinez	Minneapolis	Won KO-4
28 Oct 1938	LH	Al Gainer	New Haven, Connecticut	Won PTS-15
25 Jan 1939	H	Joe Louis	New York	Lost RSF-1

Ted 'Kid' LEWIS

Born: London, England, 24 Oct 1894
Died: London, 20 Oct 1970
World title fights: 11 (10 welterweight, 1 light-heavy) won 5, lost 4, ND 2

DATE	WEIGHT	OPPONENT	VENUE	RESULT
31 Aug 1915	W	Jack Britton	Boston	Won PTS-12
27 Sep 1915	W	Jack Britton	Boston	Won PTS-12
24 Apr 1916	W	Jack Britton	New Orleans	Lost PTS-20
25 Jun 1917	W	Jack Britton	Dayton, Ohio	Won PTS-20
4 Jul 1917	W	Johnny Griffiths	Akron, Ohio	ND-15
31 Aug 1917	W	Albert Badoud	New York	Won KO-1
17 May 1918	W	Johnny Tillman	Denver	Won RTD-20
4 Jul 1918	W	Johnny Griffiths	Akron	ND-20
17 Mar 1919	W	Jack Britton	Canton, Ohio	Lost KO-9
7 Feb 1921	W	Jack Britton	New York	Lost PTS-15
11 May 1922	LH	Georges Carpentier	London	Lost KO-1

Rafael LIMON

Born: Mexico City, Mexico, 13 Jan 1954
World title fights: 7 (all junior-light) won 3, lost 4

DATE	WEIGHT	OPPONENT	VENUE	RESULT
8 Jul 1979	JL (WBC)	Alexis Arguello	New York	Lost RSF-11
11 Dec 1980	JL (WBC)	Ildefonso Bethelmy	Los Angeles	Won RSF-15

DATE	WEIGHT	OPPONENT	VENUE	RESULT

DATE	WEIGHT	OPPONENT	VENUE	RESULT	
8 Mar 1981	JL (WBC)	Cornelius Boza-Edwards	Stockton, California	Lost	PTS–15
29 May 1982	JL (WBC)	Rolando Navarrete	Las Vegas	Won	KO–12
18 Sep 1982	JL (WBC)	Chung-Il Choi	Los Angeles	Won	KO–7
11 Dec 1982	JL (WBC)	Bobby Chacon	Sacramento, California	Lost	PTS–15
8 Aug 1983	JL (WBC)	Hector Camacho	San Juan	Lost	RSF–5

Sonny LISTON

Born: St Francis County, Arkansas, USA, 8 May 1932
Died: Las Vegas, 30 Dec 1970
World title fights: 4 (all heavyweight) won 2, lost 2

25 Sep 1962	H	Floyd Patterson	Chicago	Won	KO–1
22 Jul 1963	H	Floyd Patterson	Las Vegas	Won	KO–1
25 Feb 1964	H	Cassius Clay	Miami	Lost	RTD–6
25 May 1965	H	Muhammad Ali	Lewiston, Maine	Lost	KO–1
		(formerly Cassius Clay)			

Freddie LITTLE

Born: Picayune, Mississippi, USA, 25 Apr 1936
World title fights: 6 (all junior-middle) won 3, lost 2, NC 1

3 Oct 1967	JM	Ki-Soo Kim	Seoul	Lost	PTS–15
25 Oct 1968	JM	Sandro Mazzinghi	Rome		NC–8
17 Mar 1969	JM	Stan Hayward	Las Vegas	Won	PTS–15
9 Sep 1969	JM	Hisao Minami	Osaka, Japan	Won	KO–2
20 Mar 1970	JM	Gerhard Piaskowy	Berlin	Won	PTS–15
9 Jul 1970	JM	Carmel Bossi	Monza, Italy	Lost	PTS–15

DATE	WEIGHT	OPPONENT	VENUE	RESULT

Nicolino LOCHE

Born: Tunuyan, Mendoza, Argentina, 2 Sep 1939
World title fights: 8 (all junior-welter) won 6, lost 2

DATE	WEIGHT	OPPONENT	VENUE	RESULT	
12 Dec 1968	JW (WBA)	Paul Fujii	Tokyo	Won	RTD–9
3 May 1969	JW (WBA)	Carlos Hernandez	Buenos Aires	Won	PTS–15
11 Oct 1969	JW (WBA)	Joao Henrique	Buenos Aires	Won	PTS–15
16 May 1970	JW (WBA)	Adolph Pruitt	Buenos Aires	Won	PTS–15
3 Apr 1971	JW (WBA)	Domingo Barrera	Buenos Aires	Won	PTS–15
11 Dec 1971	JW (WBA)	Antonio Cervantes	Buenos Aires	Won	PTS–15
10 Mar 1972	JW (WBA)	Alfonso Frazer	Panama City	Lost	PTS–15
17 Mar 1973	JW (WBA)	Antonio Cervantes	Maracay, Venezuela	Lost	RTD–9

Rocky LOCKRIDGE

Born: Dallas, Texas, USA, 10 Jan 1959
World title fights: 12 (2 featherweight, 10 junior-light) won 6, lost 6

DATE	WEIGHT	OPPONENT	VENUE	RESULT	
4 Oct 1980	Fe (WBA)	Eusebio Pedroza	Great George, New Jersey	Lost	PTS–15
24 Apr 1983	Fe (WBA)	Eusebio Pedroza	San Remo, Italy	Lost	PTS–15
25 Feb 1984	JL (WBA)	Roger Mayweather	Beaumont, Texas	Won	KO–1
12 Jun 1984	JL (WBA)	Tae-Jin Moon	Anchorage, Alaska	Won	RSF–11
26 Jan 1985	JL (WBA)	Kamel Bou-Ali	River del Garda, Italy	Won	RSF–6
19 May 1985	JL (WBA)	Wilfredo Gomez	San Juan	Lost	PTS–15
3 Aug 1986	JL (WBC)	Julio Cesar Chavez	Monte Carlo	Lost	PTS–12
9 Aug 1987	JL (IBF)	Barry Michael	Windsor, England	Won	RTD–8
25 Oct 1987	JL (IBF)	Johnny de la Rosa	Tucson, Arizona	Won	RSF–10
2 Apr 1988	JL (IBF)	Harold Knight	Atlantic City	Won	PTS–15
27 Jul 1988	JL (IBF)	Tony Lopez	Sacramento, California	Lost	PTS–12
5 Mar 1989	JL (IBF)	Tony Lopez	Sacramento	Lost	PTS–12

DATE	WEIGHT	OPPONENT	VENUE	RESULT

Duilio LOI

Born: Trieste, Italy, 19 Apr 1929
World title fights: 6 (all junior-welter) won 3, lost 2, drew 1

DATE	WEIGHT	OPPONENT	VENUE	RESULT
15 Jun 1960	JW	Carlos Ortiz	San Francisco	Lost PTS-15
1 Sep 1960	JW	Carlos Ortiz	Milan	Won PTS-15
10 May 1961	JW	Carlos Ortiz	Milan	Won PTS-15
21 Oct 1961	JW	Eddie Perkins	Milan	Drew 15
14 Sep 1962	JW	Eddie Perkins	Milan	Lost PTS-15
15 Dec 1962	JW	Eddie Perkins	Milan	Won PTS-15

Falan LOOKMINGKWAN

Born: Thailand
World title fights: 3 (all strawweight) won 3, lost 0

DATE	WEIGHT	OPPONENT	VENUE	RESULT
21 Feb 1990	S (IBF)	Eric Chavez	Bangkok	Won RSF-7
15 Jun 1990	S (IBF)	Joe Constantino	Bangkok	Won PTS-12
15 Aug 1990	S (IBF)	Eric Chavez	Bangkok	Won PTS-12

Alfonso LOPEZ

Born: Taimiti, Panama, 8 Jan 1953
World title fights: 6 (4 flyweight, 2 junior-fly) won 2, lost 4

DATE	WEIGHT	OPPONENT	VENUE	RESULT
27 Feb 1976	Fl (WBA)	Erbito Salavarria	Manila	Won RSF-15
21 Apr 1976	Fl (WBA)	Shoji Oguma	Tokyo	Won PTS-15
2 Oct 1976	Fl (WBA)	Guty Espadas	Los Angeles	Lost RSF-13
30 Apr 1977	Fl (WBA)	Guty Espadas	Merida, Mexico	Lost RSF-13
8 Apr 1979	JFl (WBA)	Yoko Gushiken	Tokyo	Lost KO-7
11 Oct 1981	JFl (WBA)	Hwan-Jin Kim	Seoul	Lost PTS-15

DATE	WEIGHT	OPPONENT	VENUE	RESULT

Danny LOPEZ

Born: Fort Duchesne, Utah, USA, 6 Jul 1952
World title fights: 11 (all featherweight) won 9, lost 2

DATE	WEIGHT	OPPONENT	VENUE	RESULT	
5 Nov 1976	Fe (WBC)	David 'Poison' Kotey	Accra	Won	PTS–15
13 Sep 1977	Fe (WBC)	Jose Torres	Los Angeles	Won	RSF–7
15 Feb 1978	Fe (WBC)	David 'Poison' Kotey	Las Vegas	Won	RSF–6
22 Apr 1978	Fe (WBC)	Jose De Paula	Los Angeles	Won	RSF–6
15 Sep 1978	Fe (WBC)	Juan Malvarez	New Orleans	Won	KO–2
21 Oct 1978	Fe (WBC)	Fel Clemente	Pesaro, Italy	Won	DIS–4
10 Mar 1979	Fe (WBC)	Roberto Castanon	Salt Lake City	Won	KO–2
17 Jun 1979	Fe (WBC)	Mike Ayala	San Antonio, Texas	Won	KO–15
25 Sep 1979	Fe (WBC)	Jose Caba	Los Angeles	Won	KO–3
2 Feb 1980	Fe (WBC)	Salvador Sanchez	Phoenix	Lost	RSF–13
21 Jun 1980	Fe (WBC)	Salvador Sanchez	Las Vegas	Lost	RSF–14

Ricardo LOPEZ

Born: Mexico City, Mexico, 25 Jul 1967
World title fights: 1 (strawweight) won 1, lost 0

DATE	WEIGHT	OPPONENT	VENUE	RESULT	
25 Oct 1990	S (WBC)	Hideyuki Ohashi	Tokyo	Won	RSF–5

Tony LOPEZ

Born: Sacramento, California, USA, 24 Feb 1963
World title fights: 7 (all junior-light) won 6, lost 1

DATE	WEIGHT	OPPONENT	VENUE	RESULT	
27 Jul 1988	JL (IBF)	Rocky Lockridge	Sacramento, California	Won	PTS–12
27 Oct 1988	JL (IBF)	Juan Molina	Sacramento	Won	PTS–12
5 Mar 1989	JL (IBF)	Rocky Lockridge	Sacramento	Won	PTS–12
21 Jun 1989	JL (IBF)	Tyrone Jackson	Lake Tahoe, Nevada	Won	RSF–8

DATE	WEIGHT	OPPONENT	VENUE	RESULT

DATE	WEIGHT	OPPONENT	VENUE	RESULT
7 Oct 1989	JL (IBF)	Juan Molina	Sacramento	Lost RSF–10
20 May 1990	JL (IBF)	Juan Mohina	Reno, Nevada	Won PTS–12
22 Sep 1990	JL (IBF)	Jorge Paez	Sacramento	Won PTS–12

Sandro LOPOPOLO

Born: Milan, Italy, 18 Dec 1939
World title fights: 3 (all junior-welter) won 2, lost 1

DATE	WEIGHT	OPPONENT	VENUE	RESULT
29 Apr 1966	JW	Carlos Hernandez	Rome	Won PTS–15
21 Oct 1966	JW	Vicente Rivas	Rome	Won RSF–7
30 Apr 1967	JW	Paul Fujii	Tokyo	Lost RTD–2

Miguel 'Happy' LORA

Born: Monteria, Cordoba, Colombia, 12 Apr 1961
World title fights: 9 (all bantamweight) won 8, lost 1

DATE	WEIGHT	OPPONENT	VENUE	RESULT
9 Aug 1985	B (WBC)	Daniel Zaragoza	Miami	Won PTS–12
8 Feb 1986	B (WBC)	Wilfredo Vasquez	Miami	Won PTS–12
23 Aug 1986	B (WBC)	Enrique Sanchez	Miami	Won TKO–6
15 Nov 1986	B (WBC)	Alberto Davila	Barranquilla, Colombia	Won PTS–12
25 Jul 1987	B (WBC)	Antonio Avelar	Miami	Won RSF–4
27 Nov 1987	B (WBC)	Ray Minus, Jnr	Miami	Won PTS–12
30 Apr 1988	B (WBC)	Lucio Lopez	Cartagena, Colombia	Won PTS–12
1 Aug 1988	B (WBC)	Alberto Davila	Los Angeles	Won PTS–12
29 Oct 1988	B (WBC)	Raul Perez	Las Vegas	Lost PTS–12

DATE	WEIGHT	OPPONENT	VENUE	RESULT

Tommy LOUGHRAN

Born: Philadelphia, USA, 29 Nov 1902
Died: Altoona, Pennsylvania, USA, 7 Jul 1982
World title fights: 8 (7 light-heavy, 1 heavyweight) won 7, lost 1

DATE	WEIGHT	OPPONENT	VENUE	RESULT	
7 Oct 1927	LH	Mike McTigue	New York	Won	PTS–15
12 Dec 1927	LH	Jimmy Slattery	New York	Won	PTS–15
6 Jan 1928	LH	Leo Lomski	New York	Won	PTS–15
1 Jun 1928	LH	Pete Latzo	Brooklyn, New York	Won	PTS–15
16 Jul 1928	LH	Pete Latzo	Wilkes-Barre, Pennsylvania	Won	PTS–10
28 Mar 1929	LH	Mickey Walker	Chicago	Won	PTS–10
18 Jul 1929	LH	Jimmy Braddock	New York	Won	PTS–15
1 Mar 1934	H	Primo Carnera	Miami	Lost	PTS–15

Joe LOUIS

Born: Lafayette, Alabama, USA, 13 May 1914
Died: Las Vegas, 12 Apr 1981
World title fights: 27 (all heavyweight) won 26, lost 1

DATE	WEIGHT	OPPONENT	VENUE	RESULT	
22 Jun 1937	H	James J Braddock	Chicago	Won	KO–8
30 Aug 1937	H	Tommy Farr	New York	Won	PTS–15
23 Feb 1938	H	Nathan Mann	New York	Won	KO–3
1 Apr 1938	H	Harry Thomas	Chicago	Won	KO–5
22 Jun 1938	H	Max Schmeling	New York	Won	KO–1
25 Jan 1939	H	John Henry Lewis	New York	Won	RSF–1
17 Apr 1939	H	Jack Roper	Los Angeles	Won	KO–1
28 Jun 1939	H	Tony Galento	New York	Won	RSF–4
20 Sep 1939	H	Bob Pastor	Detroit	Won	KO–11
9 Feb 1940	H	Arturo Godoy	New York	Won	PTS–15
29 Mar 1940	H	Johnny Paychek	New York	Won	KO–2
20 Jun 1940	H	Arturo Godoy	New York	Won	RSF–8

DATE	WEIGHT	OPPONENT	VENUE	RESULT
16 Dec 1940	H	Al McCoy	Boston	Won RTD–6
31 Jan 1941	H	Red Burman	New York	Won KO–5
17 Feb 1941	H	Gus Darazio	Philadelphia	Won KO–2
21 Mar 1941	H	Abe Simon	Detroit	Won KO–13
8 Apr 1941	H	Tony Musto	St Louis	Won RSF–9
23 May 1941	H	Buddy Baer	Washington	Won DIS–7
18 Jun 1941	H	Billy Conn	New York	Won KO–13
29 Sep 1941	H	Lou Nova	New York	Won RSF–6
9 Jan 1942	H	Buddy Baer	New York	Won KO–1
27 Mar 1942	H	Abe Simon	New York	Won KO–6
19 Jun 1946	H	Billy Conn	New York	Won KO–8
18 Sep 1946	H	Tami Mauriello	New York	Won KO–1
5 Dec 1947	H	Jersey Joe Walcott	New York	Won PTS–15
25 Jun 1948	H	Jersey Joe Walcott	New York	Won KO–11
27 Sep 1950	H	Ezzard Charles	New York	Lost PTS–15

Jorge LUJAN

Born: Colon, Panama, 18 Mar 1955
World title fights: 10 (8 bantamweight, 1 junior-feather, 1 featherweight)
won 6, lost 4

DATE	WEIGHT	OPPONENT	VENUE	RESULT
19 Nov 1977	B (WBA)	Alfonso Zamora	Los Angeles	Won KO–10
18 Mar 1978	B (WBA)	Roberto Rubaldino	San Antonio, Texas	Won RTD–11
15 Sep 1978	B (WBA)	Alberto Davila	New Orleans	Won PTS–15
8 Apr 1979	B (WBA)	Cleo Garcia	Las Vegas	Won RSF–15
6 Oct 1979	B (WBA)	Roberto Rubaldino	McAllen, Texas	Won RSF–15
2 Apr 1980	B (WBA)	Shuichi Isogami	Tokyo	Won RSF–9
29 Aug 1980	B (WBA)	Julian Solis	Miami	Lost PTS–15
31 Jan 1981	B (WBA)	Jeff Chandler	Philadelphia	Lost PTS–15

DATE	WEIGHT	OPPONENT	VENUE	RESULT

DATE	WEIGHT	OPPONENT	VENUE	RESULT
15 Jan 1982	JFe (WBA)	Sergio Palma	Cordoba, Argentina	Lost PTS–15
2 Feb 1985	Fe (WBA)	Eusebio Pedroza	Panama City	Lost PTS–15

Benny LYNCH

Born: Clydesdale, Scotland, 2 Apr 1913
Died: Glasgow, 6 Aug 1946
World title fights: 5 (all flyweight) won 4, drew 1

DATE	WEIGHT	OPPONENT	VENUE	RESULT
9 Sep 1935	Fl (NBA)	Jackie Brown	Manchester	Won RTD–2
16 Sep 1936	Fl (NBA)	Pat Palmer	Glasgow	Won KO–8
19 Jan 1937	Fl	Small Montana	London	Won PTS–15
13 Oct 1937	Fl	Peter Kane	Glasgow	Won KO–13
24 Mar 1938	Fl	Peter Kane	Liverpool	Drew 15

Joe LYNCH

Born: New York City, USA, 30 Nov 1898
Died: Brooklyn, New York, 1 Aug 1965
World title fights: 5 (all bantamweight) won 3, lost 2

DATE	WEIGHT	OPPONENT	VENUE	RESULT
22 Dec 1920	B	Pete Herman	New York	Won PTS–15
25 Jul 1921	B	Pete Herman	Brooklyn, New York	Lost PTS–15
10 Jul 1922	B	Johnny Buff	New York	Won RTD–14
22 Dec 1922	B	Midget Smith	New York	Won PTS–15
21 Mar 1924	B	Abe Goldstein	New York	Lost PTS–15

Dave McAULEY

Born: Larne, Northern Ireland, 15 Jun 1961
World title fights: 6 (all flyweight) won 4, lost 2

DATE	WEIGHT	OPPONENT	VENUE	RESULT
25 Apr 1987	Fl (WBA)	Fidel Bassa	Belfast	Lost RSF–13
26 Mar 1988	Fl (WBA)	Fidel Bassa	Belfast	Lost PTS–12

DATE	WEIGHT	OPPONENT	VENUE	RESULT

DATE	WEIGHT	OPPONENT	VENUE	RESULT
7 Jun 1989	Fl (IBF)	Duke McKenzie	London	Won PTS–12
8 Nov 1989	Fl (IBF)	Dodie Penalosa	London	Won PTS–12
17 Mar 1990	Fl (IBF)	Louis Curtis	Belfast	Won PTS–12
15 Sep 1990	Fl (IBF)	Rodolfo Blanco	Belfast	Won PTS–12

Jack McAULIFFE

Born: Cork, Ireland, 24 Mar 1866
Died: Forest Hills, New York, 5 Nov 1937
World title fights: 3 (all lightweight) won 2, drew 1

16 Nov 1887	L	Jem Carney	Revere, Massachusetts	Drew 74
10 Oct 1888	L	Billy Dacey	Dover, Delaware	Won KO–10
5 Sep 1892	L	Billy Myer	New Orleans	Won KO–15

Mike McCALLUM

Born: Kingston, Jamaica, 7 Dec 1956
World title fights: 11 (7 junior-middle, 4 middleweight) won 10, lost 1

20 Oct 1984	JM (WBA)	Sean Mannion	New York	Won PTS–15
1 Dec 1984	JM (WBA)	Luigi Minchillo	Milan	Won TKO–13
28 Jul 1985	JM (WBA)	David Braxton	Miami	Won RSF–8
23 Aug 1986	JM (WBA)	Julian Jackson	Miami	Won RSF–2
25 Oct 1986	JM (WBA)	Said Skouma	Paris	Won KO–9
19 Apr 1987	JM (WBA)	Milton McCrory	Phoenix	Won RSF–10
18 Jul 1987	JM (WBA)	Don Curry	Las Vegas	Won KO–5
5 Mar 1988	M (WBA)	Sumbu Kalambay	Pesaro, Italy	Lost PTS–12
10 May 1989	M (WBA)	Herol Graham	London	Won PTS–12
3 Feb 1990	M (WBA)	Steve Collins	Boston	Won PTS–12
14 Apr 1990	M (WBA)	Michael Watson	London	Won RSF–11

DATE	WEIGHT	OPPONENT	VENUE	RESULT

Al McCOY

Born: Rosenhayn, New Jersey, USA, 23 Oct 1894
Died: Los Angeles, 22 Aug 1966
World title fights: 3 (all middleweight) won 1, lost 2

DATE	WEIGHT	OPPONENT	VENUE	RESULT
7 Apr 1914	M	George Chip	Brooklyn, New York	Won KO-1
14 Nov 1917	M	Mike O'Dowd	Brooklyn	Lost KO-6
17 Jul 1919	M	Mike O'Dowd	St Paul, Minnesota	Lost KO-3

Charles 'Kid' McCOY

Born: Rush County, Indiana, USA, 13 Oct 1872
Died: Detroit, 18 Apr 1940
World title fights: 2 (1 welterweight, 1 light-heavy) won 1, lost 1

DATE	WEIGHT	OPPONENT	VENUE	RESULT
2 Mar 1896	W	Tommy Ryan	Long Island, New York	Won KO-15
22 Apr 1903	LH	Jack Root	Detroit	Lost PTS-10

Glenn McCRORY

Born: Stanley, Co Durham, England, 23 Sep 1964
World title fights: 3 (all cruiserweight) won 2, lost 1

DATE	WEIGHT	OPPONENT	VENUE	RESULT
3 Jun 1989	C (IBF)	Patrick Lumumba	Stanley, England	Won PTS-12
21 Oct 1989	C (IBF)	Siza Makhathini	Middlesbrough	Won KO-11
22 Mar 1990	C (IBF)	Jeff Lampkin	Gateshead, England	Lost KO-3

Milton McCRORY

Born: Detroit, Michigan, USA, 7 Feb 1962
World title fights: 8 (7 welterweight, 1 junior-middle) won 5, lost 2, drew 1

DATE	WEIGHT	OPPONENT	VENUE	RESULT
19 Mar 1983	W (WBC)	Colin Jones	Reno, Nevada	Drew 12
13 Aug 1983	W (WBC)	Colin Jones	Las Vegas	Won PTS-12

DATE	WEIGHT	OPPONENT	VENUE	RESULT
14 Jan 1984	W (WBC)	Milton Guest	Detroit	Won RSF–6
15 Apr 1984	W (WBC)	Giles Elbila	Detroit	Won RSF–6
9 Mar 1985	W (WBC)	Pedro Vilella	Paris	Won PTS–12
14 Jul 1985	W (WBC)	Carlos Trujillo	Monte Carlo	Won KO–3
6 Dec 1985	W	Donald Curry	Las Vegas	Lost KO–2
19 Apr 1987	JM (WBA)	Mike McCallum	Phoenix	Lost RSF–10

James Buddy McGIRT

Born: Brentwood, New York, USA, 17 Jan 1964
World title fights: 3 (all junior-welter) won 2, lost 1

DATE	WEIGHT	OPPONENT	VENUE	RESULT
14 Feb 1988	JW (IBF)	Frankie Warren	Corpus Christi, Texas	Won RSF–14
31 Jul 1988	JW (IBF)	Howard Davis	New York	Won KO–1
3 Sep 1988	JW (IBF)	Meldrick Taylor	Atlantic City	Lost RSF–12

Terry McGOVERN

Born: Johnstown, Pennsylvania, USA, 9 Mar 1880
Died: Brooklyn, New York, 26 Feb 1918
World title fights: 10 (2 bantamweight, 8 featherweight) won 9, lost 1

DATE	WEIGHT	OPPONENT	VENUE	RESULT
12 Sep 1899	B	Pedlar Palmer	New York	Won KO–1
22 Dec 1899	B	Harry Forbes	New York	Won KO–2
9 Jan 1900	Fe	George Dixon	New York	Won KO–8
1 Feb 1900	Fe	Eddie Santry	Chicago	Won KO–5
9 Mar 1900	Fe	Oscar Gardner	New York	Won KO–3
12 Jun 1900	Fe	Tommy White	Coney Island, New York	Won KO–3
2 Nov 1900	Fe	Joe Bernstein	Louisville, Kentucky	Won KO–7
30 Apr 1901	Fe	Oscar Gardner	San Francisco	Won KO–4
29 May 1901	Fe	Aurelio Herrera	San Francisco	Won KO–5
28 Nov 1901	Fe	Young Corbett	Hartford, Connecticut	Lost KO–2

DATE	WEIGHT	OPPONENT	VENUE	RESULT

DATE	WEIGHT	OPPONENT	VENUE	RESULT

Walter McGOWAN

Born: Burnbank, Scotland, 13 Oct 1942
World title fights: 3 (all flyweight) won 1, lost 2

DATE	WEIGHT	OPPONENT	VENUE	RESULT
14 Jun 1966	Fl (WBC)	Salvatore Burruni	London	Won PTS–15
30 Dec 1966	Fl (WBC)	Chartchai Chionoi	Bangkok	Lost RSF–9
19 Sep 1967	Fl (WBC)	Chartchai Chionoi	London	Lost RSF–7

Barry McGUIGAN

Born: Clones, Monaghan, Ireland, 28 Feb 1961
World title fights: 4 (all featherweight) won 3, lost 1

DATE	WEIGHT	OPPONENT	VENUE	RESULT
8 Jun 1985	Fe (WBA)	Eusebio Pedroza	London	Won PTS–15
28 Sep 1985	Fe (WBA)	Bernard Taylor	Belfast	Won RTD–7
15 Feb 1986	Fe (WBA)	Danilo Cabrera	Dublin	Won RSF–14
23 Jun 1986	Fe (WBA)	Steve Cruz	Las Vegas	Lost PTS–15

Duke McKENZIE

Born: Croydon, England, 5 May 1963
World title fights: 3 (all flyweight) won 2, lost 1

DATE	WEIGHT	OPPONENT	VENUE	RESULT
5 Oct 1988	Fl (IBF)	Rolando Bohol	London	Won KO–11
9 Mar 1989	Fl (IBF)	Tony DeLuca	London	Won RSF–4
7 Jun 1989	Fl (IBF)	Dave McAuley	London	Lost PTS–12

Jimmy McLARNIN

Born: Inchacore, Ireland, 19 Dec 1906
World title fights: 5 (1 lightweight, 4 welterweight) won 2, lost 3

DATE	WEIGHT	OPPONENT	VENUE	RESULT
21 May 1928	L	Sammy Mandell	New York	Lost PTS–15

DATE	WEIGHT	OPPONENT	VENUE	RESULT

DATE	WEIGHT	OPPONENT	VENUE	RESULT	
29 May 1933	W	Young Corbett III	Los Angeles	Won	KO–1
28 May 1934	W	Barney Ross	New York	Lost	PTS–15
17 Sep 1934	W	Barney Ross	New York	Won	PTS–15
28 May 1935	W	Barney Ross	New York	Lost	PTS–15

Mike McTIGUE

Born: Killmonaugh Parish, County Clare, Ireland, 26 Nov 1892
Died: New York, 12 Aug 1966
World title fights: 3 (all light-heavy) won 1, lost 2

DATE	WEIGHT	OPPONENT	VENUE	RESULT	
17 Mar 1923	LH	Battling Siki	Dublin	Won	PTS–20
31 May 1925	LH	Paul Berlenbach	New York	Lost	PTS–15
7 Oct 1927	LH	Tommy Loughran	New York	Lost	PTS–15

Tacy MACALOS

Born: Tanguan, Philippines, 28 Oct 1965
World title fights: 4 (all junior-fly) won 1, lost 3

DATE	WEIGHT	OPPONENT	VENUE	RESULT	
29 Mar 1987	JFl (IBF)	Jum-Hwan Choi	Seoul	Lost	PTS–15
5 Nov 1988	JFl (IBF)	Jum-Hwan Choi	Manila	Won	PTS–12
2 May 1989	JFl (IBF)	Muangchai Kittikasem	Bangkok	Lost	PTS–12
6 Oct 1989	JFl (IBF)	Muangchai Kittikasem	Bangkok	Lost	RSF–7

Raton MACIAS

Born: Mexico City, Mexico, 28 Jul 1934
World title fights: 4 (all bantamweight) won 3, lost 1

DATE	WEIGHT	OPPONENT	VENUE	RESULT	
9 Mar 1955	B (NBA)	Chamrern Songkitrat	San Francisco	Won	KO–11
25 Mar 1956	B (NBA)	Leo Espinosa	Mexico City	Won	KO–11
15 Jun 1957	B (NBA)	Dommy Ursua	San Francisco	Won	RSF–11
6 Nov 1957	B	Alphonse Halimi	Los Angeles	Lost	PTS–15

DATE	WEIGHT	OPPONENT	VENUE	RESULT

Lupe MADERA

Born: Yucatan, Mexico, 17 Dec 1952
World title fights: 5 (all junior-fly) won 2, lost 2, drew 1

DATE	WEIGHT	OPPONENT	VENUE	RESULT	
4 Apr 1982	JFl (WBA)	Katsuo Tokashiki	Sendai, Japan	Lost	PTS-15
9 Apr 1983	JFl (WBA)	Katsuo Tokashiki	Tokyo	Drew	15
10 Jul 1983	JFl (WBA)	Katsuo Tokashiki	Tokyo	Won	RSF-4
23 Oct 1983	JFl (WBA)	Katsuo Tokashiki	Sapporo, Japan	Won	PTS-15
19 May 1984	JFl (WBA)	Francisco Quiroz	Maracaibo, Venezuela	Lost	KO-9

Charlie MAGRI

Born: Tunis, Tunisia, 20 Jul 1956
World title fights: 3 (all flyweight) won 1, lost 2

DATE	WEIGHT	OPPONENT	VENUE	RESULT	
15 Mar 1983	Fl (WBC)	Eleoncio Mercedes	London	Won	RSF-7
27 Sep 1983	Fl (WBC)	Frank Cedeno	London	Lost	RSF-6
20 Feb 1985	Fl (WBC)	Sot Chitalada	London	Lost	RSF-4

Saoul MAMBY

Born: Jamaica, West Indies, 4 Jun 1947
World title fights: 8 (all junior-welter) won 6, lost 2

DATE	WEIGHT	OPPONENT	VENUE	RESULT	
22 Oct 1977	JW (WBC)	Saensak Muangsurin	Bangkok	Lost	PTS-15
23 Feb 1980	JW (WBC)	Sang-Hyun Kim	Seoul	Won	RSF-14
7 Jul 1980	JW (WBC)	Esteban De Jesus	Minneapolis	Won	TKO-13
2 Oct 1980	JW (WBC)	Maurice Watkins	Las Vegas	Won	PTS-15
12 Jun 1981	JW (WBC)	Jo Kimpuani	Detroit	Won	PTS-15
29 Aug 1981	JW (WBC)	Thomas Americo	Jakarta	Won	PTS-15
19 Dec 1981	JW (WBC)	Obisia Nwankpa	Lagos, Nigeria	Won	PTS-15
26 Jun 1982	JW (WBC)	Leroy Haley	Highland Heights, Ohio	Lost	PTS-15

Ray MANCINI

Born: Youngstown, Ohio, USA, 4 Mar 1961
World title fights: 9 (8 lightweight, 1 junior-welter) won 5, lost 4

DATE	WEIGHT	OPPONENT	VENUE	RESULT	
3 Oct 1981	L (WBC)	Alexis Arguello	Atlantic City	Lost	RSF-14
8 May 1982	L (WBA)	Arturo Frias	Las Vegas	Won	RSF-1
24 Jul 1982	L (WBA)	Ernesto Espana	Warren, Michigan	Won	RSF-6
13 Nov 1982	L (WBA)	Duk-Koo Kim	Las Vegas	Won	RSF-14
15 Sep 1983	L (WBA)	Orlando Romero	New York	Won	KO-9
14 Jan 1984	L (WBA)	Bobby Chacon	Reno, Nevada	Won	RSF-3
1 Jun 1984	L (WBA)	Livingstone Bramble	Buffalo	Lost	RSF-14
16 Feb 1985	L (WBA)	Livingstone Bramble	Reno	Lost	PTS-15
6 Mar 1989	JW (WBO)	Hector Camacho	Reno	Lost	PTS-12

Sammy MANDELL

Born: Rockford, Illinois, USA, 5 Feb 1904
Died: Oak Park, Illinois, 7 Nov 1967
World title fights: 4 (all lightweight) won 3, lost 1

DATE	WEIGHT	OPPONENT	VENUE	RESULT	
3 Jul 1926	L	Rocky Kansas	Chicago	Won	PTS-10
21 May 1928	L	Jimmy McLarnin	New York	Won	PTS-15
2 Aug 1929	L	Tony Canzoneri	Chicago	Won	PTS-10
17 Jul 1930	L	Al Singer	New York	Lost	KO-1

Joe Louis MANLEY

Born: Lima, Ohio, USA, 11 Jun 1959
World title fights: 2 (both junior-welter) won 1, lost 1

DATE	WEIGHT	OPPONENT	VENUE	RESULT	
30 Oct 1986	JW (IBF)	Gary Hinton	Hartford, Connecticut	Won	KO-10
4 Mar 1987	JW (IBF)	Terry Marsh	Basildon, England	Lost	RSF-10

Alfredo MARCANO

Born: Sucre, Venezuela, 17 Jan 1947
World title fights: 4 (3 junior-light, 1 featherweight) won 2, lost 2

DATE	WEIGHT	OPPONENT	VENUE	RESULT
29 Jul 1971	JL (WBA)	Hiroshi Kobayashi	Aomori, Japan	Won RTD–10
6 Nov 1971	JL (WBA)	Kenji Iwata	Caracas	Won RSF–4
25 Apr 1972	JL (WBA)	Ben Villaflor	Honolulu	Lost PTS–15
7 Sep 1974	Fe (WBC)	Bobby Chacon	Los Angeles	Lost RSF–9

Ernesto MARCEL

Born: Colon, Panama, 23 May 1948
World title fights: 6 (all featherweight) won 5, drew 1

DATE	WEIGHT	OPPONENT	VENUE	RESULT
11 Nov 1971	Fe (WBC)	Kuniaki Shibata	Matsuyama, Japan	Drew 15
19 Aug 1972	Fe (WBA)	Antonio Gomez	Maracay, Venezuela	Won PTS–15
3 Dec 1972	Fe (WBA)	Enrique Garcia	Panama City	Won RSF–6
14 Jul 1973	Fe (WBA)	Antonio Gomez	Panama City	Won RTD–11
8 Sep 1973	Fe (WBA)	Shig Nimoto	Panama City	Won KO–9
16 Feb 1974	Fe (WBA)	Alexis Arguello	Panama City	Won PTS–15

Rocky MARCIANO

Born: Brockton, Massachusetts, USA, 1 Sep 1923
Died: Newton, Iowa, 31 Aug 1969
World title fights: 7 (all heavyweight) won 7, lost 0

DATE	WEIGHT	OPPONENT	VENUE	RESULT
23 Sep 1952	H	Jersey Joe Walcott	Philadelphia	Won KO–13
15 May 1953	H	Jersey Joe Walcott	Chicago	Won KO–1
24 Sep 1953	H	Roland LaStarza	New York	Won RSF–11
17 Jun 1954	H	Ezzard Charles	New York	Won PTS–15
17 Sep 1954	H	Ezzard Charles	New York	Won KO–8

16 May 1955	H	Don Cockell	San Francisco	Won RSF–9
21 Sep 1955	H	Archie Moore	New York	Won KO–9

Dado MARINO

Born: Honolulu, Hawaii, 26 Aug 1916
World title fights: 6 (5 flyweight, 1 bantamweight) won 2, lost 4

DATE	WEIGHT	OPPONENT	VENUE	RESULT
20 Oct 1947	Fl (NBA)	Rinty Monaghan	London	Lost PTS–15
1 Mar 1949	B	Manuel Ortiz	Honolulu	Lost PTS–15
1 Aug 1950	Fl	Terry Allen	Honolulu	Won PTS–15
1 Nov 1951	Fl	Terry Allen	Honolulu	Won PTS–15
19 May 1952	Fl	Yoshio Shirai	Tokyo	Lost PTS–15
15 Nov 1952	Fl	Yoshio Shirai	Tokyo	Lost PTS–15

Tony MARINO

Born: Pittsburgh, USA, 18 May 1912
Died: New York, 1 Feb 1937
World title fights: 2 (both bantamweight) won 1, lost 1

DATE	WEIGHT	OPPONENT	VENUE	RESULT
29 Jun 1936	B (NY)	Baltasar Sangchili	New York	Won KO–14
31 Aug 1936	B	Sixto Escobar	New York	Lost RSF–13

Terry MARSH

Born: Stepney, London, England, 7 Feb 1958
World title fights: 2 (both junior-welter) won 2, lost 0

DATE	WEIGHT	OPPONENT	VENUE	RESULT
4 Mar 1987	JW (IBF)	Joe Louis Manley	Basildon, England	Won RSF–10
1 Jul 1987	JW (IBF)	Akio Kameda	London	Won RSF–6

Eddie 'Cannonball' MARTIN

Born: Brooklyn, New York, USA, 3 Mar 1903
Died: Brooklyn, 27 Aug 1966
World title fights: 3 (2 bantamweight, 1 junior-light) won 1, lost 2

DATE	WEIGHT	OPPONENT	VENUE	RESULT	
19 Dec 1924	B	Abe Goldstein	New York	Won	PTS–15
20 Mar 1925	B	Charley Phil Rosenberg	New York	Lost	PTS–15
18 Jul 1928	JL	Tod Morgan	New York	Lost	PTS–15

Rodolfo MARTINEZ

Born: Tepito, Mexico, 24 Aug 1946
World title fights: 6 (all bantamweight) won 4, lost 2

DATE	WEIGHT	OPPONENT	VENUE	RESULT	
14 Apr 1973	B (WBC)	Rafael Herrera	Monterrey, Mexico	Lost	RSF–12
7 Dec 1974	B (WBC)	Rafael Herrera	Merida, Mexico	Won	RSF–4
31 May 1975	B (WBC)	Nestor Jiminez	Bogota	Won	RSF–7
8 Oct 1975	B (WBC)	Hisami Numata	Sendai, Japan	Won	PTS–15
30 Jan 1976	B (WBC)	Venice Borkorsor	Bangkok	Won	PTS–15
8 May 1976	B (WBC)	Carlos Zarate	Los Angeles	Lost	KO–9

Peter MATHEBULA

Born: Transvaal, South Africa, 3 Jul 1952
World title fights: 2 (both flyweight) won 1, lost 1

DATE	WEIGHT	OPPONENT	VENUE	RESULT	
13 Dec 1980	Fl (WBA)	Tae-Shik Kim	Los Angeles	Won	PTS–15
28 Mar 1981	Fl (WBA)	Santos Laciar	Johannesburg	Lost	KO–7

DATE	WEIGHT	OPPONENT	VENUE	RESULT

Matty MATTHEWS

Born: New York City, USA, 13 Jul 1873
Died: Brooklyn, New York, 6 Dec 1948
World title fights: 4 (all welterweight) won 2, lost 2

DATE	WEIGHT	OPPONENT	VENUE	RESULT	
25 Aug 1898	W	Mysterious Billy Smith	New York	Lost	PTS–25
16 Oct 1900	W	Rube Ferns	Detroit	Won	PTS–15
29 Apr 1901	W	Tom Couhig	Louisville, Kentucky	Won	PTS–20
24 May 1901	W	Rube Ferns	Toronto	Lost	KO–10

Rocky MATTIOLI

Born: Ripa Teatine, Italy, 20 Jul 1953
World title fights: 5 (all junior-middle) won 3, lost 2

DATE	WEIGHT	OPPONENT	VENUE	RESULT	
6 Aug 1977	JM (WBC)	Eckhard Dagge	Berlin	Won	KO–5
11 Mar 1978	JM (WBC)	Elisha Obed	Melbourne	Won	KO–7
14 May 1978	JM (WBC)	Jose Duran	Pescara, Italy	Won	RSF–5
4 Mar 1979	JM (WBC)	Maurice Hope	San Remo, Italy	Lost	RTD–8
12 Jul 1980	JM (WBC)	Maurice Hope	London	Lost	RSF–11

Joey MAXIM

Born: Cleveland, Ohio, USA, 28 Mar 1922
World title fights: 7 (6 light-heavy, 1 heavyweight) won 3, lost 4

DATE	WEIGHT	OPPONENT	VENUE	RESULT	
24 Jan 1950	LH	Freddie Mills	London	Won	KO–10
30 May 1951	H	Ezzard Charles	Chicago	Lost	PTS–15
22 Aug 1951	LH	Bob Murphy	New York	Won	PTS–15
25 Jun 1952	LH	Sugar Ray Robinson	New York	Won	RTD–14
17 Dec 1952	LH	Archie Moore	St Louis	Lost	PTS–15
24 Jun 1953	LH	Archie Moore	Ogden, Utah	Lost	PTS–15
27 Jan 1954	LH	Archie Moore	Miami	Lost	PTS–15

DATE	WEIGHT	OPPONENT	VENUE	RESULT

Roger MAYWEATHER

Born: Grand Rapids, Michigan, USA, 24 Apr 1961
World title fights: 11 (5 junior-light, 6 junior-welter) won 8, lost 3

DATE	WEIGHT	OPPONENT	VENUE	RESULT
19 Jan 1983	JL (WBA)	Sam Serrano	San Juan	Won KO–8
21 Apr 1983	JL (WBA)	Jorge Alvarado	San Jose, Costa Rica	Won RSF–8
17 Aug 1983	JL (WBA)	Ben Villablanca	Las Vegas	Won KO–1
25 Feb 1984	JL (WBA)	Rocky Lockridge	Beaumont, Texas	Lost KO–1
7 Jul 1985	JL (WBC)	Julio Cesar Chavez	Las Vegas	Lost RSF–2
12 Nov 1987	JW (WBC)	Rene Arredondo	Los Angeles	Won KO–6
24 Mar 1988	JW (WBC)	Mauricio Aceves	Los Angeles	Won KO–3
6 Jun 1988	JW (WBC)	Harold Brazier	Los Angeles	Won PTS–12
22 Sep 1988	JW (WBC)	Rodolfo Gonzalez	Los Angeles	Won PTS–12
7 Nov 1988	JW (WBC)	Vinny Pazienza	Las Vegas	Won PTS–12
13 May 1989	JW (WBC)	Julio Cesar Chavez	Los Angeles	Lost RSF–10

Sandro MAZZINGHI

Born: Pontedera, Italy, 3 Oct 1938
World title fights: 8 (all junior-middle) won 5, lost 2, NC 1

DATE	WEIGHT	OPPONENT	VENUE	RESULT
7 Sep 1963	JM	Ralph Dupas	Milan	Won KO–9
2 Dec 1963	JM	Ralph Dupas	Sydney	Won KO–13
3 Oct 1964	JM	Tony Montano	Genoa	Won RSF–12
11 Dec 1964	JM	Fortunato Manca	Rome	Won PTS–15
18 Jun 1965	JM	Nino Benvenuti	Milan	Lost KO–6
17 Dec 1965	JM	Nino Benvenuti	Rome	Lost PTS–15
26 May 1968	JM	Ki-Soo Kim	Milan	Won PTS–15
25 Oct 1968	JM	Freddie Little	Rome	NC–8

Mark MEDAL

Born: Jersey City, New Jersey, USA, 10 Jun 1957
World title fights: 3 (all junior-middle) won 1, lost 2

DATE	WEIGHT	OPPONENT	VENUE	RESULT	
11 Mar 1984	JM (IBF)	Earl Hargrove	Atlantic City	Won	RSF-5
2 Nov 1984	JM (IBF)	Carlos Santos	New York	Lost	PTS-15
23 Jun 1986	JM (WBC)	Thomas Hearns	Las Vegas	Lost	RSF-8

Honey MELLODY

Born: Charlestown, Massachusetts, USA, 15 Jan 1884
Died: Charlestown, 15 Mar 1919
World title fights: 2 (both welterweight) won 1, lost 1

DATE	WEIGHT	OPPONENT	VENUE	RESULT	
16 Oct 1906	W	Joe Walcott	Chelsea, Massachusetts	Won	PTS-15
23 Apr 1907	W	Mike Sullivan	Los Angeles	Lost	PTS-20

Luis MENDOZA

Born: San Onofre, Sucre, Colombia, 7 Apr 1965
World title fights: 4 (all junior-feather) won 2, lost 1, drew 1

DATE	WEIGHT	OPPONENT	VENUE	RESULT	
12 Jul 1989	JFe (WBA)	Juan Jose Estrada	Tijuana, Mexico	Lost	PTS-12
26 May 1990	JFe (WBA)	Ruben Palacios	Cartagena, Colombia	Drew	12
11 Sep 1990	JFe (WBA)	Ruben Palacios	Miami	Won	RSF-3
18 Oct 1990	JFe (WBA)	Fabrice Benichou	Paris	Won	PTS-12

Eleoncio MERCEDES

Born: La Romana, Dominican Republic, 12 Sep 1957
Died: La Romana, 22 Dec 1985
World title fights: 2 (both flyweight) won 1, lost 1

DATE	WEIGHT	OPPONENT	VENUE	RESULT	
7 Nov 1982	Fl (WBC)	Freddie Castillo	Los Angeles	Won	PTS-15
15 Mar 1983	Fl (WBC)	Charlie Magri	London	Lost	RSF-7

Juan 'Kid' MEZA

Born: Mexicali, Mexico, 18 Mar 1956
World title fights: 5 (all junior-feather) won 2, lost 3

DATE	WEIGHT	OPPONENT	VENUE	RESULT	
27 Mar 1982	JFe (WBC)	Wilfredo Gomez	Atlantic City	Lost	RSF-6
3 Nov 1984	JFe (WBC)	Jaime Garza	New York	Won	KO-1
19 Apr 1985	JFe (WBC)	Mike Ayala	Los Angeles	Won	RSF-6
19 Aug 1985	JFe (WBC)	Lupe Pintor	Mexico City	Lost	PTS-12
10 Dec 1986	JFe (WBC)	Samart Payakaroon	Bangkok	Lost	KO-12

Barry MICHAEL

Born: London, England, 2 Jun 1955
World title fights: 5 (all junior-light) won 4, lost 1

DATE	WEIGHT	OPPONENT	VENUE	RESULT	
12 Jul 1985	JL (IBF)	Lester Ellis	Melbourne	Won	PTS-15
18 Oct 1985	JL (IBF)	Jin-Sik Choi	Darwin, Australia	Won	RSF-4
22 May 1986	JL (IBF)	Mark Fernandez	Melbourne	Won	RSF-4
23 Aug 1986	JL (IBF)	Najib Daho	Manchester	Won	PTS-12
9 Aug 1987	JL (IBF)	Rocky Lockridge	Windsor, England	Lost	RTD-8

Tadashi MIHARA

Born: Gumma Prefecture, Japan, 3 Mar 1955
World title fights: 2 (both junior-middle) won 1, lost 1

DATE	WEIGHT	OPPONENT	VENUE	RESULT	
7 Nov 1981	JM (WBA)	Rocky Fratto	Rochester, New York	Won	PTS-15
2 Feb 1982	JM (WBA)	Davey Moore	Tokyo	Lost	RSF-6

DATE	WEIGHT	OPPONENT	VENUE	RESULT

Freddie MILLER

Born: Cincinnati, Ohio, USA, 3 Apr 1911
Died: Cincinnati, 8 May 1962
World title fights: 13 (all featherweight) won 10, lost 3

DATE	WEIGHT	OPPONENT	VENUE	RESULT
23 Jul 1931	Fe	Battling Battalino	Cincinnati	Lost PTS-10
13 Jan 1933	Fe (NBA)	Tommy Paul	Chicago	Won PTS-10
24 Feb 1933	Fe (NBA)	Baby Arizmendi	Los Angeles	Won PTS-10
21 Mar 1933	Fe (NBA)	Speedy Dado	Los Angeles	Won PTS-10
1 Jan 1934	Fe (NBA)	Little Jack Sharkey	Chicago	Won PTS-10
21 Sep 1934	Fe (NBA)	Nel Tarleton	Liverpool	Won PTS-15
17 Feb 1935	Fe (NBA)	Jose Girones	Barcelona	Won KO-1
12 Jun 1935	Fe (NBA)	Nel Tarleton	Liverpool	Won PTS-15
22 Oct 1935	Fe (NBA)	Vernon Cormier	Boston	Won PTS-15
18 Feb 1936	Fe (NBA)	Johnny Pena	Seattle	Won PTS-12
2 Mar 1936	Fe (NBA)	Petey Sarron	Miami	Won PTS-15
11 May 1936	Fe (NBA)	Petey Sarron	Washington, DC	Lost PTS-15
4 Sep 1937	Fe (NBA)	Petey Sarron	Johannesburg	Lost PTS-12

Freddie MILLS

Born: Parkstone, Dorset, England, 26 Jun 1919
Died: London, 25 Jul 1965
World title fights: 3 (all light-heavy) won 1, lost 2

DATE	WEIGHT	OPPONENT	VENUE	RESULT
14 May 1946	LH	Gus Lesnevich	London	Lost RSF-10
26 Jul 1948	LH	Gus Lesnevich	London	Won PTS-15
24 Jan 1950	LH	Joey Maxim	London	Lost KO-10

Alan MINTER

Born: Crawley, Sussex, England, 17 Aug 1951
World title fights: 3 (all middleweight) won 2, lost 1

DATE	WEIGHT	OPPONENT	VENUE	RESULT
16 Mar 1980	M	Vito Antuofermo	Las Vegas	Won PTS–15
28 Jun 1980	M	Vito Antuofermo	London	Won KO–8
27 Sep 1980	M	Marvin Hagler	London	Lost RSF–3

Brian MITCHELL

Born: Johannesburg, South Africa, 30 Aug 1961
World title fights: 13 (all junior-light) won 12, drew 1

DATE	WEIGHT	OPPONENT	VENUE	RESULT
27 Sep 1986	JL (WBA)	Alfredo Layne	Sun City, S Africa	Won RSF–10
27 Mar 1987	JL (WBA)	Jose Rivera	San Juan	Drew 15
17 May 1987	JL (WBA)	Aurelio Benitez	Sun City	Won RSF–2
1 Aug 1987	JL (WBA)	Francisco Fernandez	Panama City	Won RSF–14
3 Oct 1987	JL (WBA)	Daniel Londas	Gravelines, France	Won PTS–15
19 Dec 1987	JL (WBA)	Salvatore Curcetti	Capo D'Orlando, Italy	Won TD–9
26 Apr 1988	JL (WBA)	Jose Rivera	Madrid	Won PTS–12
2 Nov 1988	JL (WBA)	Jim McDonnell	London	Won PTS–12
10 Feb 1989	JL (WBA)	Salvatore Bottiglieri	Capo D'Orlando	Won KO–8
1 Jul 1989	JL (WBA)	Jackie Beard	Crotone, Italy	Won TKO–8
28 Sep 1989	JL (WBA)	Irving Mitchell	Lewiston, Maine	Won RSF–7
14 Mar 1990	JL (WBA)	Jackie Beard	Grosetto, Italy	Won PTS–12
29 Sep 1990	JL (WBA)	Frank Mitchell	Aosta, Italy	Won PTS–12

Kenny MITCHELL

Born: South Carolina, USA, 7 Feb 1960
World title fights: 3 (all junior-feather) won 2, lost 1

DATE	WEIGHT	OPPONENT	VENUE	RESULT
29 Apr 1989	JFe (WBO)	Julio Gervacio	San Juan	Won PTS–12
9 Sep 1989	JFe (WBO)	Simon Skosana	San Juan	Won PTS–12
9 Dec 1989	JFe (WBO)	Valerio Nati	Teramo, Italy	Lost DIS–4

Juan 'John John' MOLINA

Born: Puerto Rico, 7 Mar 1965
World title fights: 5 (all junior-light) won 3, lost 2

DATE	WEIGHT	OPPONENT	VENUE	RESULT
27 Oct 1988	JL (IBF)	Tony Lopez	Sacramento, California	Lost PTS–12
29 Apr 1989	JL (WBO)	Juan Laporte	San Juan	Won PTS–12
7 Oct 1989	JL (IBF)	Tony Lopez	Sacramento	Won RSF–10
27 Jan 1990	JL (IBF)	Lupe Suarez	Atlantic City	Won RSF–6
20 May 1990	JL (IBF)	Tony Lopez	Reno, Nevada	Lost PTS–12

Tomas MOLINARES

Born: Cartagena, Colombia, 6 Apr 1965
World title fights: 1 (welterweight) won 1, lost 0

DATE	WEIGHT	OPPONENT	VENUE	RESULT
29 Jul 1988	W (WBA)	Marlon Starling	Atlantic City	Won KO–6

Rinty MONAGHAN

Born: Belfast, Northern Ireland, 21 Aug 1920
Died: Belfast, 3 Mar 1984
World title fights: 4 (all flyweight) won 3, drew 1

DATE	WEIGHT	OPPONENT	VENUE	RESULT
20 Oct 1947	Fl (NBA)	Dado Marino	London	Won PTS–15
23 Mar 1948	Fl	Jackie Paterson	Belfast	Won KO–7

DATE	WEIGHT	OPPONENT	VENUE	RESULT
5 Apr 1949	Fl	Maurice Sandyron	Belfast	Won PTS–15
30 Sep 1949	Fl	Terry Allen	Belfast	Drew 15

Small MONTANA

Born: Philippines, 24 Feb 1913
Died: La Carlota, Philippines, 4 Aug 1976
World title fights: 2 (both flyweight) won 1, lost 1

DATE	WEIGHT	OPPONENT	VENUE	RESULT
16 Sep 1935	Fl (NY)	Midget Wolgast	Oakland, California	Won PTS–10
19 Jan 1937	Fl	Benny Lynch	London	Lost PTS–15

Bob MONTGOMERY

Born: Sumter, South Carolina, USA, 10 Feb 1919
World title fights: 6 (all lightweight) won 4, lost 2

DATE	WEIGHT	OPPONENT	VENUE	RESULT
21 May 1943	L (NY)	Beau Jack	New York	Won PTS–15
19 Nov 1943	L (NY)	Beau Jack	New York	Lost PTS–15
3 Mar 1944	L (NY)	Beau Jack	New York	Won PTS–15
28 Jun 1946	L (NY)	Allie Stolz	New York	Won KO–13
26 Nov 1946	L (NY)	Wesley Mouzon	Philadelphia	Won KO–8
4 Aug 1947	L	Ike Williams	Philadelphia	Lost KO–6

Carlos MONZON

Born: Santa Fe, Argentina, 7 Aug 1942
World title fights: 15 (all middleweight) won 15, lost 0

DATE	WEIGHT	OPPONENT	VENUE	RESULT
7 Nov 1970	M	Nino Benvenuti	Rome	Won KO–12
8 May 1971	M	Nino Benvenuti	Monte Carlo	Won RSF–3
25 Sep 1971	M	Emile Griffith	Buenos Aires	Won RSF–14
4 Mar 1972	M	Denny Moyer	Rome	Won RSF–5

DATE	WEIGHT	OPPONENT	VENUE	RESULT

DATE	WEIGHT	OPPONENT	VENUE	RESULT
17 Jun 1972	M	Jean-Claude Boutier	Paris	Won RTD–12
19 Aug 1972	M	Tom Bogs	Copenhagen	Won RSF–5
11 Nov 1972	M	Benny Briscoe	Buenos Aires	Won PTS–15
2 Jun 1973	M	Emile Griffith	Monte Carlo	Won PTS–15
29 Sep 1973	M	Jean-Claude Boutier	Paris	Won PTS–15
9 Feb 1974	M	Jose Napoles	Paris	Won RTD–7
5 Oct 1974	M (WBA)	Tony Mundine	Buenos Aires	Won KO–7
30 Jun 1975	M (WBA)	Tony Licata	New York	Won KO–10
13 Dec 1975	M (WBA)	Gratien Tonna	Paris	Won KO–5
26 Jun 1976	M	Rodrigo Valdez	Monte Carlo	Won PTS–15
30 Jul 1977	M	Rodrigo Valdez	Monte Carlo	Won PTS–15

Sung-Kil MOON

Born: Yeoung-Am, South Korea, 20 Jul 1963
World title fights: 7 (4 bantamweight, 3 junior-bantam) won 6, lost 1

DATE	WEIGHT	OPPONENT	VENUE	RESULT
14 Aug 1988	B (WBA)	Kaokor Galaxy	Pusan, S Korea	Won TD–6
27 Nov 1988	B (WBA)	Edgar Monserrat	Seoul	Won KO–7
18 Feb 1989	B (WBA)	Giaki Kobayashi	Seoul	Won KO–5
7 Jul 1989	B (WBA)	Kaokor Galaxy	Bangkok	Lost PTS–12
20 Jan 1990	JB (WBC)	Nana Yaw Konadu	Seoul	Won TD–9
9 Jun 1990	JB (WBC)	Gilberto Roman	Seoul	Won RTD–8
20 Oct 1990.	JB (WBC)	Kenji Matsumura	Seoul	Won RSF–5

Archie MOORE

Born: Benoit, Mississippi, USA, 13 Dec 1913 *or* 1916 (*year uncertain*)
World title fights: 11 (9 light-heavy, 2 heavyweight) won 9, lost 2

DATE	WEIGHT	OPPONENT	VENUE	RESULT
17 Dec 1952	LH	Joey Maxim	St Louis	Won PTS–15
24 Jun 1953	LH	Joey Maxim	Ogden, Utah	Won PTS–15

DATE	WEIGHT	OPPONENT	VENUE	RESULT

DATE	WEIGHT	OPPONENT	VENUE	RESULT
27 Jan 1954	LH	Joey Maxim	Miami	Won PTS–15
11 Aug 1954	LH	Harold Johnson	New York	Won KO–14
22 Jun 1955	LH	Carl 'Bobo' Olson	New York	Won KO–3
21 Sep 1955	H	Rocky Marciano	New York	Lost KO–9
5 Jun 1956	LH	Yolande Pompey	London	Won RSF–10
30 Nov 1956	H	Floyd Patterson	Chicago	Lost KO–5
10 Dec 1958	LH	Yvon Durelle	Montreal	Won KO–11
12 Aug 1959	LH	Yvon Durelle	Montreal	Won KO–3
10 Jun 1961	LH	Giulio Rinaldi	New York	Won PTS–15

Davey MOORE

Born: Lexington, Kentucky, USA, 1 Nov 1933
Died: Los Angeles, 23 Mar 1963*
World title fights: 7 (all featherweight) won 6, lost 1

18 Mar 1959	Fe	Hogan Bassey	Los Angeles	Won RTD–13
19 Aug 1959	Fe	Hogan Bassey	Los Angeles	Won RTD–10
29 Aug 1960	Fe	Kazuo Takayama	Tokyo	Won PTS–15
8 Apr 1961	Fe	Danny Valdez	Los Angeles	Won KO–1
13 Nov 1961	Fe	Kazuo Takayama	Tokyo	Won PTS–15
17 Aug 1962	Fe	Olli Makin	Helsinki	Won RSF–2
21 Mar 1963	Fe	Ultiminio 'Sugar' Ramos	Los Angeles	Lost RTD–10

* As a result of injuries sustained in the bout versus Ramos.

Davey MOORE

Born: Bronx, New York, USA, 9 Jun 1959
Died: Holmdel, New Jersey, 5 Jun 1988
World title fights: 5 (all junior-middle) won 4, lost 1

2 Feb 1982	JM (WBA)	Tadashi Mihara	Tokyo	Won RSF–6

DATE	WEIGHT	OPPONENT	VENUE	RESULT

DATE	WEIGHT	OPPONENT	VENUE	RESULT
26 Apr 1982	JM (WBA)	Charlie Weir	Johannesburg	Won KO–5
17 Jul 1982	JM (WBA)	Ayub Kalule	Atlantic City	Won RSF–10
29 Jan 1983	JM (WBA)	Gary Guiden	Atlantic City	Won KO–4
16 Jun 1983	JM (WBA)	Roberto Duran	New York	Lost RSF–8

Michael MOORER

Born: New York, 12 Nov 1967
World title fights: 9 (all light-heavy) won 9, lost 0

3 Dec 1988	LH (WBO)	Ramzi Hassan	Cleveland	Won RSF–5
14 Jan 1989	LH (WBO)	Victor Claudio	Auburn Hills, Michigan	Won RSF–2
19 Feb 1989	LH (WBO)	Frankie Swindell	Monessen, Pennsylvania	Won RSF–1
22 Apr 1989	LH (WBO)	Freddie Delgado	Auburn Hills	Won RSF–1
25 Jun 1989	LH (WBO)	Leslie Stewart	Atlantic City	Won RSF–8
16 Nov 1989	LH (WBO)	Jeff Thompson	Atlantic City	Won RSF–1
22 Dec 1989	LH (WBO)	Mike Sedillo	Auburn Hills	Won RSF–6
3 Feb 1990	LH (WBO)	Marcellus Allen	Atlantic City	Won TKO–9
28 Apr 1990	LH (WBO)	Mario Melo	Atlantic City	Won RSF–1

Tod MORGAN

Born: Seattle, USA, 25 Dec 1902
Died: Seattle, 3 Aug 1953
World title fights: 6 (all junior-light) won 5, lost 1

2 Dec 1925	JL	Mike Ballerino	Los Angeles	Won KO–10
19 Nov 1926	JL	Carl Duane	New York	Won PTS–15
18 Jul 1928	JL	Eddie Martin	New York	Won PTS–15
5 Apr 1929	JL	Santiago Zorilla	Los Angeles	Won PTS–10
20 May 1929	JL	Baby Salsorio	Los Angeles	Won PTS–10
19 Dec 1929	JL	Benny Bass	New York	Lost KO–2

DATE	WEIGHT	OPPONENT	VENUE	RESULT

Denny MOYER

Born: Portland, Oregon, USA, 8 Aug 1939
World title fights: 6 (1 welterweight, 4 junior-middle, 1 middleweight)
won 2, lost 4

DATE	WEIGHT	OPPONENT	VENUE	RESULT	
10 Jul 1959	W	Don Jordan	Portland, Oregon	Lost	PTS–15
20 Oct 1962	JM (WBA)	Joey Giambra	Portland	Won	PTS–15
19 Feb 1963	JM	Stan Harrington	Honolulu	Won	PTS–15
29 Apr 1963	JM	Ralph Dupas	New Orleans	Lost	PTS–15
17 Jun 1963	JM	Ralph Dupas	Baltimore	Lost	PTS–15
4 Mar 1972	M	Carlos Monzon	Rome	Lost	RSF–5

Saensak MUANGSURIN

Born: Phetchabun, Thailand, 13 Aug 1950
World title fights: 12 (all junior-welter) won 10, lost 2

DATE	WEIGHT	OPPONENT	VENUE	RESULT	
15 Jul 1975	JW (WBC)	Perico Fernandez	Bangkok	Won	RTD–8
25 Jan 1976	JW (WBC)	Tetsuo Lion Furuyama	Tokyo	Won	PTS–15
30 Jun 1976	JW (WBC)	Miguel Velasquez	Madrid	Lost	DIS–5
29 Oct 1976	JW (WBC)	Miguel Velasquez	Segovia, Spain	Won	RSF–2
15 Jan 1977	JW (WBC)	Monroe Brooks	Chian-mai, Thailand	Won	RSF–15
2 Apr 1977	JW (WBC)	Guts Ishimatsu	Tokyo	Won	KO–6
17 Jun 1977	JW (WBC)	Perico Fernandez	Madrid	Won	PTS–15
20 Aug 1977	JW (WBC)	Mike Everett	Roi-et, Thailand	Won	RSF–6
22 Oct 1977	JW (WBC)	Saoul Mamby	Bangkok	Won	PTS–15
30 Dec 1977	JW (WBC)	Jo Kimpuani	Chantaburi, Thailand	Won	RTD–13
8 Apr 1978	JW (WBC)	Francisco Moreno	Hat-yai, Thailand	Won	RSF–13
30 Dec 1978	JW (WBC)	Sang-Hyun Kim	Seoul	Lost	RSF–13

John MUGABI

Born: Kampala, Uganda, 4 Mar 1960
World title fights: 4 (1 middleweight, 3 junior-middle) won 1, lost 3

DATE	WEIGHT	OPPONENT	VENUE	RESULT
10 Mar 1986	M	Marvin Hagler	Las Vegas	Lost KO-11
5 Dec 1986	JM (WBC)	Duane Thomas	Las Vegas	Lost RSF-3
8 Jul 1989	JM (WBC)	Rene Jacquot	Miraplis, France	Won KO-1
31 Mar 1990	JM (WBC)	Terry Norris	Tampa, Florida	Lost KO-1

Takuya MUGURUMA

Born: Osaka, Japan, 16 Jan 1961
World title fights: 4 (3 bantamweight, 1 junior-feather) won 1, lost 2, drew 1

DATE	WEIGHT	OPPONENT	VENUE	RESULT
29 Mar 1987	B (WBA)	Azael Moran	Moriguchi, Japan	Won KO-5
24 May 1987	B (WBA)	Chang-Young Park	Osaka, Japan	Lost RSF-11
17 Jan 1988	B (WBA)	Wilfredo Vasquez	Osaka	Drew 12
15 Oct 1988	JFe (WBA)	Juan Jose Estrada	Moriguchi	Lost RSF-11

Eddie Mustafa MUHAMMAD
(formerly Eddie Gregory)

Born: Brooklyn, New York, USA, 30 Apr 1952
World title fights: 6 (all light-heavy) won 3, lost 3

DATE	WEIGHT	OPPONENT	VENUE	RESULT
19 Nov 1977	LH (WBA)	Victor Galindez	Turin	Lost PTS-15
31 Mar 1980	LH (WBA)	Marvin Johnson	Knoxville, Tennessee	Won RSF-11
20 Jul 1980	LH (WBA)	Jerry Martin	McAfee, New Jersey	Won RSF-10
29 Nov 1980	LH (WBA)	Rudi Koopmans	Los Angeles	Won TKO-4
18 Jul 1981	LH (WBA)	Michael Spinks	Las Vegas	Lost PTS-15
21 Dec 1985	LH (IBF)	Slobodan Kacar	Pesaro, Italy	Lost PTS-15

Matthew Saad MUHAMMAD
(formerly Matt Franklin)

Born: Philadelphia, USA, 5 Aug 1954
World title fights: 11 (all light-heavy) won 9, lost 2

DATE	WEIGHT	OPPONENT	VENUE	RESULT	
22 Apr 1979	LH (WBC)	Marvin Johnson	Indianapolis	Won	RSF–8
18 Aug 1979	LH (WBC)	John Conteh	Atlantic City	Won	PTS–15
29 Mar 1980	LH (WBC)	John Conteh	Atlantic City	Won	RSF–4
11 May 1980	LH (WBC)	Louis Pergaud	Halifax, Canada	Won	RSF–5
13 Jul 1980	LH (WBC)	Alvaro Lopez	Great George, New Jersey	Won	RSF–14
28 Nov 1980	LH (WBC)	Lottie Mwale	San Diego	Won	KO–4
28 Feb 1981	LH (WBC)	Vonzell Johnson	Atlantic City	Won	RSF–11
25 Apr 1981	LH (WBC)	Murray Sutherland	Atlantic City	Won	KO–9
26 Sep 1981	LH (WBC)	Jerry Martin	Atlantic City	Won	RSF–11
19 Dec 1981	LH (WBC)	Dwight Braxton	Atlantic City	Lost	RSF–10
8 Aug 1982	LH (WBC)	Dwight Braxton	Atlantic City	Lost	RSF–6

Billy MURPHY

Born: Auckland, New Zealand, 3 Nov 1863
Died: Auckland, 26 Jul 1939
World title fights: 1 (featherweight) won 1, lost 0

DATE	WEIGHT	OPPONENT	VENUE	RESULT	
13 Jan 1890	Fe	Ike Weir	San Francisco	Won	KO–14

Lee Roy MURPHY

Born: Chicago, Illinois, USA, 16 Jul 1958
World title fights: 5 (all cruiserweight) won 4, lost 1

DATE	WEIGHT	OPPONENT	VENUE	RESULT	
6 Oct 1984	C (IBF)	Marvin Camel	Billings, Montana	Won	RSF–14
20 Dec 1984	C (IBF)	Young Joe Louis	Chicago	Won	RSF–12

DATE	WEIGHT	OPPONENT	VENUE	RESULT
19 Oct 1985	C (IBF)	Chisanda Mutti	Monte Carlo	Won KO–12
19 Apr 1986	C (IBF)	Dorcy Gaymon	San Remo, Italy	Won KO–9
25 Oct 1986	C (IBF)	Ricky Parkey	Marsala, Italy	Lost RSF–10

Shigeo NAKAJIMA

Born: Ibaraki, Japan, 18 Jan 1954
World title fights: 3 (all junior-fly) won 1, lost 2

DATE	WEIGHT	OPPONENT	VENUE	RESULT
3 Jan 1980	JFl (WBC)	Sung-Jun Kim	Tokyo	Won PTS–15
23 Mar 1980	JFl (WBC)	Hilario Zapata	Tokyo	Lost PTS–15
17 Sep 1980	JFl (WBC)	Hilario Zapata	Tokyo	Lost RSF–11

Jose NAPOLES

Born: Santiago de Cuba, Oriente, Cuba, 13 Apr 1940
World title fights: 18 (17 welterweight, 1 middleweight) won 15, lost 3

DATE	WEIGHT	OPPONENT	VENUE	RESULT
18 Apr 1969	W	Curtis Cokes	Los Angeles	Won RSF–13
29 Jun 1969	W	Curtis Cokes	Mexico City	Won RTD–10
17 Oct 1969	W	Emile Griffith	Los Angeles	Won PTS–15
14 Feb 1970	W	Ernie Lopez	Los Angeles	Won RSF–15
3 Dec 1970	W	Billy Backus	Syracuse, New York	Lost RSF–4
4 Jun 1971	W	Billy Backus	Los Angeles	Won TKO–4
14 Dec 1971	W	Hedgemon Lewis	Los Angeles	Won PTS–15
28 Mar 1972	W	Ralph Charles	London	Won KO–7
10 Jun 1972	W	Adolph Pruitt	Monterrey, Mexico	Won RSF–2
28 Feb 1973	W	Ernie Lopez	Los Angeles	Won KO–7
23 Jun 1973	W	Roger Menetrey	Grenoble, France	Won PTS–15
22 Sep 1973	W	Clyde Gray	Toronto	Won PTS–15
9 Feb 1974	M	Carlos Monzon	Paris	Lost RTD–7
3 Aug 1974	W	Hedgemon Lewis	Mexico City	Won RSF–9

DATE	WEIGHT	OPPONENT	VENUE	RESULT

DATE	WEIGHT	OPPONENT	VENUE	RESULT
14 Dec 1974	W	Horacio Saldano	Mexico City	Won KO–3
29 Mar 1975	W	Armando Muniz	Acapulco, Mexico	Won DIS–12
12 Jul 1975	W (WBC)	Armando Muniz	Mexico City	Won PTS–15
6 Dec 1975	W (WBC)	John H Stracey	Mexico City	Lost RSF–6

Valerio NATI

Born: Dovadola, Italy, 11 Apr 1956
World title fights: 3 (all junior-feather) won 1, lost 2

DATE	WEIGHT	OPPONENT	VENUE	RESULT
26 Nov 1988	JFe (WBC)	Daniel Zaragoza	Forli, Italy	Lost KO–5
9 Dec 1989	JFe (WBO)	Kenny Mitchell	Teramo, Italy	Won DIS–4
12 May 1990	JFe (WBO)	Orlando Fernandez	Sassari, Italy	Lost RSF–10

Rolando NAVARRETE

Born: Santos City, Philippines, 14 Feb 1957
World title fights: 4 (all junior-light) won 2, lost 2

DATE	WEIGHT	OPPONENT	VENUE	RESULT
27 Apr 1980	JL (WBC)	Alexis Arguello	San Juan	Lost RSF–4
29 Aug 1981	JL (WBC)	Cornelius Boza-Edwards	Via Reggio, Italy	Won KO–5
16 Jan 1982	JL (WBC)	Chung-Il Choi	Manila	Won KO–11
29 May 1982	JL (WBC)	Rafael Limon	Las Vegas	Lost KO–12

Juan NAZARIO

Born: Guaynabo, Puerto Rico, 9 Sep 1963
World title fights: 3 (all lightweight) won 1, lost 2

DATE	WEIGHT	OPPONENT	VENUE	RESULT
11 Aug 1987	L (WBA)	Edwin Rosario	Chicago	Lost RSF–8
6 Apr 1990	L (WBA)	Edwin Rosario	New York	Won RSF–8
11 Aug 1990	L (WBC/ WBA/IBF)	Pernell Whitaker	Lake Tahoe, Nevada	Lost KO–1

DATE	WEIGHT	OPPONENT	VENUE	RESULT

Welcome NCITA

Born: South Africa, 21 Oct 1965
World title fights: 3 (all junior-featherweight) won 3, lost 0

DATE	WEIGHT	OPPONENT	VENUE	RESULT
10 Mar 1990	JFe (IBF)	Fabrice Benichou	Tel Aviv	Won PTS–12
2 Jun 1990	JFe (IBF)	Ramon Cruz	Rome	Won RSF–7
29 Sep 1990	JFe (IBF)	Gerardo Lopez	Aosta, Italy	Won RSF–8

Frankie NEIL

Born: San Francisco, USA, 25 Jul 1883
Died: Richmond, California, 6 Mar 1970
World title fights: 7 (6 bantamweight, 1 featherweight) won 3, lost 3, drew 1

DATE	WEIGHT	OPPONENT	VENUE	RESULT
23 Dec 1902	B	Harry Forbes	Oakland, California	Lost RSF–7
13 Aug 1903	B	Harry Forbes	San Francisco	Won KO–2
4 Sep 1903	B	Billy de Coursey	Los Angeles	Won KO–15
16 Oct 1903	B	Johnny Reagan	Los Angeles	Drew 20
17 Jun 1904	B	Harry Forbes	Chicago	Won KO–3
17 Oct 1904	B	Joe Bowker	London	Lost PTS–20
4 Jul 1906	Fe	Abe Attell	Los Angeles	Lost PTS–20

Azumah NELSON

Born: Accra, Ghana, 19 Jul 1958
World title fights: 15 (8 featherweight, 1 lightweight, 6 junior-light)
won 13, lost 2

DATE	WEIGHT	OPPONENT	VENUE	RESULT
21 Jul 1982	Fe (WBC)	Salvador Sanchez	New York	Lost RSF–15
8 Dec 1984	Fe (WBC)	Wilfredo Gomez	San Juan	Won RSF–11
6 Sep 1985	Fe (WBC)	Juvenal Ordenes	Miami	Won KO–5
12 Oct 1985	Fe (WBC)	Pat Cowdell	Birmingham	Won KO–1
25 Feb 1986	Fe (WBC)	Marcos Villasana	Los Angeles	Won PTS–12

DATE	WEIGHT	OPPONENT	VENUE	RESULT
22 Jun 1986	Fe (WBC)	Danilo Cabrera	San Juan	Won RSF–10
7 Mar 1987	Fe (WBC)	Mauro Gutierrez	Los Angeles	Won KO–6
30 Aug 1987	Fe (WBC)	Marcos Villasana	Los Angeles	Won PTS–12
29 Feb 1988	JL (WBC)	Mario Martinez	Los Angeles	Won PTS–12
25 Jun 1988	JL (WBC)	Lupe Suarez	Atlantic City	Won RSF–9
10 Dec 1988	JL (WBC)	Sydney Dal Rovere	Accra	Won RSF–3
25 Feb 1989	JL (WBC)	Mario Martinez	Las Vegas	Won RSF–12
5 Nov 1989	JL (WBC)	Jim McDonnell	London	Won RSF–12
19 May 1990	L (WBC/IBF)	Pernell Whitaker	Las Vegas	Lost PTS–12
13 Oct 1990	JL (WBC)	Juan Laporte	Sydney	Won PTS–12

Battling NELSON

Born: Copenhagen, Denmark, 5 Jun 1882
Died: Chicago, 7 Feb 1954
World title fights: 6 (all lightweight) won 4, lost 2

DATE	WEIGHT	OPPONENT	VENUE	RESULT
3 Sep 1906	L	Joe Gans	Goldfield, Nevada	Lost DIS–42
4 Jul 1908	L	Joe Gans	San Francisco	Won KO–17
9 Sep 1908	L	Joe Gans	Colma, California	Won KO–21
29 May 1909	L	Dick Hyland	Colma	Won KO–23
22 Jun 1909	L	Jack Clifford	Oklahoma City	Won KO–5
22 Feb 1910	L	Ad Wolgast	Port Richmond, California	Lost KO–40

George NICHOLS

Born: Sandusky, Ohio, USA, 9 Jul 1908
World title fights: 1 (light-heavy) won 1, lost 0

DATE	WEIGHT	OPPONENT	VENUE	RESULT
18 Mar 1932	LH (NBA)	Dave Maier	Chicago	Won PTS–10

DATE	WEIGHT	OPPONENT	VENUE	RESULT

Claude NOEL

Born: Port of Spain, Trinidad, 25 Jul 1948
World title fights: 3 (all lightweight) won 1, lost 2

DATE	WEIGHT	OPPONENT	VENUE	RESULT
16 Jun 1979	L (WBA)	Ernesto Espana	San Juan	Lost KO–13
12 Sep 1981	L (WBA)	Rodolfo Gonzalez	Atlantic City	Won PTS–15
5 Dec 1981	L (WBA)	Arturo Frias	Las Vegas	Lost KO–8

Terry NORRIS

Born: Campo, California, 17 Jun 1967
World title fights: 3 (all junior-middleweight) won 2, lost 1

DATE	WEIGHT	OPPONENT	VENUE	RESULT
30 Jul 1989	JM (WBA)	Julian Jackson	Atlantic City	Lost RSF–2
31 Mar 1990	JM (WBC)	John Mugabi	Tampa, Florida	Won KO–1
13 Jul 1990	JM (WBC)	Rene Jacquot	Annecy, France	Won PTS–12

Ken NORTON

Born: Jacksonville, Illinois, USA, 9 Aug 1943
World title fights: 3 (all heavyweight) won 0, lost 3

DATE	WEIGHT	OPPONENT	VENUE	RESULT
26 Mar 1974	H	George Foreman	Caracas	Lost RSF–2
28 Sep 1976	H	Muhammad Ali	New York	Lost PTS–15
10 Jun 1978	H (WBC)*	Larry Holmes	Las Vegas	Lost PTS–15

* Norton had been proclaimed champion by the WBC in 1978 after their disapproval of Muhammad Ali defending his title against Leon Spinks.

Yoshiaki NUMATA

Born: Tomikawa-cho, Hokkaido, Japan, 19 Apr 1945
World title fights: 8 (7 junior-light, 1 lightweight) won 5, lost 3

DATE	WEIGHT	OPPONENT	VENUE	RESULT
15 Jun 1967	JL	Flash Elorde	Tokyo	Won PTS–15
14 Dec 1967	JL	Hiroshi Kobayashi	Tokyo	Lost KO–12

DATE	WEIGHT	OPPONENT	VENUE	RESULT
4 Oct 1969	L	Mando Ramos	Los Angeles	Lost KO-6
5 Apr 1970	JL (WBC)	Rene Barrientos	Tokyo	Won PTS-15
27 Sep 1970	JL (WBC)	Raul Rojas	Tokyo	Won KO-5
3 Jan 1971	JL (WBC)	Rene Barrientos	Shizuoka, Japan	Won PTS-15
31 May 1971	JL (WBC)	Lionel Rose	Hiroshima, Japan	Won PTS-15
10 Oct 1971	JL (WBC)	Ricardo Arredondo	Sendai, Japan	Lost KO-10

Michael NUNN

Born: Sherman Oaks, California, USA, 14 Apr 1963
World title fights: 6 (all middleweight) won 6, lost 0

DATE	WEIGHT	OPPONENT	VENUE	RESULT
28 Jul 1988	M (IBF)	Frank Tate	Las Vegas	Won RSF-9
4 Nov 1988	M (IBF)	Juan Roldan	Las Vegas	Won KO-8
25 Mar 1989	M (IBF)	Sumbu Kalambay	Las Vegas	Won KO-1
19 Aug 1989	M (IBF)	Iran Barkley	Reno, Nevada	Won PTS-12
14 Apr 1990	M (IBF)	Marlon Starling	Las Vegas	Won PTS-12
18 Oct 1990	M (IBF)	Donald Curry	Paris	Won RSF-10

Elisha OBED

Born: Nassau, Bahamas, 21 Feb 1952
World title fights: 5 (all junior-middle) won 3, lost 2

DATE	WEIGHT	OPPONENT	VENUE	RESULT
13 Nov 1975	JM (WBC)	Miguel de Oliveira	Paris	Won RTD-10
28 Feb 1976	JM (WBC)	Tony Gardner	Nassau, Bahamas	Won KO-2
24 Apr 1976	JM (WBC)	Sea Robinson	Abidjan, Ivory Coast	Won PTS-15
18 Jun 1976	JM (WBC)	Eckhard Dagge	Berlin	Lost RTD-10
11 Mar 1978	JM (WBC)	Rocky Mattioli	Melbourne	Lost KO-7

Fulgencio OBELMEJIAS

Born: San Jose de Rio Chico, Venezuela, 11 Jan 1953
World title fights: 4 (2 middleweight, 2 super-middle) won 1, lost 3

DATE	WEIGHT	OPPONENT	VENUE	RESULT	
17 Jan 1981	M	Marvin Hagler	Boston	Lost	RSF–8
31 Oct 1982	M	Marvin Hagler	San Remo, Italy	Lost	KO–5
23 May 1988	SM (WBA)	Chong-Pal Park	Suanbao, Venezuela	Won	PTS–12
27 May 1989	SM (WBA)	In-Chul Baek	Seoul	Lost	RSF–11

Philadelphia Jack O'BRIEN

Born: Philadelphia, USA, 17 Jan 1878
Died: New York, 12 Nov 1942
World title fights: 3 (1 light-heavy, 1 heavyweight/light-heavy, 1 heavyweight)
won 1, lost 1, drew 1

DATE	WEIGHT	OPPONENT	VENUE	RESULT	
20 Dec 1905	LH	Bob Fitzsimmons	San Francisco	Won	KO–13
28 Nov 1906	H/LH	Tommy Burns	Los Angeles	Drew	20
8 May 1907	H	Tommy Burns	Los Angeles	Lost	PTS–20

Ossie OCASIO

Born: Trujillo Alto, Puerto Rico, 12 Aug 1955
World title fights: 7 (1 heavyweight, 6 cruiserweight) won 4, lost 3

DATE	WEIGHT	OPPONENT	VENUE	RESULT	
29 Mar 1979	H (WBC)	Larry Holmes	Las Vegas	Lost	RSF–7
13 Feb 1982	C (WBA)	Robbie Williams	Johannesburg	Won	PTS–15
15 Dec 1982	C (WBA)	Young Joe Louis	Chicago	Won	PTS–15
20 May 1983	C (WBA)	Randy Stephens	Las Vegas	Won	PTS–15
5 May 1984	C (WBA)	John Odhiambo	San Juan	Won	RSF–15
1 Dec 1984	C (WBA)	Piet Crous	Sun City, S Africa	Lost	PTS–15
15 Aug 1987	C (WBA/IBF)	Evander Holyfield	St Tropez, France	Lost	RSF–11

DATE	WEIGHT	OPPONENT	VENUE	RESULT

DATE	WEIGHT	OPPONENT	VENUE	RESULT

Mike O'DOWD

Born: St Paul, Minnesota, USA, 5 Apr 1895
Died: St Paul, 28 Jul 1957
World title fights: 5 (all middleweight) won 3, lost 2

DATE	WEIGHT	OPPONENT	VENUE	RESULT
14 Nov 1917	M	Al McCoy	Brooklyn, New York	Won KO–6
17 Jul 1919	M	Al McCoy	St Paul, Minnesota	Won KO–3
6 May 1920	M	Johnny Wilson	Boston	Lost PTS–12
17 Mar 1921	M	Johnny Wilson	New York	Lost PTS–15
30 Nov 1922	M (NY)	Dave Rosenberg	New York	Won DIS–8

Sean O'GRADY

Born: Oklahoma City, USA, 10 Feb 1959
World title fights: 2 (both lightweight) won 1, lost 1

DATE	WEIGHT	OPPONENT	VENUE	RESULT
1 Nov 1980	L (WBC)	Jim Watt	Glasgow	Lost RSF–12
12 Apr 1981	L (WBA)	Hilmer Kenty	Atlantic City	Won PTS–15

Shoji OGUMA

Born: Fukushima, Japan, 22 Jul 1951
World title fights: 13 (12 flyweight, 1 junior-bantam) won 5, lost 7, drew 1

DATE	WEIGHT	OPPONENT	VENUE	RESULT
1 Oct 1974	Fl (WBC)	Betulio Gonzalez	Tokyo	Won PTS–15
8 Jan 1975	Fl (WBC)	Miguel Canto	Sendai, Japan	Lost PTS–15
21 Apr 1976	Fl (WBA)	Alfonso Lopez	Tokyo	Lost PTS–15
4 Jan 1978	Fl (WBC)	Miguel Canto	Koriyama, Japan	Lost PTS–15
18 Apr 1978	Fl (WBC)	Miguel Canto	Tokyo	Lost PTS–15
29 Jan 1979	Fl (WBA)	Betulio Gonzalez	Hamamatsu, Japan	Drew 15
6 Jul 1979	Fl (WBA)	Betulio Gonzalez	Utsonomiya, Japan	Lost KO–12
18 May 1980	Fl (WBC)	Chan-Hee Park	Seoul	Won KO–9
28 Jul 1980	Fl (WBC)	Sun-Jung Kim	Tokyo	Won PTS–15

DATE	WEIGHT	OPPONENT	VENUE	RESULT

DATE	WEIGHT	OPPONENT	VENUE	RESULT	
18 Oct 1980	Fl (WBC)	Chan-Hee Park	Tokyo	Won	PTS–15
3 Feb 1981	Fl (WBC)	Chan-Hee Park	Tokyo	Won	PTS–15
12 May 1981	Fl (WBC)	Antonio Avelar	Tokyo	Lost	KO–7
11 Nov 1982	JB (WBA)	Jiro Watanabe	Hamamatsu	Lost	RTD–12

Min-Kuem OH

Born: South Korea, 15 Aug 1962
World title fights: 4 (all featherweight) won 3, lost 1

DATE	WEIGHT	OPPONENT	VENUE	RESULT	
4 Mar 1984	Fe (IBF)	Joko Arter	Seoul	Won	KO–2
10 Jun 1984	Fe (IBF)	Kelvin Lampkin	Seoul	Won	PTS–15
7 Apr 1985	Fe (IBF)	Irving Mitchell	Pusan, S Korea	Won	PTS–15
29 Nov 1985	Fe (IBF)	Ki-Yung Chung	Seoul	Lost	KO–15

Hideyuki OHASHI

Born: Yokohama, Japan, 8 Mar 1965
World title fights: 5 (3 strawweight, 2 junior-fly) won 2, lost 3

DATE	WEIGHT	OPPONENT	VENUE	RESULT	
14 Dec 1986	JFl (WBC)	Jung-Koo Chang	Inchon, S Korea	Lost	RSF–5
27 Jun 1988	JFl (WBC)	Jung-Koo Chang	Tokyo	Lost	RSF–8
7 Feb 1990	S (WBC)	Jum-Hwan Choi	Tokyo	Won	KO–9
8 Jun 1990	S (WBC)	Napa Kiatwanchai	Tokyo	Won	PTS–12
25 Oct 1990	S (WBC)	Ricardo Lopez	Tokyo	Lost	RSF–5

Masao OHBA

Born: Tokyo, Japan, 21 Oct 1949
Died: Tokyo, 24 Jan 1973
World title fights: 6 (all flyweight) won 6, lost 0

DATE	WEIGHT	OPPONENT	VENUE	RESULT	
22 Oct 1970	Fl (WBA)	Berkrerk Chartvanchai	Tokyo	Won	RSF–13

DATE	WEIGHT	OPPONENT	VENUE	RESULT

1 Apr 1971	Fl (WBA)	Betulio Gonzalez	Tokyo	Won PTS–15
23 Oct 1971	Fl (WBA)	Fernando Cabanela	Tokyo	Won PTS–15
4 Mar 1972	Fl (WBA)	Susumu Hanagata	Tokyo	Won PTS–15
20 Jun 1972	Fl (WBA)	Orlando Amores	Tokyo	Won KO–5
2 Jan 1973	Fl (WBA)	Chartchai Chionoi	Tokyo	Won RSF–12

Bob OLIN

Born: New York, USA, 4 Jul 1908
Died: New York, 16 Dec 1956
World title fights: 3 (all light-heavy) won 1, lost 2

16 Nov 1934	LH	Maxie Rosenbloom	New York	Won PTS–15
31 Oct 1935	LH	John Henry Lewis	St Louis	Lost PTS–15
3 Jun 1937	LH	John Henry Lewis	St Louis	Lost KO–8

Patrizio OLIVA

Born: Naples, Italy, 28 Jan 1959
World title fights: 4 (all junior-welter) won 3, lost 1

15 Mar 1986	JW (WBA)	Ubaldo Sacco	Monte Carlo	Won PTS–15
6 Sep 1986	JW (WBA)	Brian Brunette	Naples	Won RSF–3
10 Jan 1987	JW (WBA)	Rodolfo Gonzalez	Agrigento, Italy	Won PTS–15
4 Jul 1987	JW (WBA)	Juan Martin Coggi	Ribera, Italy	Lost KO–3

Ruben OLIVARES

Born: Mexico City, Mexico, 14 Jan 1947
World title fights: 13 (8 bantamweight, 5 featherweight) won 8, lost 5

22 Aug 1969	B	Lionel Rose	Los Angeles	Won KO–5
12 Dec 1969	B	Alan Rudkin	Los Angeles	Won RSF–2

DATE	WEIGHT	OPPONENT	VENUE	RESULT

DATE	WEIGHT	OPPONENT	VENUE	RESULT
18 Apr 1970	B	Jesus 'Chucho' Castillo	Los Angeles	Won PTS-15
16 Oct 1970	B	Jesus 'Chucho' Castillo	Los Angeles	Lost RSF-14
2 Apr 1971	B	Jesus 'Chucho' Castillo	Los Angeles	Won PTS-15
25 Oct 1971	B	Kazuyoshi Kanazawa	Nagoya, Japan	Won RSF-14
14 Dec 1971	B	Jesus Pimental	Los Angeles	Won RSF-11
19 Mar 1972	B	Rafael Herrera	Mexico City	Lost KO-8
9 Jul 1974	Fe (WBA)	Zensuke Utagawa	Los Angeles	Won RSF-7
23 Nov 1974	Fe (WBA)	Alexis Arguello	Los Angeles	Lost KO-13
20 Jun 1975	Fe (WBC)	Bobby Chacon	Los Angeles	Won RSF-2
20 Sep 1975	Fe (WBC)	David Kotey	Los Angeles	Lost PTS-15
21 Jul 1979	Fe (WBA)	Eusebio Pedroza	Houston	Lost RSF-12

Joey OLIVO

Born: Los Angeles, USA, 25 Jan 1958
World title fights: 4 (all junior-fly) won 2, lost 2

DATE	WEIGHT	OPPONENT	VENUE	RESULT
8 Feb 1981	JFl (WBC)	Hilario Zapata	Panama City	Lost RTD-13
29 Mar 1985	JFl (WBA)	Francisco Quiroz	Miami	Won PTS-15
28 Jul 1985	JFl (WBA)	Moon-Jin Choi	Seoul	Won PTS-15
8 Dec 1985	JFl (WBA)	Myung-Woo Yuh	Taegu, S Korea	Lost PTS-15

Carl 'Bobo' OLSON

Born: Honolulu, Hawaii, USA, 11 Jul 1928
World title fights: 8 (7 middleweight, 1 light-heavy) won 4, lost 4

DATE	WEIGHT	OPPONENT	VENUE	RESULT
13 Mar 1952	M	Sugar Ray Robinson	San Francisco	Lost PTS-15
21 Oct 1953	M	Randolph Turpin	New York	Won PTS-15
2 Apr 1954	M	Kid Gavilan	Chicago	Won PTS-15
20 Aug 1954	M	Rocky Castellani	San Francisco	Won PTS-15
15 Dec 1954	M	Pierre Langlois	San Francisco	Won KO-11

DATE	WEIGHT	OPPONENT	VENUE	RESULT

22 Jun 1955	LH	Archie Moore	New York	Lost	KO-3
9 Dec 1955	M	Sugar Ray Robinson	Chicago	Lost	KO-2
18 May 1956	M	Sugar Ray Robinson	Los Angeles	Lost	KO-4

Rafael ORONO

Born: Sucre, Venezuela, 30 Aug 1958
World title fights: 11 (all junior-bantam) won 7, drew 1, lost 3

2 Feb 1980	JB (WBC)	Seung-Hoon Lee	Caracas	Won	PTS-15
14 Apr 1980	JB (WBC)	Ramon Soria	Caracas	Won	PTS-15
28 Jul 1980	JB (WBC)	Willie Jensen	Caracas	Drew	15
15 Sep 1980	JB (WBC)	Jovito Rengifo	Barquisimento, Venezuela	Won	KO-3
24 Jan 1981	JB (WBC)	Chul-Ho Kim	San Cristobel, Venezuela	Lost	KO-9
28 Nov 1982	JB (WBC)	Chul-Ho Kim	Seoul	Won	RSF-6
31 Jan 1983	JB (WBC)	Pedro Romero	Caracas	Won	KO-4
9 May 1983	JB (WBC)	Raul Valdez	Caracas	Won	PTS-12
29 Oct 1983	JB (WBC)	Orlando Maldonado	Caracas	Won	KO-5
26 Nov 1983	JB (WBC)	Payao Poontarat	Bangkok	Lost	PTS-12
17 Jul 1985	JB (WBA)	Kaosai Galaxy	Bangkok	Lost	RSF-5

Rafael ORTEGA

Born: Panama City, Panama, 25 Sep 1950
World title fights: 3 (all featherweight) won 2, lost 1

15 Jan 1977	Fe (WBA)	Francisco Coronado	Panama City	Won	PTS-15
29 May 1977	Fe (WBA)	Yasutsune Uehara	Okinawa, Japan	Won	PTS-15
17 Dec 1977	Fe (WBA)	Cecilio Lastra	Torrelavega, Spain	Lost	PTS-15

Carlos ORTIZ

Born: Ponce, Puerto Rico, 9 Sep 1936
World title fights: 18 (5 junior-welter, 13 lightweight) won 14, lost 4

DATE	WEIGHT	OPPONENT	VENUE	RESULT
12 Jun 1959	JW	Kenny Lane	New York	Won RSF-2
4 Feb 1960	JW	Battling Torres	Los Angeles	Won KO-10
15 Jun 1960	JW	Duilio Loi	San Francisco	Won PTS-15
1 Sep 1960	JW	Duilio Loi	Milan	Lost PTS-15
10 May 1961	JW	Duilio Loi	Milan	Lost PTS-15
21 Apr 1962	L	Joe Brown	Las Vegas	Won PTS-15
2 Dec 1962	L	Teruo Kosaka	Tokyo	Won KO-5
7 Apr 1963	L	Doug Vaillant	San Juan	Won RSF-13
15 Feb 1964	L	Flash Elorde	Manila	Won RSF-14
11 Apr 1964	L	Kenny Lane	San Juan	Won PTS-15
10 Apr 1965	L	Ismael Laguna	Panama City	Lost PTS-15
13 Nov 1965	L	Ismael Laguna	San Juan	Won PTS-15
20 Jun 1966	L	Johnny Bizzaro	Pittsburgh	Won RSF-12
22 Oct 1966	L	Sugar Ramos	Mexico City	Won RSF-5
28 Nov 1966	L (WBA)	Flash Elorde	New York	Won KO-14
1 Jul 1967	L	Sugar Ramos	San Juan	Won RSF-4
16 Aug 1967	L	Ismael Laguna	New York	Won PTS-15
29 Jun 1968	L	Carlos Cruz	Santo Domingo	Lost PTS-15

Manuel ORTIZ

Born: Corona, California, USA, 2 Jul 1916
Died: San Diego, 31 May 1970
World title fights: 23 (all bantamweight) won 21, lost 2

DATE	WEIGHT	OPPONENT	VENUE	RESULT
7 Aug 1942	B	Lou Salica	Hollywood	Won PTS-12
1 Jan 1943	B	Kenny Lindsay	Portland, Oregon	Won PTS-10

DATE	WEIGHT	OPPONENT	VENUE	RESULT
27 Jan 1943	B	George Freitas	Oakland, California	Won RSF–10
10 Mar 1943	B	Lou Salica	Oakland	Won RSF–11
28 Apr 1943	B	Lupe Cardoza	Fort Worth, Texas	Won KO–6
26 May 1943	B	Joe Robleto	Long Beach, California	Won PTS–15
12 Jul 1943	B	Joe Robleto	Seattle	Won KO–7
1 Oct 1943	B	Leonardo Lopez	Hollywood	Won KO–4
23 Nov 1943	B	Benny Goldberg	Los Angeles	Won PTS–15
14 Mar 1944	B	Ernesto Aguilar	Los Angeles	Won PTS–15
4 Apr 1944	B	Tony Olivera	Los Angeles	Won PTS–15
12 Sep 1944	B	Luis Castillo	Los Angeles	Won RSF–4
14 Nov 1944	B	Luis Castillo	Los Angeles	Won RSF–9
25 Feb 1946	B	Luis Castillo	San Francisco	Won KO–13
26 May 1946	B	Kenny Lindsay	Los Angeles	Won KO–5
10 Jun 1946	B	Jackie Jurich	San Francisco	Won KO–11
6 Jan 1947	B	Harold Dade	San Francisco	Lost PTS–15
11 Mar 1947	B	Harold Dade	Los Angeles	Won PTS–15
30 May 1947	B	David Kui Kong Young	Honolulu	Won PTS–15
20 Dec 1947	B	Tirso Del Rosario	Manila	Won PTS–15
4 Jul 1948	B	Memo Valero	Mexicali, Mexico	Won KO–8
1 Mar 1949	B	Dado Marino	Honolulu	Won PTS–15
31 May 1950	B	Vic Toweel	Johannesburg	Lost PTS–15

Ken OVERLIN

Born: Decatur, Illinois, USA, 15 Aug 1910
Died: Reno, Nevada, 24 Jul 1969
World title fights: 5 (all middleweight) won 3, lost 2

DATE	WEIGHT	OPPONENT	VENUE	RESULT
11 Sep 1937	M	Freddie Steele	Seattle	Lost KO–4
23 May 1940	M (NY)	Ceferino Garcia	New York	Won PTS–15
1 Nov 1940	M (NY)	Larry Lane	Trenton, New Jersey	Won PTS–15

DATE	WEIGHT	OPPONENT	VENUE	RESULT
13 Dec 1940	M (NY)	Steve Belloise	New York	Won PTS–15
9 May 1941	M (NY)	Billy Soose	New York	Lost PTS–15

Jorge PAEZ

Born: Mexicali, Mexico, 27 Oct 1965
World title fights: 10 (9 featherweight, 1 junior-light) won 7, lost 1, drew 2

DATE	WEIGHT	OPPONENT	VENUE	RESULT
4 Aug 1988	Fe (IBF)	Calvin Grove	Mexicali, Mexico	Won PTS–15
30 Mar 1989	Fe (IBF)	Calvin Grove	Mexicali	Won KO–11
22 May 1989	Fe (IBF)	Louie Espinoza	Phoenix	Drew 12
6 Aug 1989	Fe (IBF)	Steve Cruz	El Paso, Texas	Won PTS–12
16 Sep 1989	Fe (IBF)	Jose Mario Lopez	Mexico City	Won KO–2
9 Dec 1989	Fe (IBF)	Lupe Gutierrez	Reno, Nevada	Won RSF–6
4 Feb 1990	Fe (IBF)	Troy Dorsey	Las Vegas	Won PTS–12
7 Apr 1990	Fe (IBF/WBO)	Louie Espinoza	Las Vegas	Won PTS–12
8 June 1990	Fe (IBF)	Troy Dorsey	Las Vegas	Drew 12
22 Sep 1990	JL (IBF)	Tony Lopez	Sacramento, California	Lost PTS–12

Greg PAGE

Born: Louisville, Kentucky, USA, 25 Oct 1958
World title fights: 3 (all heavyweight) won 1, lost 2

DATE	WEIGHT	OPPONENT	VENUE	RESULT
9 Mar 1984	H (WBC)	Tim Witherspoon	Las Vegas	Lost PTS–12
1 Dec 1984	H (WBA)	Gerrie Coetzee	Sun City, S Africa	Won KO–8
29 Apr 1985	H (WBA)	Tony Tubbs	Buffalo	Lost PTS–15

DATE	WEIGHT	OPPONENT	VENUE	RESULT

Sergio PALMA

Born: La Tigra, Chaco, Argentina, 1 Jan 1956
World title fights: 8 (all junior-feather) won 6, lost 2

DATE	WEIGHT	OPPONENT	VENUE	RESULT	
15 Dec 1979	JFe (WBA)	Ricardo Cardona	Barranquilla, Colombia	Lost	PTS–15
9 Aug 1980	JFe (WBA)	Leo Randolph	Spokane, Washington	Won	KO–5
8 Nov 1980	JFe (WBA)	Ulisses Morales	Buenos Aires	Won	KO–9
4 Apr 1981	JFe (WBA)	Leonardo Cruz	Buenos Aires	Won	PTS–15
15 Aug 1981	JFe (WBA)	Ricardo Cardona	Buenos Aires	Won	RSF–12
3 Oct 1981	JFe (WBA)	Vichit Muangroi-et	Buenos Aires	Won	PTS–15
15 Jan 1982	JFe (WBA)	Jorge Lujan	Cordoba, Argentina	Won	PTS–15
12 Jun 1982	JFe (WBA)	Leonardo Cruz	Miami	Lost	PTS–15

Carlos PALOMINO

Born: San Luis, Mexico, 10 Aug 1949
World title fights: 9 (all welterweight) won 8, lost 1

DATE	WEIGHT	OPPONENT	VENUE	RESULT	
22 Jun 1976	W (WBC)	John H Stracey	London	Won	RSF–12
22 Jan 1977	W (WBC)	Armando Muniz	Los Angeles	Won	RSF–15
14 Jun 1977	W (WBC)	Dave 'Boy' Green	London	Won	KO–11
13 Sep 1977	W (WBC)	Everaldo Costa Azevedo	Los Angeles	Won	PTS–15
10 Dec 1977	W (WBC)	Jose Palacios	Los Angeles	Won	KO–13
11 Feb 1978	W (WBC)	Ryu Sorimachi	Las Vegas	Won	KO–7
18 Mar 1978	W (WBC)	Mimoun Mohatar	Las Vegas	Won	RSF–9
27 May 1978	W (WBC)	Armando Muniz	Los Angeles	Won	PTS–15
14 Jan 1979	W (WBC)	Wilfred Benitez	San Juan	Lost	PTS–15

DATE	WEIGHT	OPPONENT	VENUE	RESULT

Billy PAPKE

Born: Spring Valley, Illinois, USA, 17 Sep 1886
Died: Newport, California, 26 Nov 1936
World title fights: 11 (all middleweight) won 6, lost 5

DATE	WEIGHT	OPPONENT	VENUE	RESULT	
4 Jun 1908	M	Stanley Ketchel	Milwaukee	Lost	PTS–10
7 Sep 1908	M	Stanley Ketchel	Vernon, California	Won	KO–12
26 Nov 1908	M	Stanley Ketchel	Colma, California	Lost	KO–11
5 Jul 1909	M	Stanley Ketchel	Colma	Lost	PTS–20
19 Mar 1910	M	Willie Lewis	Paris	Won	KO–3
11 Feb 1911	M	Johnny Thompson	Sydney	Lost	PTS–20
8 Jun 1911	M	Jim Sullivan	London	Won	KO–9
29 Jun 1912	M	Marcel Moreau	Paris	Won	RTD–15
23 Oct 1912	M	Georges Carpentier	Paris	Won	RTD–17
4 Dec 1912	M	George Bernard	Paris	Won	RTD–6
5 Mar 1913	M	Frank Klaus	Paris	Lost	DIS–15

Benny 'Kid' PARET

Born: Santa Clara, Las Villas, Cuba, 14 Mar 1937
Died: New York City, 3 Apr 1962*
World title fights: 6 (5 welterweight, 1 middleweight) won 3, lost 3

DATE	WEIGHT	OPPONENT	VENUE	RESULT	
27 May 1960	W	Don Jordan	Las Vegas	Won	PTS–15
10 Dec 1960	W	Frederico Thompson	New York	Won	PTS–15
1 Apr 1961	W	Emile Griffith	Miami	Lost	KO–13
30 Sep 1961	W	Emile Griffith	New York	Won	PTS–15
9 Dec 1961	M (NBA)	Gene Fullmer	Las Vegas	Lost	KO–10
24 Mar 1962	W	Emile Griffith	New York	Lost	RSF–12

* As a result of injuries received in the bout versus Emile Griffith.

DATE	WEIGHT	OPPONENT	VENUE	RESULT

DATE	WEIGHT	OPPONENT	VENUE	RESULT

Chan-Hee PARK

Born: Pusan, South Korea, 23 Mar 1957
World title fights: 9 (all flyweight) won 5, lost 3, drew 1

18 Mar 1979	Fl (WBC)	Miguel Canto	Pusan, S Korea	Won	PTS–15
19 May 1979	Fl (WBC)	Tsutomo Igerashi	Seoul	Won	PTS–15
9 Sep 1979	Fl (WBC)	Miguel Canto	Seoul	Drew	15
16 Dec 1979	Fl (WBC)	Guty Espadas	Pusan	Won	KO–2
10 Feb 1980	Fl (WBC)	Arnel Arrozal	Seoul	Won	PTS–15
12 Apr 1980	Fl (WBC)	Alberto Morales	Taegu, S Korea	Won	PTS–15
18 May 1980	Fl (WBC)	Shoji Oguma	Seoul	Lost	KO–9
18 Oct 1980	Fl (WBC)	Shoji Oguma	Tokyo	Lost	PTS–15
3 Feb 1981	Fl (WBC)	Shoji Oguma	Tokyo	Lost	PTS–15

Chan-Young PARK

Born: South Korea, 10 Jun 1963
World title fights: 3 (2 bantamweight, 1 junior-feather) won 1, lost 2

24 May 1987	B (WBA)	Takuya Muguruma	Osaka, Japan	Won	RSF–11
3 Oct 1987	B (WBA)	Wilfredo Vasquez	Seoul	Lost	RTD–10
3 Dec 1989	JFe (WBC)	Daniel Zaragoza	Seoul	Lost	PTS–12

Chong-Pal PARK

Born: Chon-Ra, Seoul, South Korea, 11 Aug 1960
World title fights: 12 (all super-middle) won 10, lost 1, NC 1

22 Jul 1984	SM (IBF)	Murray Sutherland	Seoul	Won	KO–11
2 Jan 1985	SM (IBF)	Roy Gumbs	Seoul	Won	KO–2
29 Jun 1985	SM (IBF)	Vinnie Curto	Seoul	Won	PTS–15
11 Apr 1986	SM (IBF)	Vinnie Curto	Los Angeles	Won	KO–15

DATE	WEIGHT	OPPONENT	VENUE	RESULT

6 Jul 1986	SM (IBF)	Lindell Holmes	Seoul		NC–2*
14 Sep 1986	SM (IBF)	Marvin Mack	Seoul	Won	PTS–15
25 Jan 1987	SM (IBF)	Doug Sam	Seoul	Won	RSF–15
2 May 1987	SM (IBF)	Lindell Holmes	Inchon, S Korea	Won	PTS–15
15 Jul 1987	SM (IBF)	Emmanuel Otti	Kwangju, S Korea	Won	KO–4
6 Dec 1987	SM (WBA)	Jesus Gallardo	Pusan, S Korea	Won	KO–2
1 Mar 1988	SM (WBA)	Polly Pesieron	Chonju, S Korea	Won	KO–5
23 May 1988	SM (WBA)	Fulgencio Obelmejias	Suanbao, Venezuela	Lost	PTS–12

* Both fighters injured, result declared a 'No Contest'

Ricky PARKEY

Born: Morristown, Tennessee, USA, 7 Nov 1956
World title fights: 3 (all cruiserweight) won 2, lost 1

25 Oct 1986	C (IBF)	Lee Roy Murphy	Marsala, Italy	Won	RSF–10
28 Mar 1987	C (IBF)	Chisanda Mutti	Lido di Camiore, Italy	Won	RSF–12
16 May 1987	C (IBF)	Evander Holyfield	Las Vegas	Lost	RSF–3

Mate PARLOV

Born: Split, Yugoslavia, 16 Nov 1948
World title fights: 5 (3 light-heavy, 2 cruiserweight) won 2, lost 2, drew 1

7 Jan 1978	LH (WBC)	Miguel Angel Cuello	Milan	Won	KO–9
17 Jun 1978	LH (WBC)	John Conteh	Belgrade	Won	PTS–15
2 Dec 1978	LH (WBC)	Marvin Johnson	Marsala, Italy	Lost	RSF–10
8 Dec 1979	C (WBC)	Marvin Camel	Split, Yugoslavia	Drew	15
31 Mar 1980	C (WBC)	Marvin Camel	Las Vegas	Lost	PTS–15

Willie PASTRANO

Born: New Orleans, USA, 27 Nov 1935
World title fights: 4 (all light-heavy) won 3, lost 1

DATE	WEIGHT	OPPONENT	VENUE	RESULT
1 Jun 1963	LH	Harold Johnson	Las Vegas	Won PTS–15
10 Apr 1964	LH	Gregorio Peralta	New Orleans	Won KO–6
30 Nov 1964	LH	Terry Downes	Manchester	Won RSF–11
30 Mar 1965	LH	Jose Torres	New York	Lost KO–9

Jackie PATERSON

Born: Springfield, Ayrshire, Scotland, 5 Sep 1920
Died: South Africa, 19 Nov 1966
World title fights: 3 (all flyweight) won 2, lost 1

DATE	WEIGHT	OPPONENT	VENUE	RESULT
19 Jun 1943	Fl	Peter Kane	Glasgow	Won KO–1
10 Jul 1946	Fl	Joe Curran	Glasgow	Won PTS–15
23 Mar 1948	Fl	Rinty Monaghan	Belfast	Lost KO–7

Floyd PATTERSON

Born: Waco, North Carolina, USA, 4 Jan 1935
World title fights: 13 (all heavyweight) won 8, lost 5

DATE	WEIGHT	OPPONENT	VENUE	RESULT
30 Nov 1956	H	Archie Moore	Chicago	Won KO–5
29 Jul 1957	H	Tommy Jackson	New York	Won RSF–10
22 Aug 1957	H	Pete Rademacher	Seattle	Won KO–6
18 Aug 1958	H	Roy Harris	Los Angeles	Won RTD–11
1 May 1959	H	Brian London	Indianapolis	Won KO–11
26 Jun 1959	H	Ingemar Johansson	New York	Lost RSF–3
20 Jun 1960	H	Ingemar Johansson	New York	Won KO–5
13 Mar 1961	H	Ingemar Johansson	Miami Beach	Won KO–6

DATE	WEIGHT	OPPONENT	VENUE	RESULT
4 Dec 1961	H	Tom McNeeley	Toronto	Won KO-4
25 Sep 1962	H	Sonny Liston	Chicago	Lost KO-1
22 Jul 1963	H	Sonny Liston	Las Vegas	Lost KO-1
22 Nov 1965	H	Muhammad Ali	Las Vegas	Lost RSF-12
14 Sep 1968	H (WBA)	Jimmy Ellis	Stockholm	Lost PTS-15

Jimmy PAUL

Born: Great Falls, South Carolina, USA, 27 Aug 1959
World title fights: 5 (all lightweight) won 4, lost 1

6 Apr 1985	L (IBF)	Harry Arroyo	Atlantic City	Won PTS-15
30 Jun 1985	L (IBF)	Robin Blake	Las Vegas	Won RSF-14
4 Jun 1986	L (IBF)	Irleis Perez	New Jersey	Won PTS-15
15 Aug 1986	L (IBF)	Darryl Tyson	Detroit	Won PTS-15
6 Dec 1986	L (IBF)	Greg Haugen	Las Vegas	Lost PTS-15

Tommy PAUL

Born: Buffalo, New York, USA, 4 Mar 1909
World title fights: 2 (both featherweight) won 1, lost 1

26 May 1932	Fe (NBA)	Johnny Pena	Detroit	Won PTS-15
13 Jan 1933	Fe (NBA)	Freddie Miller	Chicago	Lost PTS-10

Samart PAYAKAROON

Born: Chacherngsao, Thailand, 5 Dec 1962
World title fights: 3 (all junior-feather) won 2, lost 1

18 Jan 1986	JFe (WBC)	Lupe Pintor	Bangkok	Won KO-5
10 Dec 1986	JFe (WBC)	Juan 'Kid' Meza	Bangkok	Won KO-12
8 May 1987	JFe (WBC)	Jeff Fenech	Sydney	Lost RSF-4

DATE	WEIGHT	OPPONENT	VENUE	RESULT

DATE	WEIGHT	OPPONENT	VENUE	RESULT

Vinnie PAZIENZA

Born: Rhode Island, USA, 16 Dec 1962
World title fights: 5 (2 lightweight, 3 junior-welter) won 1, lost 4

7 Jun 1987	L (IBF)	Greg Haugen	Providence, Rhode Island	Won	PTS–15
6 Feb 1988	L (IBF)	Greg Haugen	Atlantic City	Lost	PTS–12
7 Nov 1988	JW (IBF)	Roger Mayweather	Las Vegas	Lost	PTS–12
3 Feb 1990	JW (WBO)	Hector Camacho	Atlantic City	Lost	PTS–12
1 Dec 1990	JW (WBA)	Loreto Garza	Sacramento, California	Lost	DIS–11

Eusebio PEDROZA

Born: Panama City, Panama, 2 Mar 1953
World title fights: 22 (21 featherweight, 1 bantamweight) won 19, lost 2, drew 1

3 Apr 1976	B (WBA)	Alfonso Zamora	Mexicali, Mexico	Lost	KO–2
15 Apr 1978	Fe (WBA)	Cecilio Lastra	Panama City	Won	KO–13
2 Jul 1978	Fe (WBA)	Ernesto Herrera	Panama City	Won	RSF–12
27 Nov 1978	Fe (WBA)	Enrique Solis	San Juan	Won	PTS–15
9 Jan 1979	Fe (WBA)	Royal Kobayashi	Tokyo	Won	RTD–13
8 Apr 1979	Fe (WBA)	Hector Carrasquilla	Panama City	Won	RSF–11
21 Jul 1979	Fe (WBA)	Ruben Olivares	Houston	Won	RSF–12
17 Nov 1979	Fe (WBA)	Johnny Aba	Port Moresby, Papua New Guinea	Won	KO–11
22 Jan 1980	Fe (WBA)	Shig Nemoto	Tokyo	Won	PTS–15
29 Mar 1980	Fe (WBA)	Juan Malvarez	Panama City	Won	KO–9
20 Jul 1980	Fe (WBA)	Sa-Wang Kim	Seoul	Won	KO–9
4 Oct 1980	Fe (WBA)	Rocky Lockridge	Great George, New Jersey	Won	PTS–15
14 Feb 1981	Fe (WBA)	Pat Ford	Panama City	Won	KO–13
1 Aug 1981	Fe (WBA)	Carlos Pinango	Caracas	Won	KO–7
5 Dec 1981	Fe (WBA)	Bashew Sibaca	Panama City	Won	KO–5
24 Jan 1982	Fe (WBA)	Juan Laporte	Atlantic City	Won	PTS–15

DATE	WEIGHT	OPPONENT	VENUE	RESULT

DATE	WEIGHT	OPPONENT	VENUE	RESULT
16 Oct 1982	Fe (WBA)	Bernard Taylor	Charlotte, N Carolina	Drew 15
24 Apr 1983	Fe (WBA)	Rocky Lockridge	San Remo, Italy	Won PTS–15
22 Oct 1983	Fe (WBA)	Jose Caba	St Vincent, West Indies	Won PTS–15
27 May 1984	Fe (WBA)	Angel Levy Meyor	Maracaibo, Venezuela	Won PTS–15
2 Feb 1985	Fe (WBA)	Jorge Lujan	Panama City	Won PTS–15
8 Jun 1985	Fe (WBA)	Barry McGuigan	London	Lost PTS–15

Rafael PEDROZA

Born: Colon, Panama, 3 Jul 1955
World title fights: 2 (both junior-bantam) won 1, lost 1

DATE	WEIGHT	OPPONENT	VENUE	RESULT
5 Dec 1981	JB (WBA)	Gustavo Ballas	Panama City	Won PTS–15
8 Apr 1982	JB (WBA)	Jiro Watanabe	Osaka, Japan	Lost PTS–15

Dodie PENALOSA

Born: San Carlos, Negros, Philippines, 19 Nov 1962
World title fights: 8 (4 junior-fly, 4 flyweight) won 5, lost 3

DATE	WEIGHT	OPPONENT	VENUE	RESULT
10 Dec 1983	JFl (IBF)	Satoshi Shingaki	Osaka, Japan	Won RSF–12
13 May 1984	JFl (IBF)	Jae-Hong Kim	Seoul	Won KO–9
16 Nov 1984	JFl (IBF)	Jum-Hwan Choi	Manila	Won PTS–15
12 Oct 1985	JFl (IBF)	Yani Dokolamo	Jakarta	Won RSF–3
5 Jul 1986	Fl (WBA)	Hilario Zapata	Manila	Lost PTS–15
22 Feb 1987	Fl (IBF)	Hi-Sup Shin	Inchon, S Korea	Won PTS–15
5 Sep 1987	Fl (IBF)	Chang-Ho Choi	Manila	Lost KO–11
8 Nov 1989	Fl (IBF)	Dave McAuley	London	Lost PTS–12

Paul PENDER

Born: Brookline, Massachusetts, USA, 20 Jun 1930
World title fights: 6 (all middleweight) won 5, lost 1

DATE	WEIGHT	OPPONENT	VENUE	RESULT	
22 Jan 1960	M	Sugar Ray Robinson	Boston	Won	PTS–15
10 Jun 1960	M	Sugar Ray Robinson	Boston	Won	PTS–15
14 Jan 1961	M	Terry Downes	Boston	Won	RSF–7
22 Apr 1961	M	Carmen Basilio	Boston	Won	PTS–15
11 Jul 1961	M	Terry Downes	London	Lost	RTD–9
7 Apr 1962	M	Terry Downes	Boston	Won	PTS–15

Willie PEP

Born: Middletown, Connecticut, USA, 19 Sep 1922
World title fights: 14 (all featherweight) won 11, lost 3

DATE	WEIGHT	OPPONENT	VENUE	RESULT	
20 Nov 1942	Fe (NY)	Chalky Wright	New York	Won	PTS–15
8 Jun 1943	Fe (NY)	Sal Bartolo	Boston	Won	PTS–15
29 Sep 1944	Fe (NY)	Chalky Wright	New York	Won	PTS–15
19 Feb 1945	Fe (NY)	Phil Terranova	New York	Won	PTS–15
7 Jun 1946	Fe	Sal Bartolo	New York	Won	KO–12
22 Aug 1947	Fe	Jock Leslie	Flint, Michigan	Won	KO–12
24 Feb 1948	Fe	Humberto Sierra	Miami	Won	RSF–10
29 Oct 1948	Fe	Sandy Saddler	New York	Lost	KO–4
11 Feb 1949	Fe	Sandy Saddler	New York	Won	PTS–15
20 Sep 1949	Fe	Eddie Compo	Waterbury, Connecticut	Won	RSF–7
16 Jan 1950	Fe	Charley Riley	St Louis	Won	KO–5
17 Mar 1950	Fe	Ray Famechon	New York	Won	PTS–15
8 Sep 1950	Fe	Sandy Saddler	New York	Lost	RTD–7
26 Sep 1951	Fe	Sandy Saddler	New York	Lost	RTD–9

DATE	WEIGHT	OPPONENT	VENUE	RESULT

Isidro PEREZ

Born: Mexico, 24 May 1964
World title fights: 4 (2 flyweight, 2 junior-fly) won 2, lost 2

13 Dec 1987	JFl (WBC)	Jung-Koo Chang	Pohang, S Korea	Lost	PTS–12
21 Oct 1989	JFl (WBO)	Jose De Jesus	San Juan	Lost	PTS–12
18 Aug 1990	Fl (WBO)	Angel Rosario	Ponce, Puerto Rico	Won	RSF–12
3 Nov 1990	Fl (WBO)	Ali Galvez	Acapulco, Mexico	Won	PTS–12

Juan Polo PEREZ

Born: Barranquilla, Colombia, 17 Oct 1963
World title fights: 2 (both junior-bantam) won 1, lost 1

14 Oct 1989	JB (IBF)	Ellyas Pical	Roanoke, Virginia	Won	PTS–12
21 Apr 1990	JB (IBF)	Roberto Quiroga	Sunderland	Lost	PTS–12

Pascual PEREZ

Born: Mendoza, Argentina, 4 Mar 1926
Died: Argentina, 22 Jan 1977
World title fights: 11 (all flyweight) won 9, lost 2

26 Nov 1954	Fl	Yoshio Shirai	Tokyo	Won	PTS–15
30 May 1955	Fl	Yoshio Shirai	Tokyo	Won	KO–5
11 Jan 1956	Fl	Leo Espinosa	Buenos Aires	Won	PTS–15
30 Jun 1956	Fl	Oscar Suarez	Montevideo	Won	RTD–11
30 Mar 1957	Fl	Dai Dower	Buenos Aires	Won	KO–1
19 Apr 1958	Fl	Ramon Arias	Caracas	Won	PTS–15
15 Dec 1958	Fl	Dommy Ursua	Manila	Won	PTS–15
10 Aug 1959	Fl	Kenji Yonekura	Tokyo	Won	PTS–15
5 Nov 1959	Fl	Sadao Yaoita	Osaka, Japan	Won	KO–13
16 Apr 1960	Fl	Pone Kingpetch	Bangkok	Lost	PTS–15
22 Sep 1960	Fl	Pone Kingpetch	Los Angeles	Lost	RSF–8

DATE	WEIGHT	OPPONENT	VENUE	RESULT

Raul PEREZ

Born: Tijuana, Mexico, 14 Feb 1967
World title fights: 7 (all bantamweight) won 6, drew 1

DATE	WEIGHT	OPPONENT	VENUE	RESULT
29 Oct 1988	B (WBC)	Miguel 'Happy' Lora	Las Vegas	Won PTS–12
10 Mar 1989	B (WBC)	Lucio Lopez	Los Angeles	Won PTS–12
26 Aug 1989	B (WBC)	Cerdenio Ulloa	Talcahuano, Chile	Won TKO–8
24 Oct 1989	B (WBC)	Diego Avila	Los Angeles	Won PTS–12
22 Jan 1990	B (WBC)	Gaby Canizales	Los Angeles	Won PTS–12
7 May 1990	B (WBC)	Gerardo Martinez	Los Angeles	Won RSF–9
14 Sep 1990	B (WBC)	Jose Valdez	Culiacan, Mexico	Drew 12

Victor 'Young' PEREZ

Born: Tunis, Tunisia, 18 Oct 1911
Died: Auschwitz, Poland, 4 Feb 1943
World title fights: 4 (2 flyweight, 2 bantamweight) won 1, lost 3

DATE	WEIGHT	OPPONENT	VENUE	RESULT
27 Oct 1931	Fl (NBA)	Frankie Genaro	Paris	Won KO–2
31 Oct 1932	Fl (NBA)	Jackie Brown	Manchester	Lost RSF–13
19 Feb 1934	B	Panama Al Brown	Paris	Lost PTS–15
1 Nov 1934	B	Panama Al Brown	Tunis	Lost KO–10

Eddie PERKINS

Born: Clarksdale, Mississippi, USA, 3 Mar 1937
World title fights: 7 (all junior-welter) won 4, lost 2, drew 1

DATE	WEIGHT	OPPONENT	VENUE	RESULT
21 Oct 1961	JW	Duilio Loi	Milan	Drew 15
14 Sep 1962	JW	Duilio Loi	Milan	Won PTS–15
15 Dec 1962	JW	Duilio Loi	Milan	Lost PTS–15
15 Jun 1963	JW	Roberto Cruz	Manila	Won PTS–15

4 Jan 1964	JW	Yoshinori Takahashi	Tokyo	Won RSF–13
19 Apr 1964	JW	Bunny Grant	Kingston, Jamaica	Won PTS–15
18 Jan 1965	JW	Carlos Hernandez	Caracas	Lost PTS–15

Ellyas PICAL

Born: Maluku, Indonesia, 24 Mar 1960
World title fights: 11 (all junior-bantam) won 8, lost 3

DATE	WEIGHT	OPPONENT	VENUE	RESULT
3 May 1985	JB (IBF)	Joo-Do Chun	Jakarta	Won KO–8
25 Aug 1985	JB (IBF)	Wayne Mulholland	Jakarta	Won RSF–3
15 Feb 1986	JB (IBF)	Cesar Polanco	Jakarta	Lost PTS–15
6 Jul 1986	JB (IBF)	Cesar Polanco	Jakarta	Won KO–3
3 Dec 1986	JB (IBF)	Dong-Chun Lee	Jakarta	Won KO–10
28 Feb 1987	JB (WBA)	Kaosai Galaxy	Jakarta	Lost KO–14
17 Oct 1987	JB (IBF)	Tae-Il Chang	Jakarta	Won PTS–15
20 Feb 1988	JB (IBF)	Raul Diaz	Pontianak, Colombia	Won PTS–15
9 Sep 1988	JB (IBF)	Chang-Ki Kim	Urabaya, Indonesia	Won PTS–12
25 Feb 1989	JB (IBF)	Mike Phelps	Singapore	Won PTS–12
14 Oct 1989	JB (IBF)	Juan Polo Perez	Roanoke, Virginia	Lost PTS–12

Bernardo PINANGO

Born: Caracas, Venezuela, 9 Feb 1960
World title fights: 6 (4 bantamweight, 2 junior-feather) won 5, lost 1

DATE	WEIGHT	OPPONENT	VENUE	RESULT
4 Jun 1986	B (WBA)	Gaby Canizales	East Rutherford, New Jersey	Won PTS–15
4 Oct 1986	B (WBA)	Ciro de Leva	Turin	Won TKO–10
22 Nov 1986	B (WBA)	Simon Skosana	Johannesburg	Won TKO–15
3 Feb 1987	B (WBA)	Frankie Duarte	Los Angeles	Won PTS–15
27 Feb 1988	JFe (WBA)	Julio Gervacio	San Juan	Won PTS–12
28 May 1988	JFe (WBA)	Juan Jose Estrada	Tijuana, Mexico	Lost PTS–12

Enrique PINDER

Born: Panama City, Panama, 7 Aug 1947
World title fights: 3 (all bantamweight) won 1, lost 2

DATE	WEIGHT	OPPONENT	VENUE	RESULT
29 Jul 1972	B	Rafael Herrera	Panama City	Won PTS–15
20 Jan 1973	B (WBA)	Romeo Anaya	Panama City	Lost KO–3
18 Aug 1973	B (WBA)	Romeo Anaya	Los Angeles	Lost KO–3

Lupe PINTOR

Born: Cuajimalpa, Mexico, 13 Apr 1955
World title fights: 12 (9 bantamweight, 3 junior-feather) won 9, lost 2, drew 1

DATE	WEIGHT	OPPONENT	VENUE	RESULT
3 Jun 1979	B (WBC)	Carlos Zarate	Las Vegas	Won PTS–15
9 Feb 1980	B (WBC)	Alberto Sandoval	Los Angeles	Won RSF–12
11 Jun 1980	B (WBC)	Eijiro Murata	Tokyo	Drew 15
19 Sep 1980	B (WBC)	Johnny Owen	Los Angeles	Won KO–12
19 Dec 1980	B (WBC)	Alberto Davila	Los Angeles	Won PTS–15
22 Feb 1981	B (WBC)	Jose Uziga	Houston	Won PTS–15
26 Jul 1981	B (WBC)	Jovito Rengifo	Las Vegas	Won RSF–8
22 Sep 1981	B (WBC)	Hurricane Teru	Tokyo	Won KO–15
3 Jun 1982	B (WBC)	Seung-Hoon Lee	Los Angeles	Won RSF–11
3 Dec 1982	JFe (WBC)	Wilfredo Gomez	New Orleans	Lost RSF–14
19 Aug 1985	JFe (WBC)	Juan 'Kid' Meza	Mexico City	Won PTS–12
18 Jan 1986	JFe (WBC)	Samart Payakaroon	Bangkok	Lost KO–5

Emile PLADNER

Born: Clermont-Ferrand, France, 2 Sep 1906
Died: Auch, France, 15 Mar 1960
World title fights: 3 (2 flyweight, 1 bantamweight) won 1, lost 2

DATE	WEIGHT	OPPONENT	VENUE	RESULT	
2 Mar 1929	Fl (NBA)	Frankie Genaro	Paris	Won	KO–1
18 Apr 1929	Fl (NBA)	Frankie Genaro	Paris	Lost	DIS–5
19 Sep 1932	B	Panama Al Brown	Toronto	Lost	KO–1

Cesar POLANCO

Born: Santiago, Dominican Republic, 29 Nov 1967
World title fights: 2 (both junior-bantam) won 1, lost 1

DATE	WEIGHT	OPPONENT	VENUE	RESULT	
15 Feb 1986	JB (IBF)	Ellyas Pical	Jakarta	Won	PTS–15
6 Jul 1986	JB (IBF)	Ellyas Pical	Jakarta	Lost	KO–3

Payao POONTARAT

Born: Prachuap Khiri Khan, Thailand, 1956
World title fights: 4 (all junior-bantam) won 2, lost 2

DATE	WEIGHT	OPPONENT	VENUE	RESULT	
26 Nov 1983	JB (WBC)	Rafael Orono	Bangkok	Won	PTS–12
28 Mar 1984	JB (WBC)	Guty Espadas	Bangkok	Won	TKO–10
5 Jul 1984	JB (WBC)	Jiro Watanabe	Osaka, Japan	Lost	PTS–12
29 Nov 1984	JB (WBC)	Jiro Watanabe	Kumamoto, Japan	Lost	RSF–11

Aaron PRYOR

Born: Cincinnati, Ohio, USA, 20 Oct 1955
World title fights: 11 (all junior-welter) won 11, lost 0

DATE	WEIGHT	OPPONENT	VENUE	RESULT
2 Aug 1980	JW (WBA)	Antonio Cervantes	Cincinnati	Won KO–4
22 Nov 1980	JW (WBA)	Gaetan Hart	Cincinnati	Won RSF–6
27 Jun 1981	JW (WBA)	Lennox Blackmore	Las Vegas	Won RSF–2
14 Nov 1981	JW (WBA)	Dujuan Johnson	Cleveland	Won RSF–7
21 Mar 1982	JW (WBA)	Miguel Montilla	Atlantic City	Won RSF–12
4 Jul 1982	JW (WBA)	Akio Kameda	Cincinnati	Won RSF–6
12 Nov 1982	JW (WBA)	Alexis Arguello	Miami	Won RSF–14
2 Apr 1983	JW (WBA)	Sang-Hyun Kim	Atlantic City	Won RSF–3
9 Sep 1983	JW (WBA)	Alexis Arguello	Las Vegas	Won KO–10
22 Jun 1984	JW (IBF)	Nicky Furlano	Toronto	Won PTS–15
2 Mar 1985	JW (IBF)	Gary Hinton	Atlantic City	Won PTS–15

Richard PULTZ

Born: Washington, USA, 28 Nov 1959
World title fights: 2 (both cruiserweight) won 1, lost 1

DATE	WEIGHT	OPPONENT	VENUE	RESULT
3 Dec 1989	C (WBO)	Magne Havnaa	Copenhagen	Won PTS–12
13 May 1990	C (WBO)	Magne Havnaa	Aars, Denmark	Lost RSF–5

Dwight Muhammad QAWI
(formerly Dwight Braxton)

Born: Baltimore, USA, 5 Jan 1953
World title fights: 10 (5 light-heavy, 5 cruiserweight) won 6, lost 4

DATE	WEIGHT	OPPONENT	VENUE	RESULT
19 Dec 1981	LH (WBC)	Matt Saad Muhammad	Atlantic City	Won RSF–10
21 Mar 1982	LH (WBC)	Jerry Martin	Las Vegas	Won RSF–6

DATE	WEIGHT	OPPONENT	VENUE	RESULT
8 Aug 1982	LH (WBC)	Matt Saad Muhammad	Philadelphia	Won RSF-6
20 Nov 1982	LH (WBC)	Eddie Davis	Atlantic City	Won RSF-11
18 Mar 1983	LH	Michael Spinks	Atlantic City	Lost PTS-15
28 Jul 1985	C (WBA)	Piet Crous	Sun City, S Africa	Won KO-11
23 Mar 1986	C (WBA)	Leon Spinks	Reno, Nevada	Won RSF-6
12 Jul 1986	C (WBA)	Evander Holyfield	Atlanta	Lost PTS-15
5 Dec 1987	C (IBF)	Evander Holyfield	Atlantic City	Lost KO-4
28 Nov 1989	C (WBA)	Robert Daniels	Paris	Lost PTS-12

Roberto QUIROGA

Born: San Antonio, Texas, USA, 1968
World title fights: 2 (both junior-bantam) won 2, lost 0

DATE	WEIGHT	OPPONENT	VENUE	RESULT
21 Apr 1990	JB (IBF)	Juan Polo Perez	Sunderland	Won PTS-12
6 Oct 1990	JB (IBF)	Vuyani Nene	Pagliara, Italy	Won RSF-6

Francisco QUIROZ

Born: Moca, Dominican Republic, 4 Jun 1957
World title fights: 3 (all junior-fly) won 2, lost 1

DATE	WEIGHT	OPPONENT	VENUE	RESULT
19 May 1984	JFl (WBA)	Lupe Madera	Maracaibo, Venezuela	Won KO-9
18 Aug 1984	JFl (WBA)	Victor Sierra	Panama City	Won KO-2
29 Mar 1985	JFl (WBA)	Joey Olivo	Miami	Lost PTS-15

Jose Luis RAMIREZ

Born: Huatabampo, Sonora, Mexico, 3 Dec 1958
World title fights: 9 (8 lightweight, 1 junior-welter) won 4, lost 5

DATE	WEIGHT	OPPONENT	VENUE	RESULT
2 May 1983	L (WBC)	Edwin Rosario	San Juan	Lost PTS-12
3 Nov 1984	L (WBC)	Edwin Rosario	San Juan	Won RSF-4

DATE	WEIGHT	OPPONENT	VENUE	RESULT

DATE	WEIGHT	OPPONENT	VENUE	RESULT
10 Aug 1985	L (WBC)	Hector Camacho	Las Vegas	Lost PTS–12
19 Jul 1987	L (WBC)	Terrence Alli	St Tropez, France	Won PTS–12
10 Oct 1987	L (WBC)	Cornelius Boza-Edwards	Paris	Won KO–5
12 Mar 1988	L (WBC)	Pernell Whitaker	Paris	Won PTS–12
29 Oct 1988	L (WBC/WBA)	Julio Cesar Chavez	Las Vegas	Lost TD–11
20 Aug 1989	L (WBC/IBF)	Pernell Whitaker	Norfolk, Virginia	Lost PTS–12
24 Mar 1990	JW (WBA)	Juan Martin Loggi	Ajaccio, Corsica	Lost PTS–12

Mando RAMOS

Born: Long Beach, California, USA, 15 Nov 1948
World title fights: 8 (all lightweight) won 4, lost 4

27 Sep 1968	L	Carlos Cruz	Los Angeles	Lost PTS–15
18 Feb 1969	L	Carlos Cruz	Los Angeles	Won RSF–11
4 Oct 1969	L	Yoshiaki Numata	Los Angeles	Won KO–6
3 Mar 1970	L	Ismael Laguna	Los Angeles	Lost RTD–9
5 Nov 1971	L (WBC)	Pedro Carrasco	Madrid	Lost DIS–11
18 Feb 1972	L (WBC)	Pedro Carrasco	Los Angeles	Won PTS–15
28 Jun 1972	L (WBC)	Pedro Carrasco	Madrid	Won PTS–15
15 Sep 1972	L (WBC)	Chango Carmona	Los Angeles	Lost RSF–8

Ultiminio 'Sugar' RAMOS

Born: Matanzas, Cuba, 2 Dec 1941
World title fights: 7 (5 featherweight, 2 lightweight) won 4, lost 3

21 Mar 1963	Fe	Davey Moore	Los Angeles	Won RTD–10
13 Jul 1963	Fe	Rafiu King	Mexico City	Won PTS–15
28 Feb 1964	Fe	Mitsunori Seki	Tokyo	Won RTD–6
9 May 1964	Fe	Floyd Robertson	Accra	Won PTS–15
26 Sep 1964	Fe	Vicente Saldivar	Mexico City	Lost RTD–11

DATE	WEIGHT	OPPONENT	VENUE	RESULT

DATE	WEIGHT	OPPONENT	VENUE	RESULT
22 Oct 1966	L	Carlos Ortiz	Mexico City	Lost RSF-5
1 Jul 1967	L	Carlos Ortiz	San Juan	Lost RSF-4

Leo RANDOLPH

Born: Tacoma, Washington, USA, 27 Feb 1958
World title fights: 2 (both junior-feather) won 1, lost 1

4 May 1980	JFe (WBA)	Ricardo Cardona	Seattle	Won RSF-15
9 Aug 1980	JFe (WBA)	Sergio Palma	Spokane, Washington	Lost KO-5

Alfonso RATLIFF

Born: Chicago, Illinois, USA, 18 Feb 1956
World title fights: 2 (both cruiserweight) won 1, lost 1

6 Jun 1985	C (WBC)	Carlos DeLeon	Las Vegas	Won PTS-12
22 Sep 1985	C (WBC)	Bernard Benton	Las Vegas	Lost PTS-12

Rigoberto RIASCO

Born: Panama City, Panama, 11 Jan 1953
World title fights: 5 (1 featherweight, 4 junior-feather) won 3, lost 2

31 May 1975	Fe (WBA)	Alexis Arguello	Granada, Nicaragua	Lost RSF-2
3 Apr 1976	JFe (WBC)	Waruinge Nakayama	Panama City	Won RTD-8
12 Jun 1976	JFe (WBC)	Livio Nolasco	Panama City	Won RSF-10
1 Aug 1976	JFe (WBC)	Dong-Kyun Yum	Pusan, S Korea	Won PTS-15
9 Oct 1976	JFe (WBC)	Royal Kobayashi	Tokyo	Lost RSF-8

DATE	WEIGHT	OPPONENT	VENUE	RESULT

Jaime RIOS

Born: Panama City, Panama, 14 Aug 1953
World title fights: 5 (all junior-fly) won 2, lost 3

DATE	WEIGHT	OPPONENT	VENUE	RESULT	
23 Aug 1975	JFl (WBA)	Rigoberto Marcano	Panama City	Won	PTS–15
3 Jan 1976	JFl (WBA)	Kazunori Tenryu	Kogoshima, Japan	Won	PTS–15
1 Jul 1976	JFl (WBA)	Juan Guzman	Santo Domingo	Lost	PTS–15
30 Jan 1977	JFl (WBA)	Yoko Gushiken	Tokyo	Lost	PTS–15
7 May 1978	JFl (WBA)	Yoko Gushiken	Tokyo	Lost	RSF–13

Ed 'Babe' RISKO

Born: Syracuse, New York, USA, 14 Jul 1911
Died: Syracuse, 7 Mar 1957
World title fights: 4 (all middleweight) won 2, lost 2

DATE	WEIGHT	OPPONENT	VENUE	RESULT	
19 Sep 1935	M (NY)	Teddy Yarosz	Pittsburgh	Won	PTS–15
10 Feb 1936	M (NY)	Tony Fisher	Newark, New Jersey	Won	PTS–15
11 Jul 1936	M (NY)	Freddie Steele	Seattle	Lost	PTS–15
19 Feb 1937	M	Freddie Steele	New York	Lost	PTS–15

Willie RITCHIE

Born: San Francisco, USA, 13 Feb 1891
Died: Burlingame, California, 24 Mar 1975
World title fights: 4 (all lightweight) won 3, lost 1

DATE	WEIGHT	OPPONENT	VENUE	RESULT	
28 Nov 1912	L	Ad Wolgast	Daly City, California	Won	DIS–16
4 Jul 1913	L	Joe Rivers	San Francisco	Won	KO–11
17 Apr 1914	L	Tommy Murphy	San Francisco	Won	PTS–20
7 Jul 1914	L	Freddie Welsh	London	Lost	PTS–20

Antonio RIVERA

Born: Rio Piedras, Puerto Rico, 5 Dec 1963
World title fights: 3 (2 featherweight, 1 junior-light) won 1, lost 2

DATE	WEIGHT	OPPONENT	VENUE	RESULT
30 Aug 1986	Fe (IBF)	Ki-Yung Chung	Seoul	Won RTD–10
23 Jan 1988	Fe (IBF)	Calvin Grove	Gamaches, France	Lost RSF–4
9 Dec 1989	JL (WBO)	Kamel Bou-Ali	Teramo, Italy	Lost KO–8

Sugar Ray ROBINSON

Born: Detroit, Michigan, USA, 3 May 1921
Died: Los Angeles, 12 Apr 1989
World title fights: 22 (6 welterweight, 15 middleweight, 1 light-heavy)
won 14, lost 7, drew 1

DATE	WEIGHT	OPPONENT	VENUE	RESULT
20 Dec 1946	W	Tommy Bell	New York	Won PTS–15
24 Jun 1947	W	Jimmy Doyle	Cleveland	Won KO–8
19 Dec 1947	W	Chuck Taylor	Detroit	Won KO–6
28 Jun 1948	W	Bernard Docusen	Chicago	Won PTS–15
11 Jul 1949	W	Kid Gavilan	Philadelphia	Won PTS–15
9 Aug 1950	W	Charley Fusari	Jersey City, New Jersey	Won PTS–15
14 Feb 1951	M	Jake La Motta	Chicago	Won RSF–13
10 Jul 1951	M	Randolph Turpin	London	Lost PTS–15
12 Sep 1951	M	Randolph Turpin	New York	Won RSF–10
13 Mar 1952	M	Carl 'Bobo' Olson	San Francisco	Won PTS–15
16 Apr 1952	M	Rocky Graziano	Chicago	Won KO–3
25 Jun 1952	LH	Joey Maxim	New York	Lost RTD–14
9 Dec 1955	M	Carl 'Bobo' Olson	Chicago	Won KO–2
18 May 1956	M	Carl 'Bobo' Olson	Los Angeles	Won KO–4
2 Jan 1957	M	Gene Fullmer	New York	Lost PTS–15
1 May 1957	M	Gene Fullmer	Chicago	Won KO–5

DATE	WEIGHT	OPPONENT	VENUE	RESULT

DATE	WEIGHT	OPPONENT	VENUE	RESULT
23 Sep 1957	M	Carmen Basilio	New York	Lost PTS-15
25 Mar 1958	M	Carmen Basilio	Chicago	Won PTS-15
22 Jan 1960	M	Paul Pender	Boston	Lost PTS-15
10 Jun 1960	M	Paul Pender	Boston	Lost PTS-15
3 Dec 1960	M (NBA)	Gene Fullmer	Los Angeles	Drew 15
4 Mar 1961	M (NBA)	Gene Fullmer	Las Vegas	Lost PTS-15

Graciano ROCCHIGIANI

Born: Rheinhausen, West Germany, 29 Dec 1963
World title fights: 4 (all super-middle) won 4, lost 0

DATE	WEIGHT	OPPONENT	VENUE	RESULT
12 Mar 1988	SM (IBF)	Vincent Boulware	Dusseldorf	Won RSF-8
3 Jun 1988	SM (IBF)	Nicky Walker	Berlin	Won PTS-15
7 Oct 1988	SM (IBF)	Chris Reid	Berlin	Won RSF-11
27 Jan 1989	SM (IBF)	Sugar Boy Malinga	Berlin	Won PTS-12

Leo RODAK

Born: Chicago, Illinois, USA, 5 Jun 1913
World title fights: 2 (both featherweight) won 1, lost 1

DATE	WEIGHT	OPPONENT	VENUE	RESULT
29 Dec 1938	Fe (NBA)	Leone Efrati	Chicago	Won PTS-10
18 Apr 1939	Fe	Joey Archibald	Providence, Rhode Island	Lost PTS-15

Luis RODRIGUEZ

Born: Camaguey, Cuba, 17 Jun 1937
World title fights: 4 (3 welterweight, 1 middleweight) won 1, lost 3

DATE	WEIGHT	OPPONENT	VENUE	RESULT
21 Mar 1963	W	Emile Griffith	Los Angeles	Won PTS-15
8 Jun 1963	W	Emile Griffith	New York	Lost PTS-15

DATE	WEIGHT	OPPONENT	VENUE	RESULT

DATE	WEIGHT	OPPONENT	VENUE	RESULT
12 Jun 1964	W	Emile Griffith	Las Vegas	Lost PTS–15
22 Nov 1969	M	Nino Benvenuti	Rome	Lost KO–11

Baby ROJAS

Born: Barranquilla, Colombia, 1 Feb 1961
World title fights: 5 (all junior-bantam) won 2, lost 3

DATE	WEIGHT	OPPONENT	VENUE	RESULT
8 Aug 1987	JB (WBC)	Santos Laciar	Miami	Won PTS–12
24 Oct 1987	JB (WBC)	Gustavo Ballas	Miami	Won RSF–4
8 Apr 1988	JB (WBC)	Gilberto Roman	Miami	Lost PTS–12
7 Nov 1988	JB (WBC)	Gilberto Roman	Las Vegas	Lost PTS–12
29 Apr 1989	JB (WBO)	Jose Ruiz	San Juan	Lost PTS–12

Jesus ROJAS

Born: Rio Caribe, Sucre, Venezuela, 31 Jan 1964
World title fights: 2 (both flyweight) won 1, drew 1

DATE	WEIGHT	OPPONENT	VENUE	RESULT
30 Sep 1989	Fl (WBA)	Fidel Bassa	Barranquilla, Colombia	Won PTS–12
6 Dec 1990	Fl (WBA)	Yukito Tamakuma	Aomori, Japan	Drew 12

Raul ROJAS

Born: San Pedro, California, USA, 5 Nov 1941
World title fights: 4 (3 featherweight, 1 junior-lightweight) won 1, lost 3

DATE	WEIGHT	OPPONENT	VENUE	RESULT
7 May 1965	Fe	Vicente Saldivar	Los Angeles	Lost RSF–15
28 Mar 1968	Fe (WBA)	Enrique Higgins	Los Angeles	Won PTS–15
28 Sep 1968	Fe (WBA)	Sho Saijyo	Los Angeles	Lost PTS–15
27 Sep 1970	JL (WBC)	Yoshiaki Numata	Tokyo	Lost KO–5

DATE	WEIGHT	OPPONENT	VENUE	RESULT

Gilberto ROMAN

Born: Mexicali, Mexico, 29 Nov 1961
Died: Mexico, 6 Jul 1990
World title fights: 16 (all junior-bantam) won 12, drew 1, lost 3

DATE	WEIGHT	OPPONENT	VENUE	RESULT
30 Mar 1986	JB (WBC)	Jiro Watanabe	Osaka, Japan	Won PTS–12
15 May 1986	JB (WBC)	Edgar Monserrat	Paris	Won PTS–12
18 Jul 1986	JB (WBC)	Ruben Condori	Salta, Argentina	Won PTS–12
30 Aug 1986	JB (WBC)	Santos Laciar	Cordoba, Mexico	Drew 12
15 Dec 1986	JB (WBC)	Kongtoranee Payakaroon	Bangkok	Won PTS–12
31 Jan 1987	JB (WBC)	Antoine Montero	Montpellier, France	Won RSF–9
19 Mar 1987	JB (WBC)	Frank Cedeno	Mexicali, Mexico	Won PTS–12
16 May 1987	JB (WBC)	Santos Laciar	Reims, France	Lost RSF–11
8 Apr 1988	JB (WBC)	Baby Rojas	Miami	Won PTS–12
9 Jul 1988	JB (WBC)	Yoshiyuki Uchida	Kawagoe, Japan	Won RSF–5
3 Sep 1988	JB (WBC)	Kiyoshi Hatanaka	Nagoya, Japan	Won PTS–12
7 Nov 1988	JB (WBC)	Baby Rojas	Las Vegas	Won PTS–12
5 Jun 1989	JB (WBC)	Juan Carazo	Los Angeles	Won PTS–12
12 Sep 1989	JB (WBC)	Santos Laciar	Los Angeles	Won PTS–12
7 Nov 1989	JB (WBC)	Nana Yaw Konadu	Mexico City	Lost PTS–12
9 Jun 1990	JB (WBC)	Sung-Kil Moon	Seoul	Lost RTD–8

Vicente Paul RONDON

Born: San Jose de Rio Chico, Miranda, Venezuela, 29 Jul 1938
World title fights: 6 (all light-heavy) won 5, lost 1

DATE	WEIGHT	OPPONENT	VENUE	RESULT
27 Feb 1971	LH (WBA)	Jimmy Dupree	Caracas	Won RSF–6
5 Jun 1971	LH (WBA)	Piero del Papa	Caracas	Won KO–1
21 Aug 1971	LH (WBA)	Eddie Jones	Caracas	Won PTS–15
26 Oct 1971	LH (WBA)	Gomeo Brennan	Miami	Won RSF–12

DATE	WEIGHT	OPPONENT	VENUE	RESULT
15 Dec 1971	LH (WBA)	Doyle Baird	Cleveland	Won KO–8
7 Apr 1972	LH	Bob Foster	Miami	Lost KO–2

Jack ROOT

Born: Austria, 26 May 1876
Died: Los Angeles, California, USA, 10 Jun 1963
World title fights: 3 (2 light-heavy, 1 heavyweight) won 1, lost 2

DATE	WEIGHT	OPPONENT	VENUE	RESULT
22 Apr 1903	LH	George 'Kid' McCoy	Detroit	Won PTS–10
4 Jul 1903	LH	George Gardner	Fort Erie, Canada	Lost KO–12
3 Jul 1905	H	Marvin Hart	Reno, Nevada	Lost RSF–12

Edwin ROSARIO

Born: San Juan, Puerto Rico, 15 Mar 1963
World title fights: 10 (all lightweight) won 6, lost 4

DATE	WEIGHT	OPPONENT	VENUE	RESULT
2 May 1983	L (WBC)	Jose Luis Ramirez	San Juan	Won PTS–12
17 Mar 1984	L (WBC)	Roberto Elizondo	San Juan	Won RSF–1
23 Jun 1984	L (WBC)	Howard Davis	San Juan	Won PTS–12
3 Nov 1984	L (WBC)	Jose Luis Ramirez	San Juan	Lost RSF–4
13 Jun 1986	L (WBC)	Hector Camacho	New York	Lost PTS–12
26 Sep 1986	L (WBA)	Livingstone Bramble	Miami	Won KO–2
11 Aug 1987	L (WBA)	Juan Nazario	Chicago	Won RSF–8
22 Nov 1987	L (WBA)	Julio Cesar Chavez	Las Vegas	Lost RSF–11
9 Jul 1989	L (WBA)	Anthony Jones	Atlantic City	Won RSF–6
6 Apr 1990	L (WBA)	Juan Nazario	New York	Lost RSF–8

DATE	WEIGHT	OPPONENT	VENUE	RESULT

Lionel ROSE

Born: Victoria, Australia, 21 Jun 1948
World title fights: 6 (5 bantamweight, 1 junior-light) won 4, lost 2

DATE	WEIGHT	OPPONENT	VENUE	RESULT
26 Feb 1968	B	Fighting Harada	Tokyo	Won PTS–15
2 Jul 1968	B	Takao Sakurai	Tokyo	Won PTS–15
6 Dec 1968	B	Chucho Castillo	Los Angeles	Won PTS–15
8 Mar 1969	B	Alan Rudkin	Melbourne	Won PTS–15
22 Aug 1969	B	Ruben Olivares	Los Angeles	Lost KO–5
31 May 1971	JL (WBC)	Yoshiaki Numata	Hiroshima, Japan	Lost PTS–15

Charley Phil ROSENBERG

Born: New York City, USA, 15 Aug 1902
Died: New York City, 12 Mar 1976
World title fights: 4 (all bantamweight) won 4, lost 0

DATE	WEIGHT	OPPONENT	VENUE	RESULT
20 Mar 1925	B	Eddie 'Cannonball' Martin	New York	Won PTS–15
23 Jul 1925	B	Eddie Shea	New York	Won KO–4
2 Mar 1926	B	George Butch	St Louis	Won PTS–10
4 Feb 1927	B	Bushy Graham	New York	Won PTS–15

Dave ROSENBERG

Born: New York City, USA, 15 May 1901
World title fights: 2 (both middleweight) won 1, lost 1

DATE	WEIGHT	OPPONENT	VENUE	RESULT
14 Aug 1922	M (NY)	Phil Krug	New York	Won PTS–15
30 Nov 1922	M (NY)	Mike O'Dowd	New York	Lost DIS–8

Maxie ROSENBLOOM

Born: Leonard's Bridge, New York, USA, 6 Sep 1904
Died: South Pasadena, California, 6 Mar 1976
World title fights: 11 (all light-heavy) won 8, lost 2, drew 1

DATE	WEIGHT	OPPONENT	VENUE	RESULT
30 Aug 1927	LH (NBA)	Jimmy Slattery	Hartford, Connecticut	Lost PTS–10
25 Jun 1930	LH (NY)	Jimmy Slattery	Buffalo	Won PTS–15
22 Oct 1930	LH (NY)	Abe Bain	New York	Won KO–11
5 Aug 1931	LH (NY)	Jimmy Slattery	New York	Won PTS–15
14 Jul 1932	LH	Lou Scozza	Buffalo	Won PTS–15
22 Feb 1933	LH	Al Stillman	St Louis	Won PTS–10
10 Mar 1933	LH	Ad Heuser	New York	Won PTS–15
24 Mar 1933	LH	Bob Godwin	New York	Won KO–4
3 Nov 1933	LH	Mickey Walker	New York	Won PTS–15
5 Feb 1934	LH	Joe Knight	Miami	Drew 15
16 Nov 1934	LH	Bob Olin	New York	Lost PTS–15

Gianfranco ROSI

Born: Assisi, Italy, 5 Aug 1957
World title fights: 8 (all junior-middle) won 7, lost 1

DATE	WEIGHT	OPPONENT	VENUE	RESULT
2 Oct 1987	JM (WBC)	Lupe Aquino	Perugia, Italy	Won PTS–12
3 Jan 1988	JM (WBC)	Duane Thomas	Genoa	Won RSF–7
8 Jul 1988	JM (WBC)	Don Curry	San Remo, Italy	Lost RTD–9
16 Jul 1989	JM (IBF)	Darrin Van Horn	Atlantic City	Won PTS–12
27 Oct 1989	JM (IBF)	Troy Waters	St Vincent, West Indies	Won PTS–12
14 Apr 1990	JM (IBF)	Kevin Daigle	Monte Carlo	Won RSF–7
21 Jul 1990	JM (IBF)	Darrin Van Horn	Marino, Italy	Won PTS–12
30 Nov 1990	JM (IBF)	Rene Jacquot	Marsala, Italy	Won PTS–12

Barney ROSS

Born: New York City, USA, 23 Dec 1909
Died: Chicago, 17 Jan 1967
World title fights: 14 (1 lightweight/junior-welter, 1 lightweight,
6 junior-welter, 6 welterweight) won 11, lost 2, drew 1

DATE	WEIGHT	OPPONENT	VENUE	RESULT
23 Jun 1933	L/JW	Tony Canzoneri	Chicago	Won PTS–10
12 Sep 1933	L	Tony Canzoneri	New York	Won PTS–15
17 Nov 1933	JW	Sammy Fuller	Chicago	Won PTS–10
7 Feb 1934	JW	Peter Nebo	Kansas City	Won PTS–12
5 Mar 1934	JW	Frankie Klick	San Francisco	Drew 10
28 May 1934	W	Jimmy McLarnin	New York	Won PTS–15
17 Sep 1934	W	Jimmy McLarnin	New York	Lost PTS–15
10 Dec 1934	JW	Bobby Pacho	Cleveland	Won PTS–12
28 Jan 1935	JW	Frankie Klick	Miami	Won PTS–10
9 Apr 1935	JW	Henry Woods	Seattle	Won PTS–12
28 May 1935	W	Jimmy McLarnin	New York	Won PTS–15
27 Nov 1936	W	Izzy Jannazzo	New York	Won PTS–15
23 Sep 1937	W	Ceferino Garcia	New York	Won PTS–15
31 May 1938	W	Henry Armstrong	New York	Lost PTS–15

Mike ROSSMAN

Born: Turnersville, New Jersey, USA, 1 Jul 1956
World title fights: 3 (all light-heavy) won 2, lost 1

DATE	WEIGHT	OPPONENT	VENUE	RESULT
15 Sep 1978	LH (WBA)	Victor Galindez	New Orleans	Won RSF–13
5 Dec 1978	LH (WBA)	Aldo Traversaro	Philadelphia	Won RSF–6
14 Apr 1979	LH (WBA)	Victor Galindez	New Orleans	Lost RTD–10

Andre ROUTIS

Born: Bordeaux, France, 16 Jul 1900
Died: Paris, 16 Jul 1969
World title fights: 3 (all featherweight) won 2, lost 1

DATE	WEIGHT	OPPONENT	VENUE	RESULT
28 Sep 1928	Fe	Tony Canzoneri	New York	Won PTS–15
27 May 1929	Fe	Buster Brown	Baltimore	Won KO–3
23 Sep 1929	Fe	Battling Battalino	Hartford, Connecticut	Lost PTS–15

Jose RUIZ

Born: Trujillo, Puerto Rico, 24 Oct 1966
World title fights: 5 (all junior-bantam) won 5, lost 0

DATE	WEIGHT	OPPONENT	VENUE	RESULT
29 Apr 1989	JB (WBO)	Baby Rojas	San Juan	Won PTS–12
9 Sep 1989	JB (WBO)	Juan Carazo	San Juan	Won RSF–1
21 Oct 1989	JB (WBO)	Angel Rosario	San Juan	Won RSF–10
18 Aug 1990	JB (WBO)	Wilfredo Vargas	Ponce, Puerto Rico	Won KO–8
3 Nov 1990	JB (WBO)	Armando Velasco	Acapulco, Mexico	Won PTS–12

Tommy RYAN

Born: Redwood, New York, USA, 31 Mar 1870
Died: Van Nuys, California, 3 Aug 1948
World title fights: 10 (4 welterweight, 6 middleweight) won 8, lost 1, drew 1

DATE	WEIGHT	OPPONENT	VENUE	RESULT
26 Jul 1894	W	Mysterious Billy Smith	Minneapolis	Won PTS–20
18 Jan 1895	W	Jack Dempsey	New York	Won KO–3
27 May 1895	W	Mysterious Billy Smith	New York	Drew 18*
2 Mar 1896	W	Charles 'Kid' McCoy	Long Island, New York	Lost KO–15
25 Feb 1898	M	George Green	San Francisco	Won KO–18
24 Oct 1898	M	Jack Bonner	Coney Island, New York	Won PTS–20
18 Sep 1899	M	Frank Craig	Coney Island	Won KO–10

* Police stopped fight

4 Mar 1901	M	Tommy West	Louisville, Kentucky	Won KO–17
15 Sep 1902	M	Kid Carter	Fort Erie, Canada	Won KO–6
3 Nov 1903	M	Johnny Gorman	London	Won KO–3

Ubaldo SACCO

Born: Buenos Aires, Argentina, 28 Jul 1955
World title fights: 3 (all junior-welter) won 1, lost 2

15 Dec 1984	JW (WBA)	Gene Hatcher	Fort Worth, Texas	Lost PTS–15
21 Jul 1985	JW (WBA)	Gene Hatcher	Campione d'Italia, Italy	Won RSF–9
15 Mar 1986	JW (WBA)	Patrizio Oliva	Monte Carlo	Lost PTS–15

Sandy SADDLER

Born: Boston, Massachusetts, USA, 23 Jun 1926
World title fights: 6 (all featherweight) won 5, lost 1

29 Oct 1948	Fe	Willie Pep	New York	Won KO–4
11 Feb 1949	Fe	Willie Pep	New York	Lost PTS–15
8 Sep 1950	Fe	Willie Pep	New York	Won RTD–7
26 Sep 1951	Fe	Willie Pep	New York	Won RTD–9
25 Feb 1955	Fe	Teddy 'Red Top' Davis	New York	Won PTS–15
18 Jan 1956	Fe	Flash Elorde	San Francisco	Won RSF–13

Sho SAIJYO

Born: Kit-adachi-Gun, Japan, 28 Jan 1947
World title fights: 7 (all featherweight) won 6, lost 1

28 Sep 1968	Fe (WBA)	Raul Rojas	Los Angeles	Won PTS–15
9 Feb 1969	Fe (WBA)	Pedro Gomez	Tokyo	Won PTS–15
7 Sep 1969	Fe (WBA)	Jose Luis Pimental	Sapporo, Japan	Won KO–2

DATE	WEIGHT	OPPONENT	VENUE	RESULT
8 Feb 1970	Fe (WBA)	Godfrey Stevens	Tokyo	Won PTS–15
5 Jul 1970	Fe (WBA)	Frankie Crawford	Sendai, Japan	Won PTS–15
28 Feb 1971	Fe (WBA)	Frankie Crawford	Utsunomaya, Japan	Won PTS–15
2 Sep 1971	Fe (WBA)	Antonio Gomez	Tokyo	Lost RSF–5

Lauro SALAS

Born: Monterrey, Nuevo Leon, Mexico, 18 Aug 1928
World title fights: 3 (all lightweight) won 1, lost 2

DATE	WEIGHT	OPPONENT	VENUE	RESULT
1 Apr 1952	L	Jimmy Carter	Los Angeles	Lost PTS–15
14 May 1952	L	Jimmy Carter	Los Angeles	Won PTS–15
15 Oct 1952	L	Jimmy Carter	Chicago	Lost PTS–15

Erbito SALAVARRIA

Born: Manila, Philippines, 20 Jan 1946
World title fights: 7 (all flyweight) won 4, lost 2, drew 1

DATE	WEIGHT	OPPONENT	VENUE	RESULT
7 Dec 1970	Fl (WBC)	Chartchai Chionoi	Bangkok	Won RSF–2
30 Apr 1971	Fl (WBC)	Susumu Hanagata	Manila	Won PTS–15
20 Nov 1971	Fl (WBC)	Betulio Gonzalez	Maracaibo, Venezuela	Drew 15
9 Feb 1973	Fl (WBC)	Venice Borkorsor	Bangkok	Lost PTS–15
1 Apr 1975	Fl (WBA)	Susumu Hanagata	Toyama, Japan	Won PTS–15
17 Oct 1975	Fl (WBA)	Susumu Hanagata	Yokohama, Japan	Won PTS–15
27 Feb 1976	Fl (WBA)	Alfonso Lopez	Manila	Lost RSF–15

Vicente SALDIVAR

Born: Mexico City, Mexico, 3 May 1943
Died: Mexico, 18 Jul 1985
World title fights: 11 (all featherweight) won 9, lost 2

DATE	WEIGHT	OPPONENT	VENUE	RESULT	
26 Sep 1964	Fe	Ultiminio 'Sugar' Ramos	Mexico City	Won	RTD–11
7 May 1965	Fe	Raul Rojas	Los Angeles	Won	RSF–15
7 Sep 1965	Fe	Howard Winstone	London	Won	PTS–15
12 Feb 1966	Fe	Floyd Robertson	Mexico City	Won	KO–2
7 Aug 1966	Fe	Mitsunori Seki	Mexico City	Won	PTS–15
29 Jan 1967	Fe	Mitsunori Seki	Mexico City	Won	RSF–7
15 Jun 1967	Fe	Howard Winstone	Cardiff	Won	PTS–15
14 Oct 1967	Fe	Howard Winstone	Mexico City	Won	RTD–12
9 May 1970	Fe (WBC)	Johnny Famechon	Rome	Won	PTS–15
11 Dec 1970	Fe (WBC)	Kuniaki Shibata	Tijuana, Mexico	Lost	RSF–12
21 Oct 1973	Fe (WBC)	Eder Jofre	Salvador, Brazil	Lost	KO–4

Lou SALICA

Born: New York, USA, 26 Jul 1913
World title fights: 10 (all bantamweight) won 5, lost 4, drew 1

DATE	WEIGHT	OPPONENT	VENUE	RESULT	
26 Aug 1935	B (NBA)	Sixto Escobar	New York	Won	PTS–15
15 Nov 1935	B (NBA)	Sixto Escobar	New York	Lost	PTS–15
21 Feb 1937	B	Sixto Escobar	San Juan	Lost	PTS–15
4 Mar 1940	B (NBA)	Georgie Pace	Toronto	Drew	15
24 Sep 1940	B	Georgie Pace	New York	Won	PTS–15
13 Jan 1941	B	Tommy Forte	Philadelphia	Won	PTS–15
25 Apr 1941	B	Lou Transparenti	Baltimore	Won	PTS–15
16 Jun 1941	B	Tommy Forte	Philadelphia	Won	PTS–15
7 Aug 1942	B	Manuel Ortiz	Hollywood	Lost	PTS–12
10 Mar 1943	B	Manuel Ortiz	Oakland, California	Lost	RSF–11

Jesus SALUD

Born: Waianae, Hawaii, USA, 3 May 1963
World title fights: 1 (junior-feather) won 1, lost 0

DATE	WEIGHT	OPPONENT	VENUE	RESULT	
11 Dec 1989	JFe (WBA)	Juan Jose Estrada	Los Angeles	Won	DIS–9

Jose SANABRIA

Born: Mormon, Venezuela, 16 Feb 1963
World title fights: 6 (all junior-feather) won 4, lost 2

DATE	WEIGHT	OPPONENT	VENUE	RESULT	
27 Dec 1987	JFe (IBF)	Seung-Hoon Lee	Pohang, S Korea	Lost	PTS–15
21 May 1988	JFe (IBF)	Moises Fuentes	Bucaramanga, Venezuela	Won	KO–5
21 Aug 1988	JFe (IBF)	Vincenzo Belcastro	Capo D'Orlando, Italy	Won	PTS–12
26 Sep 1988	JFe (IBF)	Fabrice Benichou	Nogent-sur-Marne, France	Won	RSF–10
11 Nov 1988	JFe (IBF)	Thierry Jacob	Gravelines, France	Won	RSF–6
10 Mar 1989	JFe (IBF)	Fabrice Benichou	Limoges, France	Lost	PTS–12

Clemente SANCHEZ

Born: Monterrey, Mexico, 9 Jul 1947
Died: Monterrey, 25 Dec 1978
World title fights: 2 (both featherweight) won 1, lost 1

DATE	WEIGHT	OPPONENT	VENUE	RESULT	
19 May 1972	Fe (WBC)	Kuniaki Shibata	Tokyo	Won	KO–3
16 Dec 1972	Fe (WBC)	Jose Legra	Monterrey, Mexico	Lost	RSF–10

Salvador SANCHEZ

Born: Santiago Tianguistenco, Mexico, 26 Jan 1959
Died: Queretaro, Mexico, 12 Aug 1982
World title fights: 10 (all featherweight) won 10, lost 0

DATE	WEIGHT	OPPONENT	VENUE	RESULT	
2 Feb 1980	Fe (WBC)	Danny Lopez	Phoenix	Won	RSF–13

DATE	WEIGHT	OPPONENT	VENUE	RESULT	
12 Apr 1980	Fe (WBC)	Ruben Castillo	Tucson, Arizona	Won	PTS–15
21 Jun 1980	Fe (WBC)	Danny Lopez	Las Vegas	Won	RSF–14
13 Sep 1980	Fe (WBC)	Pat Ford	San Antonio, Texas	Won	PTS–15
13 Dec 1980	Fe (WBC)	Juan Laporte	El Paso, Texas	Won	PTS–15
22 Mar 1981	Fe (WBC)	Roberto Castanon	Las Vegas	Won	RSF–10
21 Aug 1981	Fe (WBC)	Wilfredo Gomez	Las Vegas	Won	RSF–8
12 Dec 1981	Fe (WBC)	Pat Cowdell	Houston	Won	PTS–15
8 May 1982	Fe (WBC)	Jorge 'Rocky' Garcia	Dallas	Won	PTS–15
21 Jul 1982	Fe (WBC)	Azumah Nelson	New York	Won	RSF–15

Richie SANDOVAL

Born: Pomona, California, USA, 18 Oct 1960
World title fights: 4 (all bantamweight) won 3, lost 1

7 Apr 1984	B (WBA)	Jeff Chandler	Atlantic City	Won	RSF–15
22 Sep 1984	B (WBA)	Edgar Roman	Monte Carlo	Won	PTS–15
15 Dec 1984	B (WBA)	Gardeno Villoa	Miami	Won	RSF–8
10 Mar 1986	B (WBA)	Gaby Canizales	Las Vegas	Lost	KO–7

Baltasar SANGCHILLI

Born: Valencia, Spain, 15 Oct 1911
World title fights: 2 (both bantamweight) won 1, lost 1

1 Jun 1935	B (NY)	Panama Al Brown	Valencia	Won	PTS–15
29 Jun 1936	B (NY)	Tony Marino	New York	Lost	KO–14

Carlos SANTOS

Born: Santurce, Puerto Rico, 1 Oct 1955
World title fights: 4 (all junior-middle) won 2, lost 2

DATE	WEIGHT	OPPONENT	VENUE	RESULT
14 Nov 1981	JM (WBC)	Wilfred Benitez	Las Vegas	Lost PTS–15
2 Nov 1984	JM (IBF)	Mark Medal	New York	Won PTS–15
1 Jun 1985	JM (IBF)	Louis Acaries	Paris	Won PTS–15
4 Jun 1986	JM (IBF)	Buster Drayton	East Rutherford, New Jersey	Lost PTS–15

Petey SARRON

Born: Birmingham, Alabama, USA, 21 Nov 1908
World title fights: 5 (all featherweight) won 3, lost 2

DATE	WEIGHT	OPPONENT	VENUE	RESULT
2 Mar 1936	Fe (NBA)	Freddie Miller	Miami	Lost PTS–15
11 May 1936	Fe (NBA)	Freddie Miller	Washington DC	Won PTS–15
22 Jul 1936	Fe (NBA)	Baby Manuel	Dallas	Won PTS–15
4 Sep 1937	Fe (NBA)	Freddie Miller	Johannesburg	Won PTS–12
29 Oct 1937	Fe	Henry Armstrong	New York	Lost KO–6

Johnny SAXTON

Born: Newark, New Jersey, USA, 4 Jul 1930
World title fights: 5 (all welterweight) won 2, lost 3

DATE	WEIGHT	OPPONENT	VENUE	RESULT
20 Oct 1954	W	Kid Gavilan	Philadelphia	Won PTS–15
1 Apr 1955	W	Tony DeMarco	Boston	Lost RSF–14
14 Mar 1956	W	Carmen Basilio	Chicago	Won PTS–15
12 Sep 1956	W	Carmen Basilio	Syracuse, New York	Lost KO–9
22 Feb 1957	W	Carmen Basilio	Cleveland	Lost KO–2

Petey SCALZO

Born: New York City, USA, 1 Aug 1917
World title fights: 3 (all featherweight) won 2, lost 1

DATE	WEIGHT	OPPONENT	VENUE	RESULT
10 Jul 1940	Fe (NBA)	Bobby 'Poison' Ivy	Hartford, Connecticut	Won RSF–15
19 May 1941	Fe (NBA)	Phil Zwick	Milwaukee	Won PTS–15
1 Jul 1941	Fe (NBA)	Richie Lemos	Los Angeles	Lost KO–5

Max SCHMELING

Born: Klein Luckaw, Brandenburg, Germany, 28 Sep 1905
World title fights: 4 (all heavyweight) won 2, lost 2

DATE	WEIGHT	OPPONENT	VENUE	RESULT
12 Jun 1930	H	Jack Sharkey	New York	Won DIS–4
3 Jul 1931	H	Young Stribling	Cleveland	Won RSF–15
21 Jun 1932	H	Jack Sharkey	Long Island, New York	Lost PTS–15
22 Jun 1938	H	Joe Louis	New York	Lost KO–1

Izzy SCHWARTZ

Born: New York City, USA, 23 Oct 1902
World title fights: 5 (4 flyweight, 1 bantamweight) won 4, lost 1

DATE	WEIGHT	OPPONENT	VENUE	RESULT
16 Dec 1927	Fl (NY)	Newsboy Brown	New York	Won PTS–15
9 Apr 1928	Fl (NY)	Routtier Para	New York	Won PTS–15
23 May 1928	B (NY)	Bushy Graham	Brooklyn, New York	Lost PTS–15
20 Jul 1928	Fl (NY)	Frisco Grande	New York	Won DIS–4
12 Mar 1929	Fl (NY)	Albert 'Frenchie' Belanger	Toronto	Won PTS–12

DATE	WEIGHT	OPPONENT	VENUE	RESULT

Kelvin SEABROOKS

Born: Charlotte, North Carolina, USA, 10 Mar 1963
World title fights: 6 (all bantamweight) won 4, lost 2

DATE	WEIGHT	OPPONENT	VENUE	RESULT
16 May 1987	B (IBF)	Miguel Maturana	Cartagena, Colombia	Won KO–5
4 Jul 1987	B (IBF)	Thierry Jacob	Calais, France	Won RTD–9
18 Nov 1987	B (IBF)	Ernie Cataluna	San Cataldo, Philippines	Won RSF–4
6 Feb 1988	B (IBF)	Fernando Beltran	Paris	Won RSF–2
9 Jul 1988	B (IBF)	Orlando Canizales	Atlantic City	Lost RSF–15
24 Jun 1989	B (IBF)	Orlando Canizales	Atlantic City	Lost RSF–11

Sam SERRANO

Born: Toa Alta, Puerto Rico, 7 Nov 1952
World title fights: 18 (all junior-light) won 15, lost 2, drew 1

DATE	WEIGHT	OPPONENT	VENUE	RESULT
13 Apr 1976	JL (WBA)	Ben Villaflor	Honolulu	Drew 15
16 Oct 1976	JL (WBA)	Ben Villaflor	San Juan	Won PTS–15
15 Jan 1977	JL (WBA)	Alberto Herrera	Guyaquil, Ecuador	Won KO–11
26 Jun 1977	JL (WBA)	Leonel Hernandez	Puerto de la Cruz, Venezuela	Won PTS–15
27 Aug 1977	JL (WBA)	Apollo Yoshio	San Juan	Won PTS–15
19 Nov 1977	JL (WBA)	Tae-Ho Kim	San Juan	Won RSF–10
18 Feb 1978	JL (WBA)	Mario Martinez	San Juan	Won PTS–15
8 Jul 1978	JL (WBA)	Young-Ho Oh	San Juan	Won RSF–9
29 Nov 1978	JL (WBA)	Takao Muruki	Nagoya, Japan	Won PTS–15
18 Feb 1979	JL (WBA)	Julio Valdez	San Juan	Won PTS–15
15 Apr 1979	JL (WBA)	Nkosana Mgxaji	Capetown, S Africa	Won RSF–8
3 Apr 1980	JL (WBA)	Kiyoshi Kazama	Nara, Japan	Won RSF–13
2 Aug 1980	JL (WBA)	Yasutsune Uehara	Detroit	Lost KO–6
9 Apr 1981	JL (WBA)	Yasutsune Uehara	Wakayama, Japan	Won PTS–15

DATE	WEIGHT	OPPONENT	VENUE	RESULT

DATE	WEIGHT	OPPONENT	VENUE	RESULT
29 Jun 1981	JL (WBA)	Leonel Hernandez	Caracas	Won PTS–15
10 Dec 1981	JL (WBA)	Hikaru Tomonari	San Juan	Won RSF–12
5 Jun 1982	JL (WBA)	Ben Villablanca	Santiago	Won TKO–10
19 Jan 1983	JL (WBA)	Roger Mayweather	San Juan	Lost KO–8

Marty SERVO

Born: Schenectady, New York, USA, 3 Nov 1919
Died: Pueblo, Colorado, 9 Feb 1969
World title fights: 1 (welterweight) won 1, lost 0

DATE	WEIGHT	OPPONENT	VENUE	RESULT
1 Feb 1946	W	Freddie Cochrane	New York	Won KO–4

Jack SHARKEY

Born: Binghampton, New York, USA, 26 Oct 1902
World title fights: 3 (all heavyweight) won 1, lost 2

DATE	WEIGHT	OPPONENT	VENUE	RESULT
12 Jun 1930	H	Max Schmeling	New York	Lost DIS–4
21 Jun 1932	H	Max Schmeling	Long Island, New York	Won PTS–15
29 Jun 1933	H	Primo Carnera	Long Island	Lost KO–6

Battling SHAW

Born: Nuevo Laredo, Tampaulipas, Mexico, 21 Oct 1910
World title fights: 2 (both junior-welter) won 1, lost 1

DATE	WEIGHT	OPPONENT	VENUE	RESULT
20 Feb 1933	JW	Johnny Jadick	New Orleans	Won PTS–10
21 May 1933	JW	Tony Canzoneri	New Orleans	Lost PTS–10

DATE	WEIGHT	OPPONENT	VENUE	RESULT

Kuniaki SHIBATA

Born: Hitachi, Ibaraki, Japan, 29 Mar 1947
World title fights: 12 (4 featherweight, 8 junior-light) won 8, lost 3, drew 1

DATE	WEIGHT	OPPONENT	VENUE	RESULT
11 Dec 1970	Fe (WBC)	Vicente Saldivar	Tijuana, Mexico	Won RSF–12
3 Jun 1971	Fe (WBC)	Raul Cruz	Tokyo	Won KO–1
11 Nov 1971	Fe (WBC)	Ernesto Marcel	Matsuyama, Japan	Drew 15
19 May 1972	Fe (WBC)	Clemente Sanchez	Tokyo	Lost KO–3
12 Mar 1973	JL (WBA)	Ben Villaflor	Honolulu	Won PTS–15
19 Jun 1973	JL (WBA)	Victor Echegaray	Tokyo	Won PTS–15
17 Oct 1973	JL (WBA)	Ben Villaflor	Honolulu	Lost KO–1
28 Feb 1974	JL (WBC)	Ricardo Arredondo	Tokyo	Won PTS–15
27 Jun 1974	JL (WBC)	Antonio Amaya	Tokyo	Won PTS–15
3 Oct 1974	JL (WBC)	Ramiro Bolanos	Tokyo	Won RSF–15
27 Mar 1975	JL (WBC)	Ould Makloufi	Fukuoka, Japan	Won PTS–15
5 Jul 1975	JL (WBC)	Alfredo Escalera	Mito, Japan	Lost KO–2

Hi-Sup SHIN

Born: Seoul, South Korea, 29 Jul 1964
World title fights: 3 (all flyweight) won 2, lost 1

DATE	WEIGHT	OPPONENT	VENUE	RESULT
17 Jul 1983	Fl (WBA)	Santos Laciar	Cheju, S Korea	Lost RSF–1
2 Aug 1986	Fl (IBF)	Bi-Won Chung	Inchon, S Korea	Won KO–15
22 Nov 1986	Fl (IBF)	Henry Brent	Chunchon, S Korea	Won KO–13

Satoshi SHINGAKI

Born: Okinawa, Japan, 21 Feb 1964
World title fights: 5 (1 junior-fly, 4 bantamweight) won 2, lost 3

DATE	WEIGHT	OPPONENT	VENUE	RESULT
10 Dec 1983	JFl (IBF)	Dodie Penalosa	Osaka, Japan	Lost RSF–12

DATE	WEIGHT	OPPONENT	VENUE	RESULT

DATE	WEIGHT	OPPONENT	VENUE	RESULT
15 Apr 1984	B (IBF)	Elmer Magallano	Kashiwara, Japan	Won KO–8
4 Aug 1984	B (IBF)	Jorves de la Puz	Naha, Japan	Won PTS–15
26 Apr 1985	B (IBF)	Jeff Fenech	Sydney	Lost RSF–9
23 Aug 1985	B (IBF)	Jeff Fenech	Sydney	Lost RSF–3

Yoshio SHIRAI

Born: Tokyo, Japan, 23 Nov 1923
World title fights: 7 (all flyweight) won 5, lost 2

DATE	WEIGHT	OPPONENT	VENUE	RESULT
19 May 1952	Fl	Dado Marino	Tokyo	Won PTS–15
15 Nov 1952	Fl	Dado Marino	Tokyo	Won PTS–15
18 May 1953	Fl	Tanny Campo	Tokyo	Won PTS–15
27 Oct 1953	Fl	Terry Allen	Tokyo	Won PTS–15
24 May 1954	Fl	Leo Espinosa	Tokyo	Won PTS–15
26 Nov 1954	Fl	Pascual Perez	Tokyo	Lost PTS–15
30 May 1955	Fl	Pascual Perez	Tokyo	Lost KO–5

Battling SIKI

Born: St Louis, Senegal, 16 Sep 1897
Died: New York, 15 Dec 1925
World title fights: 2 (both light-heavy) won 1, lost 1

DATE	WEIGHT	OPPONENT	VENUE	RESULT
24 Sep 1922	LH	Georges Carpentier	Paris	Won KO–6
17 Mar 1923	LH	Mike McTigue	Dublin	Lost PTS–20

Al SINGER

Born: New York City, USA, 6 Sep 1909
Died: New York City, 20 Apr 1961
World title fights: 2 (both lightweight) won 1, lost 1

DATE	WEIGHT	OPPONENT	VENUE	RESULT	
17 Jul 1930	L	Sammy Mandell	New York	Won	KO–1
14 Nov 1930	L	Tony Canzoneri	New York	Lost	KO–1

Mahasamuth SITHNARUEPOL

Born: Chonburi, Thailand, 17 May 1959
World title fights: 4 (all strawweight) won 2, lost 1, drew 1

DATE	WEIGHT	OPPONENT	VENUE	RESULT	
24 Mar 1988	S (IBF)	Pretty Boy Lucas	Bangkok	Won	RSF–11
29 Aug 1988	S (IBF)	In-Kyu Hwang	Bangkok	Won	PTS–15
23 Mar 1989	S (IBF)	Nico Thomas	Jakarta	Drew	12
17 Jun 1989	S (IBF)	Nico Thomas	Jakarta	Lost	PTS–12

Jimmy SLATTERY

Born: Buffalo, USA, 24 Aug 1904
Died: Buffalo, 30 Aug 1960
World title fights: 6 (all light-heavy) won 2, lost 4

DATE	WEIGHT	OPPONENT	VENUE	RESULT	
11 Sep 1925	LH	Paul Berlenbach	New York	Lost	RSF–11
30 Aug 1927	LH (NBA)	Maxie Rosenbloom	Hartford, Connecticut	Won	PTS–10
12 Dec 1927	LH	Tommy Loughran	New York	Lost	PTS–15
10 Feb 1930	LH (NY)	Lou Scozza	Buffalo	Won	PTS–15
25 Jun 1930	LH (NY)	Maxie Rosenbloom	Buffalo	Lost	PTS–15
5 Aug 1931	LH (NY)	Maxie Rosenbloom	New York	Lost	PTS–15

DATE	WEIGHT	OPPONENT	VENUE	RESULT

James SMITH

Born: Magnolia, North Carolina, USA, 3 Apr 1955
World title fights: 3 (all heavyweight) won 1, lost 2

9 Nov 1984	H (IBF)	Larry Holmes	Las Vegas	Lost RSF–12
12 Dec 1986	H (WBA)	Tim Witherspoon	New York	Won RSF–1
7 Mar 1987	H (WBC/WBA)	Mike Tyson	Las Vegas	Lost PTS–12

Lonnie SMITH

Born: Pueblo, Colorado, USA, 25 Nov 1962
World title fights: 2 (both junior-welter) won 1, lost 1

22 Aug 1985	JW (WBC)	Billy Costello	New York	Won RSF–8
5 May 1986	JW (WBC)	Rene Arredondo	Los Angeles	Lost KO–5

Mysterious Billy SMITH

Born: Nova Scotia, Canada, 15 May 1871
Died: Portland, Oregon, 15 Oct 1937
World title fights: 12 (all welterweight) won 8, lost 2, drew 2

14 Dec 1892	W	Danny Needham	San Francisco	Won KO–14
17 Apr 1893	W	Tom Williams	New York	Won KO–2
26 Jul 1894	W	Tommy Ryan	Minneapolis	Lost PTS–20
27 May 1895	W	Tommy Ryan	New York	Drew 18*
25 Aug 1898	W	Matty Matthews	New York	Won PTS–25
7 Oct 1898	W	Charlie McKeever	New York	Won PTS–25
6 Dec 1898	W	Joe Walcott	New York	Won PTS–20
23 Jan 1899	W	Billy Edwards	New York	Won KO–15
10 Mar 1899	W	George Kid Lavigne	San Francisco	Won RSF–14
30 Jun 1899	W	Charlie McKeever	New York	Drew 20

* Police stopped contest

DATE	WEIGHT	OPPONENT	VENUE	RESULT

| 8 Nov 1899 | W | Charlie McKeever | New York | Won PTS–20 |
| 15 Jan 1900 | W | Rube Ferns | Buffalo | Lost DIS–21 |

Solly SMITH

Born: Los Angeles, USA, 1871
Died: Culver City, California, 29 Aug 1933
World title fights: 3 (all featherweight) won 1, lost 2

25 Sep 1893	Fe	George Dixon	Coney Island, New York	Lost KO–7
4 Oct 1897	Fe	George Dixon	San Francisco	Won PTS–20
26 Sep 1898	Fe	Dave Sullivan	Coney Island	Lost RTD–5

Wallace 'Bud' SMITH

Born: Cincinnati, Ohio, USA, 2 Apr 1929
Died: Cincinnati, 11 Jul 1973
World title fights: 4 (all lightweight) won 2, lost 2

29 Jun 1955	L	Jimmy Carter	Boston	Won PTS–15
19 Oct 1955	L	Jimmy Carter	Cincinnati	Won PTS–15
24 Aug 1956	L	Joe Brown	New Orleans	Lost PTS–15
13 Feb 1957	L	Joe Brown	Miami	Lost KO–11

Julian SOLIS

Born: Rio Piedras, Puerto Rico, 7 Jan 1957
World title fights: 3 (all bantamweight) won 1, lost 2

29 Aug 1980	B (WBA)	Jorge Lujan	Miami	Won PTS–15
14 Nov 1980	B (WBA)	Jeff Chandler	Miami	Lost RSF–14
25 Jul 1981	B (WBA)	Jeff Chandler	Atlantic City	Lost KO–7

DATE	WEIGHT	OPPONENT	VENUE	RESULT

Billy SOOSE

Born: Farrell, Pennsylvania, USA, 2 Aug 1915
World title fights: 1 (middleweight) won 1, lost 0

DATE	WEIGHT	OPPONENT	VENUE	RESULT
9 May 1941	M (NY)	Ken Overlin	New York	Won PTS–15

Leon SPINKS

Born: St Louis, Missouri, USA, 11 Jul 1953
World title fights: 4 (3 heavyweight, 1 cruiserweight) won 1, lost 3

DATE	WEIGHT	OPPONENT	VENUE	RESULT
15 Feb 1978	H	Muhammad Ali	Las Vegas	Won PTS–15
15 Sep 1978	H (WBA)	Muhammad Ali	New Orleans	Lost PTS–15
12 Jun 1981	H (WBC)	Larry Holmes	Detroit	Lost RSF–3
23 Mar 1986	C (WBA)	Dwight Qawi	Reno, Nevada	Lost RSF–6

Michael SPINKS

Born: St Louis, Missouri, USA, 13 Jul 1956
World title fights: 15 (11 light-heavy, 4 heavyweight) won 14, lost 1

DATE	WEIGHT	OPPONENT	VENUE	RESULT
18 Jul 1981	LH (WBA)	Eddie Mustafa Muhammad	Las Vegas	Won PTS–15
7 Nov 1981	LH (WBA)	Vonzell Johnson	Atlantic City	Won KO–7
13 Feb 1982	LH (WBA)	Mustafa Wasajja	Atlantic City	Won RSF–6
11 Apr 1982	LH (WBA)	Murray Sutherland	Atlantic City	Won KO–8
12 Jun 1982	LH (WBA)	Jerry Celestine	Atlantic City	Won RSF–8
18 Sep 1982	LH (WBA)	Johnny Davis	Atlantic City	Won KO–9
18 Mar 1983	LH	Dwight Qawi	Atlantic City	Won PTS–15
25 Nov 1983	LH	Oscar Rivadeneyra	Vancouver	Won RSF–10
25 Feb 1984	LH	Eddie Davis	Atlantic City	Won PTS–12
23 Feb 1985	LH	David Sears	Atlantic City	Won RSF–3
6 Jun 1985	LH	Jim McDonald	Las Vegas	Won RSF–8

DATE	WEIGHT	OPPONENT	VENUE	RESULT	
21 Sep 1985	H (IBF)	Larry Holmes	Las Vegas	Won	PTS–15
19 Apr 1986	H (IBF)	Larry Holmes	Las Vegas	Won	PTS–15
6 Sep 1986	H (IBF)	Steffen Tangstad	Las Vegas	Won	RSF–4
27 Jun 1988	H	Mike Tyson	Atlantic City	Lost	KO–1

Marlon STARLING

Born: Hartford, Connecticut, USA, 29 Aug 1958
World title fights: 9 (8 welterweight, 1 middleweight) won 4, lost 4, drew 1

DATE	WEIGHT	OPPONENT	VENUE	RESULT	
4 Feb 1984	W (WBA)	Donald Curry	Atlantic City	Lost	PTS–15
22 Aug 1987	W (WBA)	Mark Breland	Columbia, South Carolina	Won	RSF–11
6 Feb 1988	W (WBA)	Fujio Ozaki	Atlantic City	Won	PTS–12
16 Apr 1988	W (WBA)	Mark Breland	Las Vegas	Drew	12
29 Jul 1988	W (WBA)	Tomas Molinares	Atlantic City	Lost	KO–6
4 Feb 1989	W (WBC)	Lloyd Honeyghan	Las Vegas	Won	RSF–9
15 Sep 1989	W (WBC)	Yung-Kil Chung	Hartford, Connecticut	Won	PTS–12
14 Apr 1990	M (IBF)	Michael Nunn	Las Vegas	Lost	PTS–12
19 Aug 1990	W (WBC)	Maurice Blocker	Reno, Nevada	Lost	PTS–12

Loris STECCA

Born: San Arcangelo di Romagna, Italy, 30 Mar 1960
World title fights: 3 (all junior-feather) won 1, lost 2

DATE	WEIGHT	OPPONENT	VENUE	RESULT	
22 Feb 1984	JFe (WBA)	Leonardo Cruz	Milan	Won	RSF–12
26 May 1984	JFe (WBA)	Victor Callejas	Guaynabo, Puerto Rico	Lost	KO–8
8 Nov 1985	JFe (WBA)	Victor Callejas	Rimini, Italy	Lost	TKO–7

Maurizio STECCA

Born: San Arcangelo di Romagna, Italy, 9 Mar 1963
World title fights: 3 (all featherweight) won 2, lost 1

DATE	WEIGHT	OPPONENT	VENUE	RESULT	
28 Jan 1989	Fe (WBO)	Pedro Nolasco	Milan	Won	RSF–6
16 Jun 1989	Fe (WBO)	Angel Levi Mayor	Milan	Won	RSF–9
11 Nov 1989	Fe (WBO)	Louie Espinoza	Rimini, Italy	Lost	RSF–7

Freddie STEELE

Born: Tacoma, Washington, USA, 18 Dec 1912
Died: Aberdeen, Washington, 23 Aug 1984
World title fights: 7 (all middleweight) won 6, lost 1

DATE	WEIGHT	OPPONENT	VENUE	RESULT	
11 Jul 1936	M (NBA)	Babe Risko	Seattle	Won	PTS–15
1 Jan 1937	M (NBA)	Gorilla Jones	Milwaukee	Won	PTS–10
19 Feb 1937	M (NBA)	Babe Risko	New York	Won	PTS–15
11 May 1937	M (NBA)	Frank Battaglia	Seattle	Won	KO–3
11 Sep 1937	M (NBA)	Ken Overlin	Seattle	Won	KO–4
19 Feb 1938	M (NBA)	Carmen Barth	Cleveland	Won	KO–7
26 Jul 1938	M (NBA)	Al Hostak	Seattle	Lost	KO–1

Leslie STEWART

Born: Laventille, Trinidad, 21 Mar 1961
World title fights: 5 (all light-heavy) won 1, lost 4

DATE	WEIGHT	OPPONENT	VENUE	RESULT	
9 Feb 1986	LH (WBA)	Marvin Johnson	Indianapolis	Lost	RSF–7
23 May 1987	LH (WBA)	Marvin Johnson	Port of Spain, Trinidad	Won	RSF–8
5 Sep 1987	LH (WBA)	Virgil Hill	Atlantic City	Lost	RSF–4
29 May 1988	LH (WBC)	Donny Lalonde	Port of Spain	Lost	RSF–5
25 Jun 1989	LH (WBO)	Michael Moorer	Atlantic City	Lost	RSF–8

John H STRACEY

Born: Bethnal Green, London, England, 22 Sep 1950
World title fights: 3 (all welterweight) won 2, lost 1

DATE	WEIGHT	OPPONENT	VENUE	RESULT	
6 Dec 1975	W (WBC)	Jose Napoles	Mexico City	Won	RSF–6
20 Mar 1976	W (WBC)	Hedgemon Lewis	London	Won	RSF–10
22 Jun 1976	W (WBC)	Carlos Palomino	London	Lost	RSF–12

Seung-Il SUH

Born: South Korea, 18 Jul 1959
World title fights: 5 (all junior-feather) won 2, lost 3

DATE	WEIGHT	OPPONENT	VENUE	RESULT	
4 Dec 1983	JFe (IBF)	Bobby Berna	Seoul	Lost	KO–9
15 Apr 1984	JFe (IBF)	Bobby Berna	Seoul	Won	KO–10
8 Jul 1984	JFe (IBF)	Cleo Garcia	Seoul	Won	KO–4
3 Jan 1985	JFe (IBF)	Chi-Won Kim	Seoul	Lost	KO–10
9 Oct 1985	JFe (IBF)	Chi-Won Kim	Chunju, S Korea	Lost	KO–1

Dave SULLIVAN

Born: Cork, Ireland, 19 May 1877
Died: Cork, 1929
World title fights: 2 (both featherweight) won 1, lost 1

DATE	WEIGHT	OPPONENT	VENUE	RESULT	
26 Sep 1898	Fe	Solly Smith	Coney Island, New York	Won	RTD–5
11 Nov 1898	Fe	George Dixon	New York	Lost	DIS–10

Mike 'Twin' SULLIVAN

Born: Cambridge, Massachusetts, USA, 23 Sep 1878
Died: Cambridge, 31 Oct 1937
World title fights: 2 (1 welterweight, 1 middleweight) won 1, lost 1

DATE	WEIGHT	OPPONENT	VENUE	RESULT	
23 Apr 1907	W	Honey Mellody	Los Angeles	Won	PTS–20
22 Feb 1908	M	Stanley Ketchel	Colma, California	Lost	KO–1

Steve 'Kid' SULLIVAN

Born: Brooklyn, New York, USA, 21 May 1897
World title fights: 3 (all junior-light) won 2, lost 1

DATE	WEIGHT	OPPONENT	VENUE	RESULT	
20 Jun 1924	JL	Johnny Dundee	New York	Won	PTS–10
15 Oct 1924	JL	Mike Ballerino	New York	Won	KO–5
1 Apr 1925	JL	Mike Ballerino	Philadelphia	Lost	PTS–10

Murray SUTHERLAND

Born: Edinburgh, Scotland, 10 Apr 1954
World title fights: 4 (2 light-heavy, 2 super-middle) won 1, lost 3

DATE	WEIGHT	OPPONENT	VENUE	RESULT	
25 Apr 1981	LH (WBC)	Matt Saad Muhammad	Atlantic City	Lost	KO–9
11 Apr 1982	LH (WBA)	Michael Spinks	Atlantic City	Lost	KO–8
28 Mar 1984	SM (IBF)	Ernie Singletary	Atlantic City	Won	PTS–15
22 Jul 1984	SM (IBF)	Chong-Pal Park	Seoul	Lost	KO–11

Ishimatsu SUZUKI
see Guts ISHIMATSU

Yukito TAMAKUMA

Born: Aomori, Japan, 25 Jan 1964
World title fights: 3 (all flyweight) won 1, drew 1, lost 1

DATE	WEIGHT	OPPONENT	VENUE	RESULT
5 Mar 1989	Fl (WBC)	Yung-Kang Kim	Aomori, Japan	Lost PTS–12
28 Jul 1990	Fl (WBA)	Yul-Woo Lee	Mito, Japan	Won RSF–10
6 Dec 1990	Fl (WBA)	Jesus Rojas	Aomori	Drew 12

Frank TATE

Born: Detroit, Michigan, USA, 27 Aug 1964
World title fights: 4 (3 middleweight, 1 super-middle) won 2, lost 2

DATE	WEIGHT	OPPONENT	VENUE	RESULT
10 Oct 1987	M (IBF)	Michael Olijade	Las Vegas	Won PTS–15
7 Feb 1988	M (IBF)	Tony Sibson	Stafford, England	Won KO–10
28 Jul 1988	M (IBF)	Michael Nunn	Las Vegas	Lost RSF–9
27 Jan 1990	SM (IBF)	Lindell Holmes	New Orleans	Lost PTS–12

John TATE

Born: Marion City, Arkansas, USA, 29 Jan 1955
World title fights: 2 (both heavyweight) won 1, lost 1

DATE	WEIGHT	OPPONENT	VENUE	RESULT
20 Oct 1979	H (WBA)	Gerrie Coetzee	Johannesburg	Won PTS–15
31 Mar 1980	H (WBA)	Mike Weaver	Knoxville, Tennessee	Lost KO–15

Arnold TAYLOR

Born: Johannesburg, South Africa, 21 July 1945
Died: Johannesburg, 22 Nov 1981
World title fights: 2 (both bantamweight) won 1, lost 1

DATE	WEIGHT	OPPONENT	VENUE	RESULT
3 Nov 1973	B (WBA)	Romeo Anaya	Johannesburg	Won KO–14
3 Jul 1974	B (WBA)	Soo-Hwan Hong	Durban	Lost PTS–15

Charles 'Bud' TAYLOR

Born: Terre Haute, Indiana, USA, 22 Jul 1903
Died: Los Angeles, 8 Mar 1962
World title fights: 2 (both bantamweight) won 1, drew 1

DATE	WEIGHT	OPPONENT	VENUE	RESULT
26 Mar 1927	B (NBA)	Tony Canzoneri	Chicago	Drew 10
24 Jun 1927	B (NBA)	Tony Canzoneri	Chicago	Won PTS–10

Meldrick TAYLOR

Born: Philadelphia, USA, 19 Oct 1966
World title fights: 5 (all junior-welter) won 4, lost 1

DATE	WEIGHT	OPPONENT	VENUE	RESULT
3 Sep 1988	JW (IBF)	James Buddy McGirt	Atlantic City	Won RSF–12
21 Jan 1989	JW (IBF)	John Meekins	Atlantic City	Won RSF–7
11 Sep 1989	JW (IBF)	Courtney Hooper	Atlantic City	Won PTS–12
17 Mar 1990	JW (WBC/IBF)	Julio Cesar Chavez	Las Vegas	Lost RSF–12
11 Aug 1990	JW (IBF)	Primo Ramos	Lake Tahoe, Nevada	Won PTS–12

Phil TERRANOVA

Born: New York City, USA, 4 Sep 1919
World title fights: 5 (all featherweight) won 2, lost 3

DATE	WEIGHT	OPPONENT	VENUE	RESULT
16 Aug 1943	Fe (NBA)	Jackie Callura	New Orleans	Won KO–8
27 Dec 1943	Fe (NBA)	Jackie Callura	New Orleans	Won KO–6
10 Mar 1944	Fe (NBA)	Sal Bartolo	Boston	Lost PTS–15
5 May 1944	Fe (NBA)	Sal Bartolo	Boston	Lost PTS–15
19 Feb 1945	Fe (NY)	Willie Pep	New York	Lost PTS–15

DATE	WEIGHT	OPPONENT	VENUE	RESULT

DATE	WEIGHT	OPPONENT	VENUE	RESULT

Ernie TERRELL

Born: Chicago, Illinois, USA, 4 Apr 1939
World title fights: 4 (all heavyweight) won 3, lost 1

DATE	WEIGHT	OPPONENT	VENUE	RESULT
5 Mar 1965	H (WBA)	Eddie Machen	Chicago	Won PTS–15
1 Nov 1965	H (WBA)	George Chuvalo	Toronto	Won PTS–15
28 Jun 1966	H (WBA)	Doug Jones	Houston	Won PTS–15
6 Feb 1967	H	Muhammad Ali	Houston	Lost PTS–15

Marcel THIL

Born: Saint-Dizier, France, 25 May 1904
Died: Cannes, France, 14 Aug 1968
World title fights: 10 (all middleweight) won 9, drew 1

DATE	WEIGHT	OPPONENT	VENUE	RESULT
11 Jun 1932	M (NBA)	Gorilla Jones	Paris	Won DIS–11
4 Jul 1932	M (NBA)	Len Harvey	London	Won PTS–15
2 Oct 1933	M (NBA)	Kid Tunero	Paris	Won PTS–15
26 Feb 1934	M (NBA)	Ignacio Ara	Paris	Won PTS–15
3 May 1934	M (NBA)	Gustav Roth	Paris	Won PTS–15
15 Oct 1934	M (NBA)	Carmelo Candel	Paris	Drew 15
4 May 1935	M (NBA)	Vilda Jacks	Paris	Won RSF–14
1 Jun 1935	M (NBA)	Ignacio Ara	Madrid	Won PTS–15
28 Jun 1935	M (NBA)	Carmelo Candel	Paris	Won PTS–10
20 Jan 1936	M (NBA)	Lou Brouillard	Paris	Won DIS–4

Dingaan THOBELA

Born: South Africa, 26 Sep 1966
World title fights: 1 (lightweight) won 1, lost 0

DATE	WEIGHT	OPPONENT	VENUE	RESULT
22 Sep 1990	L (WBO)	Mauricio Aceves	Brownsville, Texas	Won PTS–12

DATE	WEIGHT	OPPONENT	VENUE	RESULT

Duane THOMAS

Born: Detroit, Michigan, USA, 1 Feb 1961
World title fights: 3 (all junior-middle) won 1, lost 2

DATE	WEIGHT	OPPONENT	VENUE	RESULT	
5 Dec 1986	JM (WBC)	John Mugabi	Las Vegas	Won	RSF–3
12 Jul 1987	JM (WBC)	Lupe Aquino	Bordeaux	Lost	PTS–12
3 Jan 1988	JM (WBC)	Gianfranco Rosi	Genoa	Lost	RSF–7

Nico THOMAS

Born: Tonsco, Indonesia, 10 Jun 1966
World title fights: 3 (all strawweight) won 1, lost 1, drew 1

DATE	WEIGHT	OPPONENT	VENUE	RESULT	
23 Mar 1988	S (IBF)	Mahasamuth Sithnaruepol	Jakarta	Drew	12
17 Jun 1989	S (IBF)	Mahasamuth Sithnaruepol	Jakarta	Won	PTS–12
21 Sep 1989	S (IBF)	Eric Chavez	Jakarta	Lost	KO–4

Pinklon THOMAS

Born: Pontiac, Michigan, USA, 10 Feb 1958
World title fights: 4 (all heavyweight) won 2, lost 2

DATE	WEIGHT	OPPONENT	VENUE	RESULT	
31 Aug 1984	H (WBC)	Tim Witherspoon	Las Vegas	Won	PTS–12
15 Jun 1985	H (WBC)	Mike Weaver	Las Vegas	Won	RSF–8
22 Mar 1986	H (WBC)	Trevor Berbick	Las Vegas	Lost	PTS–12
30 May 1987	H (WBC/WBA)	Mike Tyson	Las Vegas	Lost	RSF–6

Johnny 'Cyclone' THOMPSON

Born: Ogle County, Illinois, USA, 20 Jun 1876
Died: Sycamore, Illinois, 28 May 1951
World title fights: 1 (middleweight) won 1, lost 0

DATE	WEIGHT	OPPONENT	VENUE	RESULT	
11 Feb 1911	M	Billy Papke	Sydney	Won	PTS–20

Young Jack THOMPSON

Born: Los Angeles, USA, 17 Aug 1904
Died: Los Angeles, 9 Apr 1946
World title fights: 5 (all welterweight) won 2, lost 3

DATE	WEIGHT	OPPONENT	VENUE	RESULT	
25 Mar 1929	W	Jackie Fields	Chicago	Lost	PTS–10
9 May 1930	W	Jackie Fields	Detroit	Won	PTS–15
5 Sep 1930	W	Tommy Freeman	Cleveland	Lost	PTS–15
14 Apr 1931	W	Tommy Freeman	Cleveland	Won	KO–12
23 Oct 1931	W	Lou Brouillard	Boston	Lost	PTS–15

Dick TIGER

Born: Amaigbo, Orlu, Nigeria, 14 Aug 1929
Died: Nigeria, 14 Dec 1971
World title fights: 10 (6 middleweight, 4 light-heavy) won 6, lost 3, drew 1

DATE	WEIGHT	OPPONENT	VENUE	RESULT	
23 Oct 1962	M (NBA)	Gene Fullmer	San Francisco	Won	PTS–15
23 Feb 1963	M	Gene Fullmer	Las Vegas	Drew 15	
10 Aug 1963	M	Gene Fullmer	Ibadan, Nigeria	Won	KO–7
7 Dec 1963	M	Joey Giardello	New York	Lost	PTS–15
21 Oct 1965	M	Joey Giardello	New York	Won	PTS–15
25 Apr 1966	M	Emile Griffith	New York	Lost	PTS–15
16 Dec 1966	LH	Jose Torres	New York	Won	PTS–15
16 May 1967	LH	Jose Torres	New York	Won	PTS–15
17 Nov 1967	LH	Roger Rouse	Las Vegas	Won	KO–12
24 May 1968	LH	Bob Foster	New York	Lost	KO–4

Christophe TIOZZO

Born: St Denis, France, 1 Jun 1963
World title fights: 3 (all super-middle) won 3, lost 0

DATE	WEIGHT	OPPONENT	VENUE	RESULT
30 Mar 1990	SM (WBA)	In-Chul Baek	Lyons	Won RSF–10
20 Jul 1990	SM (WBA)	Paul Whittaker	Arles, France	Won RSF–8
23 Nov 1990	SM (WBA)	Danny Morgan	Paris	Won RSF–2

Katsuo TOKASHIKI

Born: Okinawa, Japan, 27 Jul 1960
World title fights: 9 (all junior-fly) won 5, lost 3, drew 1

DATE	WEIGHT	OPPONENT	VENUE	RESULT
16 Dec 1981	JFl (WBA)	Hwan-Jin Kim	Sendai, Japan	Won PTS–15
4 Apr 1982	JFl (WBA)	Lupe Madera	Sendai	Won PTS–15
7 Jul 1982	JFl (WBA)	Masaharu Inami	Tokyo	Won KO–8
10 Oct 1982	JFl (WBA)	Sung-Nam Kim	Tokyo	Won PTS–15
9 Jan 1983	JFl (WBA)	Hwan-Jin Kim	Kyoto, Japan	Won PTS–15
9 Apr 1983	JFl (WBA)	Lupe Madera	Tokyo	Drew 15
10 Jul 1983	JFl (WBA)	Lupe Madera	Tokyo	Lost RSF–4
23 Oct 1983	JFl (WBA)	Lupe Madera	Sapporo, Japan	Lost PTS–15
18 Aug 1984	JFl (WBC)	Jung-Koo Chang	Pohang, S Korea	Lost RSF–9

Tadashi TOMORI

Born: Okinawa, Japan, 28 Dec 1959
World title fights: 3 (all junior-fly) won 1, lost 2

DATE	WEIGHT	OPPONENT	VENUE	RESULT
13 Apr 1982	JFl (WBC)	Amado Ursua	Tokyo	Won PTS–15
20 Jul 1982	JFl (WBC)	Hilario Zapata	Kanazawa, Japan	Lost PTS–15
30 Nov 1982	JFl (WBC)	Hilario Zapata	Tokyo	Lost RSF–8

Efren TORRES

Born: Michoacan, Mexico, 29 Nov 1943
World title fights: 5 (all flyweight) won 2, lost 3

DATE	WEIGHT	OPPONENT	VENUE	RESULT	
10 Dec 1966	Fl (WBA)	Horacio Accavallo	Buenos Aires	Lost	PTS–15
28 Jan 1968	Fl (WBC)	Chartchai Chionoi	Mexico City	Lost	RSF–13
23 Feb 1969	Fl (WBC)	Chartchai Chionoi	Mexico City	Won	RSF–8
28 Nov 1969	Fl (WBC)	Susumu Hanagata	Guadalajara, Mexico	Won	PTS–15
20 Mar 1970	Fl (WBC)	Chartchai Chionoi	Bangkok	Lost	PTS–15

German TORRES

Born: Celeya Guanajato, Mexico, 28 May 1957
World title fights: 6 (all junior-fly) won 1, lost 5

DATE	WEIGHT	OPPONENT	VENUE	RESULT	
15 Aug 1981	JFl (WBC)	Hilario Zapata	Panama City	Lost	PTS–15
10 Sep 1983	JFl (WBC)	Jung-Koo Chang	Taejon, S Korea	Lost	PTS–12
27 Apr 1985	JFl (WBC)	Jung-Koo Chang	Ulsan, S Korea	Lost	PTS–12
13 Apr 1986	JFl (WBC)	Jung-Koo Chang	Seoul	Lost	PTS–12
11 Dec 1988	JFl (WBC)	Soon-Jung Kang	Seoul	Won	PTS–12
19 Mar 1989	JFl (WBC)	Yul-Woo Lee	Seoul	Lost	RSF–9

Jose TORRES

Born: Playa Ponce, Puerto Rico, 3 May 1936
World title fights: 6 (all light-heavy) won 4, lost 2

DATE	WEIGHT	OPPONENT	VENUE	RESULT	
30 Mar 1965	LH	Willie Pastrano	New York	Won	KO–9
21 May 1966	LH	Wayne Thornton	New York	Won	PTS–15
15 Aug 1966	LH	Eddie Cotton	Las Vegas	Won	PTS–15
15 Oct 1966	LH	Chic Calderwood	San Juan	Won	KO–2

DATE	WEIGHT	OPPONENT	VENUE	RESULT	
16 Dec 1966	LH	Dick Tiger	New York	Lost	PTS–15
16 May 1967	LH	Dick Tiger	New York	Lost	PTS–15

Rafael TORRES

Born: Dominican Republic, 17 Apr 1964
World title fights: 2 (both strawweight) won 2, lost 0

30 Aug 1989	S (WBO)	Yamil Caraballo	Santo Domingo	Won	PTS–12
31 Jul 1990	S (WBO)	Hunsi Ray	Jakarta	Won	PTS–12

Vic TOWEEL

Born: Benoni, Transvaal, South Africa, 12 Jan 1928
World title fights: 6 (all bantamweight) won 4, lost 2

31 May 1950	B	Manuel Ortiz	Johannesburg	Won	PTS–15
2 Dec 1950	B	Danny O'Sullivan	Johannesburg	Won	RTD–10
17 Nov 1951	B	Luis Romero	Johannesburg	Won	PTS–15
26 Jan 1952	B	Peter Keenan	Johannesburg	Won	PTS–15
15 Nov 1952	B	Jimmy Carruthers	Johannesburg	Lost	KO–1
21 Mar 1953	B	Jimmy Carruthers	Johannesburg	Lost	KO–10

Tony TUBBS

Born: Cincinnati, Ohio, USA, 15 Feb 1959
World title fights: 3 (all heavyweight) won 1, lost 2

29 Apr 1985	H (WBA)	Greg Page	Buffalo	Won	PTS–15
17 Jan 1986	H (WBA)	Tim Witherspoon	Atlanta	Lost	PTS–15
21 Mar 1988	H	Mike Tyson	Tokyo	Lost	RSF–2

Tony TUCKER

Born: Grand Rapids, Michigan, USA, 27 Dec 1958
World title fights: 2 (both heavyweight) won 1, lost 1

DATE	WEIGHT	OPPONENT	VENUE	RESULT
30 May 1987	H (IBF)	James 'Buster' Douglas	Las Vegas	Won KO–10
2 Aug 1987	H	Mike Tyson	Las Vegas	Lost PTS–12

Gene TUNNEY

Born: New York City, USA, 25 May 1897
Died: Greenwich, Connecticut, 7 Nov 1978
World title fights: 3 (all heavyweight) won 3, lost 0

DATE	WEIGHT	OPPONENT	VENUE	RESULT
23 Sep 1926	H	Jack Dempsey	Philadelphia	Won PTS–10
22 Sep 1927	H	Jack Dempsey	Chicago	Won PTS–10
23 Jul 1928	H	Tom Heeney	New York	Won RSF–11

Randolph TURPIN

Born: Leamington, Warwickshire, England, 7 Jun 1928
Died: Leamington, 17 May 1966
World title fights: 3 (all middleweight) won 1, lost 2

DATE	WEIGHT	OPPONENT	VENUE	RESULT
10 Jul 1951	M	Sugar Ray Robinson	London	Won PTS–15
12 Sep 1951	M	Sugar Ray Robinson	New York	Lost RSF–10
21 Oct 1953	M	Carl 'Bobo' Olson	New York	Lost PTS–15

Mike TYSON

Born: Brooklyn, New York, USA, 30 Jun 1966
World title fights: 11 (all heavyweight) won 10, lost 1

DATE	WEIGHT	OPPONENT	VENUE	RESULT
22 Nov 1986	H (WBC)	Trevor Berbick	Las Vegas	Won RSF–2

DATE	WEIGHT	OPPONENT	VENUE	RESULT
7 Mar 1987	H (WBC/WBA)	James Smith	Las Vegas	Won PTS–12
30 May 1987	H (WBC/WBA)	Pinklon Thomas	Las Vegas	Won RSF–6
2 Aug 1987	H	Tony Tucker	Las Vegas	Won PTS–12
19 Oct 1987	H	Tyrrell Biggs	Atlantic City	Won KO–7
22 Jan 1988	H	Larry Holmes	Atlantic City	Won RSF–4
21 Mar 1988	H	Tony Tubbs	Tokyo	Won RSF–2
27 Jun 1988	H	Michael Spinks	Atlantic City	Won KO–1
25 Feb 1989	H	Frank Bruno	Las Vegas	Won RSF–5
21 Jul 1989	H (WBC/WBA/ IBF)	Carl Williams	Atlantic City	Won RSF–1
11 Feb 1990	H (WBC/WBA/ IBF)	James 'Buster' Douglas	Tokyo	Lost KO–10

Franco UDELLA

Born: Cagliari, Italy, 25 Feb 1947
World title fights: 3 (1 flyweight, 2 junior-fly) won 1, lost 2

DATE	WEIGHT	OPPONENT	VENUE	RESULT
20 Jul 1974	Fl (WBC)	Betulio Gonzalez	Sabbiadoro, Italy	Lost RSF–10
4 Apr 1975	JFl (WBC)	Valentin Martinez	Milan	Won DIS–12
18 Jul 1976	JFl (WBC)	Luis Estaba	Caracas	Lost KO–3

Yasutsune UEHARA

Born: Okinawa, Japan, 12 Oct 1949
World title fights: 6 (4 junior-light, 2 featherweight) won 2, lost 4

DATE	WEIGHT	OPPONENT	VENUE	RESULT
24 Aug 1974	JL (WBA)	Ben Villaflor	Honolulu	Lost RSF–2
6 Mar 1976	Fe (WBC)	David Kotey	Accra	Lost RSF–12
29 May 1977	Fe (WBA)	Rafael Ortega	Okinawa, Japan	Lost PTS–15
2 Aug 1980	JL (WBA)	Sam Serrano	Detroit	Won KO–6

DATE	WEIGHT	OPPONENT	VENUE	RESULT

20 Nov 1980	JL (WBA)	Leonel Hernandez	Tokyo	Won	PTS–15
9 Apr 1981	JL (WBA)	Sam Serrano	Wakayama, Japan	Lost	PTS–15

Amado URSUA

Born: Mexico City, Mexico, 13 Sep 1956
World title fights: 2 (both junior-fly) won 1, lost 1

6 Feb 1982	JFl (WBC)	Hilario Zapata	Panama City	Won	KO–2
13 Apr 1982	JFl (WBC)	Tadashi Tomori	Tokyo	Lost	PTS–15

Jorge VACA

Born: Guadalajara, Mexico, 14 Dec 1959
World title fights: 3 (all welterweight) won 1, lost 2

28 Oct 1987	W (WBC)	Lloyd Honeyghan	London	Won	TD–8
28 Mar 1988	W (WBC)	Lloyd Honeyghan	London	Lost	KO–3
16 Jul 1988	W (IBF)	Simon Brown	Kingston, Jamaica	Lost	RSF–3

Rodrigo VALDEZ

Born: Rocha, Bolivar, Colombia, 22 Dec 1946
World title fights: 10 (all middleweight) won 6, lost 4

24 May 1974	M (WBC)	Benny Briscoe	Monte Carlo	Won	KO–7
13 Nov 1974	M (WBC)	Gratien Tonna	Paris	Won	KO–11
31 May 1975	M (WBC)	Ramon Mendez	Cali, Colombia	Won	KO–8
16 Aug 1975	M (WBC)	Rudy Robles	Cartagena, Colombia	Won	PTS–15
28 Mar 1976	M (WBC)	Max Cohen	Paris	Won	KO–4
26 Jun 1976	M	Carlos Monzon	Monte Carlo	Lost	PTS–15
30 Jul 1977	M	Carlos Monzon	Monte Carlo	Lost	PTS–15
5 Nov 1977	M	Bennie Briscoe	Campione, Italy	Won	PTS–15

DATE	WEIGHT	OPPONENT	VENUE	RESULT
22 Apr 1978	M	Hugo Corro	San Remo, Italy	Lost PTS–15
11 Nov 1978	M	Hugo Corro	Buenos Aires	Lost PTS–15

Darrin VAN HORN

Born: Morgan City, Louisiana, USA, 7 Sep 1968
World title fights: 3 (all junior-middle) won 1, lost 2

DATE	WEIGHT	OPPONENT	VENUE	RESULT
4 Feb 1989	JM (IBF)	Robert Hines	Atlantic City	Won PTS–12
16 Jul 1989	JM (IBF)	Gianfranco Rosi	Atlantic City	Lost PTS–12
21 Jul 1990	JM (IBF)	Gianfranco Rosi	Marino, Italy	Lost PTS–12

Wilfredo VASQUEZ

Born: Rio Piedras, Puerto Rico, 2 Aug 1960
World title fights: 4 (all bantamweight) won 1, lost 2, drew 1

DATE	WEIGHT	OPPONENT	VENUE	RESULT
8 Feb 1986	B (WBC)	Miguel 'Happy' Lora	Miami	Lost PTS–12
3 Oct 1987	B (WBA)	Chan-Young Park	Seoul	Won RTD–10
17 Jan 1988	B (WBA)	Takuya Muguruma	Osaka, Japan	Drew 12
9 May 1988	B (WBA)	Kaokor Galaxy	Bangkok	Lost PTS–12

Miguel VELASQUEZ

Born: Santa Cruz de Tenerife, Spain, 27 Dec 1944
World title fights: 2 (both junior-welter) won 1, lost 1

DATE	WEIGHT	OPPONENT	VENUE	RESULT
30 Jun 1976	JW (WBC)	Saensak Muangsurin	Madrid	Won DIS–5
29 Oct 1976	JW (WBC)	Saensak Muangsurin	Segovia, Spain	Lost RSF–2

DATE	WEIGHT	OPPONENT	VENUE	RESULT
7 May 1972	JM	Domenico Tiberia	Fukuoka, Japan	Won KO–1
3 Oct 1972	JM	Matt Donovan	Tokyo	Won KO–3
9 Jan 1973	JM	Miguel de Oliveira	Tokyo	Drew 15
20 Apr 1973	JM	Ryu Sorimachi	Tokyo	Won PTS–15
14 Aug 1973	JM	Silvano Bertini	Sapporo, Japan	Won RTD–13
5 Feb 1974	JM	Miguel de Oliveira	Tokyo	Won PTS–15
4 Jun 1974	JM	Oscar Albarado	Tokyo	Lost KO–15
21 Jan 1975	JM	Oscar Albarado	Tokyo	Won PTS–15
7 Jun 1975	JM (WBA)	Jae-Do Yuh	Kitsakyushu, Japan	Lost KO–7
17 Feb 1976	JM (WBA)	Jae-Do Yuh	Tokyo	Won KO–15
18 May 1976	JM (WBA)	Jose Duran	Tokyo	Lost KO–14
7 Jun 1977	JM (WBA)	Eddie Gazo	Tokyo	Lost RSF–11

Jersey Joe WALCOTT

Born: Merchantville, New Jersey, USA, 31 Jan 1914
World title fights: 8 (all heavyweight) won 2, lost 6

DATE	WEIGHT	OPPONENT	VENUE	RESULT
5 Dec 1947	H	Joe Louis	New York	Lost PTS–15
25 Jun 1948	H	Joe Louis	New York	Lost KO–11
22 Jun 1949	H (NBA)	Ezzard Charles	Chicago	Lost PTS–15
7 Mar 1951	H	Ezzard Charles	Detroit	Lost PTS–15
18 Jul 1951	H	Ezzard Charles	Pittsburgh	Won KO–7
5 Jun 1952	H	Ezzard Charles	Philadelphia	Won PTS–15
23 Sep 1952	H	Rocky Marciano	Philadelphia	Lost KO–13
15 May 1953	H	Rocky Marciano	Chicago	Lost KO–1

DATE	WEIGHT	OPPONENT	VENUE	RESULT

Joe WALCOTT

Born: Barbados, British West Indies, 13 Mar 1873
Died: Massillon, Ohio, Oct 1935
World title fights: 7 (1 lightweight, 6 welterweight) won 2, lost 4, drew 1

DATE	WEIGHT	OPPONENT	VENUE	RESULT	
29 Oct 1897	L	George 'Kid' Lavigne	San Francisco	Lost	PTS–12
6 Dec 1898	W	Billy Smith	New York	Lost	PTS–20
18 Dec 1901	W	Rube Ferns	Fort Erie, Canada	Won	KO–5
23 Jun 1902	W	Tommy West	London	Won	PTS–15
30 Apr 1904	W	Dixie Kid	San Francisco	Lost	DIS–20
12 May 1904	W	Dixie Kid	San Francisco	Drew	20
16 Oct 1906	W	Honey Mellody	Chelsea, Massachusetts	Lost	PTS–15

Mickey WALKER

Born: Elizabeth, New Jersey, USA, 13 Jul 1901
Died: Freehold, New Jersey, 28 Apr 1981
World title fights: 13 (6 welterweight, 5 middleweight, 2 light-heavy)
won 8, lost 4, ND 1

DATE	WEIGHT	OPPONENT	VENUE	RESULT	
1 Nov 1922	W	Jack Britton	New York	Won	PTS–15
22 Mar 1923	W	Pete Latzo	Newark, New Jersey		ND–12
2 Jun 1924	W	Lew Tendler	Philadelphia	Won	PTS–10
12 Oct 1924	W	Bobby Barrett	Philadelphia	Won	KO–6
2 Jul 1925	M	Harry Greb	New York	Lost	PTS–15
21 Sep 1925	W	Dave Shade	New York	Won	PTS–15
20 May 1926	W	Pete Latzo	Scranton, Pennsylvania	Lost	PTS–10
3 Dec 1926	M	Tiger Flowers	Chicago	Won	PTS–10
30 Jun 1927	M	Tommy Milligan	London	Won	KO–10
21 Jun 1928	M	Ace Hudkins	Chicago	Won	PTS–10
28 Mar 1929	LH	Tommy Loughran	Chicago	Lost	PTS–10

DATE	WEIGHT	OPPONENT	VENUE	RESULT
29 Oct 1929	M	Ace Hudkins	Los Angeles	Won PTS–10
3 Nov 1933	LH	Maxie Rosenbloom	New York	Lost PTS–15

Jimmy WALSH

Born: Newton, Massachusetts, USA, 18 Jul 1886
Died: Newton, 23 Nov 1964
World title fights: 3 (1 bantamweight, 2 featherweight) won 1, lost 1, drew 1

DATE	WEIGHT	OPPONENT	VENUE	RESULT
20 Oct 1905	B	Digger Stanley	Chelsea, Massachusetts	Won PTS–15
7 Dec 1906	Fe	Abe Attell	Los Angeles	Lost KO–8
21 May 1912	Fe	Johnny Kilbane	Boston	Drew 12

Jiro WATANABE

Born: Osaka, Japan, 16 Mar 1955
World title fights: 14 (all junior-bantam) won 12, lost 2

DATE	WEIGHT	OPPONENT	VENUE	RESULT
22 Apr 1981	JB (WBC)	Chul-Ho Kim	Seoul	Lost PTS–15
8 Apr 1982	JB (WBA)	Rafael Pedroza	Osaka, Japan	Won PTS–15
29 Jul 1982	JB (WBA)	Gustavo Ballas	Osaka	Won RSF–9
11 Nov 1982	JB (WBA)	Shoji Oguma	Hamamatsu, Japan	Won RTD–12
24 Feb 1983	JB (WBA)	Luis Ibanez	Hamamatsu	Won KO–8
23 Jun 1983	JB (WBA)	Roberto Ramirez	Miyagi-Kew, Japan	Won PTS–15
5 Oct 1983	JB (WBA)	Soo-Chun Kwon	Osaka	Won TD–11
15 Mar 1984	JB (WBA)	Celso Chavez	Osaka	Won RSF–15
5 Jul 1984	JB (WBC)	Payao Poontarat	Osaka	Won PTS–12
29 Nov 1984	JB (WBC)	Payao Poontarat	Kumamoto, Japan	Won RSF–11
9 May 1985	JB (WBC)	Julio Soto Solano	Tokyo	Won PTS–12
17 Sep 1985	JB (WBC)	Kazuo Katsuma	Osaka	Won RSF–7
12 Dec 1985	JB (WBC)	Suk-Huan Yun	Seoul	Won RSF–5
30 Mar 1986	JB (WBC)	Gilberto Roman	Osaka	Lost PTS–12

DATE	WEIGHT	OPPONENT	VENUE	RESULT

DATE	WEIGHT	OPPONENT	VENUE	RESULT

Jim WATT

Born: Glasgow, Scotland, 18 Jul 1948
World title fights: 6 (all lightweight) won 5, lost 1

DATE	WEIGHT	OPPONENT	VENUE	RESULT	
17 Apr 1979	L (WBC)	Alfredo Pitalua	Glasgow	Won	RSF–12
3 Nov 1979	L (WBC)	Roberto Vasquez	Glasgow	Won	RSF–9
14 Mar 1980	L (WBC)	Charlie Nash	Glasgow	Won	RSF–4
7 Jun 1980	L (WBC)	Howard Davis	Glasgow	Won	PTS–15
1 Nov 1980	L (WBC)	Sean O'Grady	Glasgow	Won	RSF–12
20 Jun 1981	L (WBC)	Alexis Arguello	London	Lost	PTS–15

Mike WEAVER

Born: Gatesville, Texas, USA, 14 Jun 1952
World title fights: 7 (all heavyweight) won 3, lost 3, drew 1

DATE	WEIGHT	OPPONENT	VENUE	RESULT	
22 Jun 1979	H (WBC)	Larry Holmes	New York	Lost	RSF–12
31 Mar 1980	H (WBA)	John Tate	Knoxville, Tennessee	Won	KO–15
25 Oct 1980	H (WBA)	Gerrie Coetzee	Sun City, S Africa	Won	KO–13
3 Oct 1981	H (WBA)	James Tillis	Rosemont, Illinois	Won	PTS–15
10 Dec 1982	H (WBA)	Michael Dokes	Las Vegas	Lost	RSF–1
20 May 1983	H (WBA)	Michael Dokes	Las Vegas	Drew	15
15 Jun 1985	H (WBC)	Pinklon Thomas	Las Vegas	Lost	RSF–8

Freddie WELSH

Born: Pontypridd, Wales, 5 Mar 1886
Died: New York City, 29 Jul 1929
World title fights: 4 (all lightweight) won 3, lost 1

DATE	WEIGHT	OPPONENT	VENUE	RESULT	
7 Jul 1914	L	Willie Ritchie	London	Won	PTS–20
4 Jul 1916	L	Ad Wolgast	Denver	Won	DIS–11

DATE	WEIGHT	OPPONENT	VENUE	RESULT

Date	Weight	Opponent	Venue	Result	
4 Sep 1916	L	Charley White	Colorado Springs	Won	PTS–20
28 May 1917	L	Benny Leonard	New York	Lost	KO–9

Pernell WHITAKER

Born: Norfolk, Virginia, USA, 2 Jan 1964
World title fights: 7 (all lightweight) won 6, lost 1

Date	Weight	Opponent	Venue	Result	
12 Mar 1988	L (WBC)	Jose Luis Ramirez	Paris	Lost	PTS–12
20 Feb 1989	L (IBF)	Greg Haugen	Hampton, Virginia	Won	PTS–12
1 May 1989	L (IBF)	Louie Lomeli	Norfolk, Virginia	Won	RSF–3
20 Aug 1989	L (WBC/IBF)	Jose Luis Ramirez	Norfolk	Won	PTS–12
3 Feb 1990	L (WBC/IBF)	Freddie Pendleton	Atlantic City	Won	PTS–12
19 May 1990	L (WBC/IBF)	Azumah Nelson	Las Vegas	Won	PTS–12
11 Aug 1990	L (WBC/WBA/IBF)	Juan Nazario	Lake Tahoe, Nevada	Won	KO–1

Jimmy WILDE

Born: Tylorstown, Wales, 15 May 1892
Died: Cardiff, 10 Mar 1969
World title fights: 3 (all flyweight) won 2, lost 1

Date	Weight	Opponent	Venue	Result	
18 Dec 1916	Fl	Young Zulu Kid	London	Won	KO–11
12 Mar 1917	Fl	George Clark	London	Won	RTD–4
18 Jun 1923	Fl	Pancho Villa	New York	Lost	KO–7

Jess WILLARD

Born: Pottawatomie County, Kansas, USA, 29 Dec 1881
Died: Los Angeles, 15 Dec 1968
World title fights: 3 (all heavyweight) won 1, lost 1, NC 1

DATE	WEIGHT	OPPONENT	VENUE	RESULT
5 Apr 1915	H	Jack Johnson	Havana	Won KO–26
25 Mar 1916	H	Frank Moran	New York	NC–10
4 Jul 1919	H	Jack Dempsey	Toledo, Ohio	Lost RTD–3

Ike WILLIAMS

Born: Brunswick, Georgia, USA, 2 Aug 1923
World title fights: 9 (all lightweight) won 8, lost 1

DATE	WEIGHT	OPPONENT	VENUE	RESULT
18 Apr 1945	L (NBA)	Juan Zurita	Mexico City	Won KO–2
4 Sep 1946	L (NBA)	Ronnie James	Cardiff	Won KO–9
4 Aug 1947	L	Bob Montgomery	Philadelphia	Won KO–6
25 May 1948	L	Enrique Bolanos	Los Angeles	Won PTS–15
12 Jul 1948	L	Beau Jack	Philadelphia	Won KO–6
23 Sep 1948	L	Jesse Flores	New York	Won KO–10
21 Jul 1949	L	Enrique Bolanos	Los Angeles	Won KO–4
5 Dec 1949	L	Freddie Dawson	Philadelphia	Won PTS–15
25 May 1951	L	Jimmy Carter	New York	Lost RSF–14

Kid WILLIAMS

Born: Copenhagen, Denmark, 5 Dec 1893
Died: Baltimore, 18 Oct 1963
World title fights: 6 (all bantamweight) won 1, lost 2, drew 2, ND 1

DATE	WEIGHT	OPPONENT	VENUE	RESULT
18 Oct 1912	B	Johnny Coulon	New York	ND–10
3 Jun 1914	B	Johnny Coulon	Los Angeles	Won KO–3

DATE	WEIGHT	OPPONENT	VENUE	RESULT

DATE	WEIGHT	OPPONENT	VENUE	RESULT
10 Sep 1915	B	Johnny Ertle	St Paul, Minnesota	Lost DIS-5*
6 Dec 1915	B	Frankie Burns	New Orleans	Drew 20
7 Feb 1916	B	Pete Herman	New Orleans	Drew 20
9 Jan 1917	B	Pete Herman	New Orleans	Lost PTS-20

* Williams argued that the bout took place in a town where decisions were prohibited. Consequently he claimed he could not be disqualified and continued to be regarded as the champion

Prince Charles WILLIAMS

Born: Columbus, Mississippi, USA, 2 Jun 1962
World title fights: 5 (all light-heavy) won 5, lost 0

DATE	WEIGHT	OPPONENT	VENUE	RESULT
29 Oct 1987	LH (IBF)	Bobby Czyz	Las Vegas	Won TKO-9
10 Jun 1988	LH (IBF)	Richard Caramanolis	Annecy, France	Won RTD-11
21 Oct 1988	LH (IBF)	Rufino Angulo	Villenave D'Ornon, France	Won RSF-3
25 Jun 1989	LH (IBF)	Bobby Czyz	Atlantic City	Won TKO-10
7 Jan 1990	LH (IBF)	Frankie Swindell	Atlantic City	Won RSF-8

J B WILLIAMSON

Born: Indianapolis, USA, 18 Dec 1956
World title fights: 2 (both light-heavy) won 1, lost 1

DATE	WEIGHT	OPPONENT	VENUE	RESULT
11 Dec 1985	LH (WBC)	Prince Mohammed	Los Angeles	Won PTS-12
30 Apr 1986	LH (WBC)	Dennis Andries	London	Lost PTS-12

Jackie WILSON

Born: Arkansas, USA, 1909
Died: Torrance, Pennsylvania, 2 Dec 1966
World title fights: 4 (all featherweight) won 2, lost 2

DATE	WEIGHT	OPPONENT	VENUE	RESULT
18 Nov 1941	Fe (NBA)	Richie Lemos	Los Angeles	Won PTS-12
12 Dec 1941	Fe (NBA)	Richie Lemos	Los Angeles	Won PTS-12

DATE	WEIGHT	OPPONENT	VENUE	RESULT

DATE	WEIGHT	OPPONENT	VENUE	RESULT
18 Jan 1943	Fe (NBA)	Jackie Callura	Providence, Rhode Island	Lost PTS–15
18 Mar 1943	Fe (NBA)	Jackie Callura	Boston	Lost PTS–15

Johnny WILSON

Born: New York City, USA, 23 Mar 1893
Died: Boston, Massachusetts, 8 Dec 1985
World title fights: 6 (all middleweight) won 2, lost 2, ND 2

DATE	WEIGHT	OPPONENT	VENUE	RESULT
6 May 1920	M	Mike O'Dowd	Boston	Won PTS–12
17 Jan 1921	M	George Chip	Pittsburgh	ND–12
17 Mar 1921	M	Mike O'Dowd	New York	Won PTS–15
5 Sep 1921	M	Bryan Downey	Jersey City, New Jersey	ND–12
31 Aug 1923	M	Harry Greb	New York	Lost PTS–15
18 Jan 1924	M	Harry Greb	New York	Lost PTS–15

Howard WINSTONE

Born: Merthyr Tydfil, Wales, 15 Apr 1939
World title fights: 5 (all featherweight) won 1, lost 4

DATE	WEIGHT	OPPONENT	VENUE	RESULT
7 Sep 1965	Fe	Vicente Saldivar	London	Lost PTS–15
15 Jun 1967	Fe	Vicente Saldivar	Cardiff	Lost PTS–15
14 Oct 1967	Fe	Vicente Saldivar	Mexico City	Lost RTD–12
23 Jan 1968	Fe (WBC)	Mitsunori Seki	London	Won RSF–9
24 Jul 1968	Fe (WBC)	Jose Legra	Porthcawl, Wales	Lost RSF–5

Tim WITHERSPOON

Born: Philadelphia, USA, 27 Dec 1957
World title fights: 6 (all heavyweight) won 3, lost 3

DATE	WEIGHT	OPPONENT	VENUE	RESULT
20 May 1983	H (WBC)	Larry Holmes	Las Vegas	Lost PTS–12

DATE	WEIGHT	OPPONENT	VENUE	RESULT

DATE	WEIGHT	OPPONENT	VENUE	RESULT
9 Mar 1984	H (WBC)	Greg Page	Las Vegas	Won PTS–12
31 Aug 1984	H (WBC)	Pinklon Thomas	Las Vegas	Lost PTS–12
17 Jan 1986	H (WBA)	Tony Tubbs	Atlanta	Won PTS–15
20 Jul 1986	H (WBA)	Frank Bruno	London	Won KO–11
12 Dec 1986	H (WBA)	James Smith	New York	Lost RSF–1

Ad WOLGAST

Born: Cadillac, Michigan, USA, 8 Feb 1888
Died: Camarillo, California, 14 Apr 1955
World title fights: 6 (all lightweight) won 4, lost 2

22 Feb 1910	L	Battling Nelson	Port Richmond, California	Won KO–40
27 May 1911	L	Frankie Burns	San Francisco	Won KO–16
4 Jul 1911	L	Owen Moran	San Francisco	Won KO–13
4 Jul 1912	L	Joe Rivers	Vernon, California	Won TKO–13
28 Nov 1912	L	Willie Ritchie	Daly City, California	Lost DIS–16
4 Jul 1916	L	Freddie Welsh	Denver	Lost DIS–11

Midget WOLGAST

Born: Philadelphia, USA, 18 Jul 1910
Died: Philadelphia, 19 Oct 1955
World title fights: 5 (all flyweight) won 3, lost 1, drew 1

21 Mar 1930	Fl (NY)	Black Bill	New York	Won PTS–15
16 May 1930	Fl (NY)	Willie La Morte	New York	Won RTD–5
13 Jul 1930	Fl (NY)	Ruby Bradley	New York	Won PTS–15
26 Dec 1930	Fl (NBA)	Frankie Genaro	New York	Drew 15
16 Sep 1935	Fl (NY)	Small Montana	Oakland, California	Lost PTS–10

DATE	WEIGHT	OPPONENT	VENUE	RESULT

Albert 'Chalky' WRIGHT

Born: Durango, Mexico, 10 Feb 1912
Died: Los Angeles, 12 Aug 1957
World title fights: 5 (all featherweight) won 3, lost 2

DATE	WEIGHT	OPPONENT	VENUE	RESULT	
11 Sep 1941	Fe (NY)	Joey Archibald	Washington DC	Won	KO–11
19 Jun 1942	Fe (NY)	Harry Jeffra	Baltimore	Won	KO–10
25 Sep 1942	Fe (NY)	Charlie Costantino	New York	Won	PTS–15
20 Nov 1942	Fe (NY)	Willie Pep	New York	Lost	PTS–15
29 Sep 1944	Fe (NY)	Willie Pep	New York	Lost	PTS–15

Teddy YAROSZ

Born: Pittsburgh, USA, 24 Jun 1910
Died: Monaca, Pennsylvania, 29 Mar 1974
World title fights: 2 (both middleweight) won 1, lost 1

DATE	WEIGHT	OPPONENT	VENUE	RESULT	
11 Sep 1934	M (NY)	Vince Dundee	Pittsburgh	Won	PTS–15
19 Sep 1935	M (NY)	Ed 'Babe' Risko	Pittsburgh	Lost	PTS–15

Hwan-Kil YUH

Born: Kyongnam, South Korea, 23 Sep 1962
World title fights: 3 (all junior-light) won 2, lost 1

DATE	WEIGHT	OPPONENT	VENUE	RESULT	
22 Apr 1984	JL (IBF)	Rod Sequenan	Seoul	Won	PTS–15
16 Sep 1984	JL (IBF)	Sakda Galaxy	Pohang, S Korea	Won	KO–6
15 Feb 1985	JL (IBF)	Lester Ellis	Melbourne	Lost	PTS–15

Jae-Do YUH

Born: Chumra-Nam-Do, South Korea, 25 Apr 1948
World title fights: 3 (all junior-middle) won 2, lost 1

DATE	WEIGHT	OPPONENT	VENUE	RESULT
7 Jun 1975	JM (WBA)	Koichi Wajima	Kitsakyushu, Japan	Won KO–7
11 Nov 1975	JM (WBA)	Masashiro Misako	Shizuoko, Japan	Won KO–6
17 Feb 1976	JM (WBA)	Koichi Wajima	Tokyo	Lost KO–15

Myung-Woo YUH

Born: Seoul, South Korea, 10 Jan 1964
World title fights: 17 (all junior-fly) won 17, lost 0

DATE	WEIGHT	OPPONENT	VENUE	RESULT
8 Dec 1985	JFl (WBA)	Joey Olivo	Taegu, S Korea	Won PTS–15
9 Mar 1986	JFl (WBA)	Jose De Jesus	Suwo, S Korea	Won PTS–15
14 Jun 1986	JFl (WBA)	Tomohiro Kiyuna	Inchon, S Korea	Won KO–12
30 Nov 1986	JFl (WBA)	Mario De Marco	Seoul	Won PTS–15
1 Mar 1987	JFl (WBA)	Eduardo Tunon	Seoul	Won KO–1
7 Jun 1987	JFl (WBA)	Benedicto Murillo	Pusan, S Korea	Won RSF–15
20 Sep 1987	JFl (WBA)	Ricardo Blanco	Pohang, S Korea	Won KO–8
7 Feb 1988	JFl (WBA)	Wilibardo Salazar	Seoul	Won PTS–12
12 Jun 1988	JFl (WBA)	Jose De Jesus	Seoul	Won PTS–12
28 Aug 1988	JFl (WBA)	Putt Ohyuthanakorn	Pusan	Won KO–6
6 Nov 1988	JFl (WBA)	Bahar Udin	Seoul	Won KO–7
11 Feb 1989	JFl (WBA)	Katsumi Komiyama	Chongjo, S Korea	Won RSF–10
11 Jun 1989	JFl (WBA)	Mario De Marco	Inchon	Won PTS–12
24 Sep 1989	JFl (WBA)	Taiho Kenbun	Seoul	Won KO–11
14 Jan 1990	JFl (WBA)	Hisashi Takashima	Seoul	Won RSF–7
29 Apr 1990	JFl (WBA)	Leo Gamez	Seoul	Won PTS–12
10 Nov 1990	JFl (WBA)	Leo Gamez	Seoul	Won PTS–12

Dong-Kyun YUM

Born: Chung-Buk-Do, South Korea, 17 Jan 1952
World title fights: 4 (all junior-feather) won 2, lost 2

DATE	WEIGHT	OPPONENT	VENUE	RESULT	
1 Aug 1976	JFe (WBC)	Rigoberto Riasco	Pusan, S Korea	Lost	PTS–15
24 Nov 1976	JFe (WBC)	Royal Kobayashi	Seoul	Won	PTS–15
13 Feb 1977	JFe (WBC)	Jose Cervantes	Seoul	Won	PTS–15
21 May 1977	JFe (WBC)	Wilfredo Gomez	San Juan	Lost	KO–12

Tony ZALE

Born: Gary, Indiana, USA, 29 May 1913
World title fights: 8 (all middleweight) won 6, lost 2

DATE	WEIGHT	OPPONENT	VENUE	RESULT	
19 Jul 1940	M (NBA)	Al Hostak	Seattle	Won	KO–13
21 Feb 1941	M (NBA)	Steve Mamakos	Chicago	Won	KO–14
28 May 1941	M (NBA)	Al Hostak	Chicago	Won	KO–2
28 Nov 1941	M	Georgie Abrams	New York	Won	PTS–15
27 Sep 1946	M	Rocky Graziano	New York	Won	KO–6
16 Jul 1947	M	Rocky Graziano	Chicago	Lost	KO–6
10 Jun 1948	M	Rocky Graziano	Newark, New Jersey	Won	KO–3
21 Sep 1948	M	Marcel Cerdan	Jersey City, New Jersey	Lost	KO–12

Alfonso ZAMORA

Born: Mexico City, Mexico, 9 Feb 1954
World title fights: 7 (all bantamweight) won 6, lost 1

DATE	WEIGHT	OPPONENT	VENUE	RESULT	
14 Mar 1975	B (WBA)	Soo-Hwan Hong	Los Angeles	Won	KO–4
30 Aug 1975	B (WBA)	Thanomjit Sukothai	Anaheim, California	Won	KO–4
6 Dec 1975	B (WBA)	Socrates Batoto	Mexico City	Won	KO–2
3 Apr 1976	B (WBA)	Eusebio Pedroza	Mexicali, Mexico	Won	KO–2

10 Jul 1976	B (WBA)	Gilberto Illeuca	Juarez, Mexico	Won	KO–3
16 Oct 1976	B (WBA)	Soo-Hwan Hong	Inchon, S Korea	Won	RSF–12
19 Nov 1977	B (WBA)	Jorge Lujan	Los Angeles	Lost	KO–10

Hilario ZAPATA

Born: Colon, Panama, 19 Aug 1958
World title fights: 23 (14 junior-fly, 9 flyweight) won 18, lost 4, drew 1

23 Mar 1980	JFl (WBC)	Shigeo Nakajima	Tokyo	Won	PTS–15
7 Jun 1980	JFl (WBC)	Chi-Bok Kim	Seoul	Won	PTS–15
4 Aug 1980	JFl (WBC)	Hector Ray Melendez	Caracas	Won	PTS–15
17 Sep 1980	JFl (WBC)	Shigeo Nakajima	Tokyo	Won	RSF–11
1 Dec 1980	JFl (WBC)	Reinaldo Becerra	Caracas	Won	PTS–15
8 Feb 1981	JFl (WBC)	Joey Olivo	Panama City	Won	RTD–13
24 Apr 1981	JFl (WBC)	Rudy Crawford	San Francisco	Won	PTS–15
15 Aug 1981	JFl (WBC)	German Torres	Panama City	Won	PTS–15
7 Nov 1981	JFl (WBC)	Netrnoi Vorasingh	Korat, Thailand	Won	RSF–10
6 Feb 1982	JFl (WBC)	Amado Ursua	Panama City	Lost	KO–2
20 Jul 1982	JFl (WBC)	Tadashi Tomori	Kanazawa, Japan	Won	PTS–15
18 Sep 1982	JFl (WBC)	Jung-Koo Chang	Seoul	Won	PTS–15
30 Nov 1982	JFl (WBC)	Tadashi Tomori	Tokyo	Won	RSF–8
26 Mar 1983	JFl (WBC)	Jung-Koo Chang	Seoul	Lost	RSF–3
8 Dec 1984	Fl (WBA)	Santos Laciar	Buenos Aires	Lost	PTS–15
5 Oct 1985	Fl (WBA)	Alonso Gonzalez	Panama City	Won	PTS–15
31 Jan 1986	Fl (WBA)	Javier Lucas	Panama City	Won	PTS–15
7 Apr 1986	Fl (WBA)	Shuichi Hozumi	Hirasaki, Japan	Won	PTS–15
5 Jul 1986	Fl (WBA)	Dodie Penalosa	Manila	Won	PTS–15
13 Sep 1986	Fl (WBA)	Alberto Castro	Panama City	Won	PTS–15
6 Dec 1986	Fl (WBA)	Claudemir Dias	Salvador, Brazil	Won	PTS–15

13 Feb 1987	Fl (WBA)	Fidel Bassa	Barranquilla, Colombia	Lost	PTS–15
15 Aug 1987	Fl (WBA)	Fidel Bassa	Panama City	Drew	15

Daniel ZARAGOZA

Born: Mexico City, Mexico, 11 Dec 1959
World title fights: 9 (2 bantamweight, 7 junior-feather) won 6, lost 2, drew 1

4 May 1985	B (WBC)	Freddie Jackson	Aruba, Dutch West Indies	Won	DIS–7
9 Aug 1985	B (WBC)	Miguel 'Happy' Lora	Miami	Lost	PTS–12
29 Feb 1988	JFe (WBC)	Carlos Zarate	Los Angeles	Won	RSF–10
29 May 1988	JFe (WBC)	Seung-Hoon Lee	Seoul	Drew	12
26 Nov 1988	JFe (WBC)	Valerio Nati	Forli, Italy	Won	KO–5
24 Jun 1989	JFe (WBC)	Paul Banke	Los Angeles	Won	PTS–12
31 Aug 1989	JFe (WBC)	Frankie Duarte	Los Angeles	Won	RSF–10
3 Dec 1989	JFe (WBC)	Chan-Young Park	Seoul	Won	PTS–12
23 Apr 1990	JFe (WBC)	Paul Banke	Los Angeles	Lost	RSF–9

Carlos ZARATE

Born: Tepito, Mexico, 23 May 1951
World title fights: 14 (11 bantamweight, 3 junior-feather) won 10, lost 4

8 May 1976	B (WBC)	Rodolfo Martinez	Los Angeles	Won	KO–9
28 Aug 1976	B (WBC)	Paul Ferreri	Los Angeles	Won	RSF–12
13 Nov 1976	B (WBC)	Waruinge Nakayama	Culiacan, Mexico	Won	KO–4
5 Feb 1977	B (WBC)	Fernando Cabanela	Mexico City	Won	RSF–3
29 Oct 1977	B (WBC)	Danilo Batista	Los Angeles	Won	RSF–6
2 Dec 1977	B (WBC)	Juan Rodriguez	Madrid	Won	RSF–5
25 Feb 1978	B (WBC)	Alberto Davila	Los Angeles	Won	RSF–8
22 Apr 1978	B (WBC)	Andres Hernandez	San Juan	Won	RSF–13

DATE	WEIGHT	OPPONENT	VENUE	RESULT	
10 Jun 1978	B (WBC)	Emilio Hernandez	Las Vegas	Won	KO–4
28 Oct 1978	JFe (WBC)	Wilfredo Gomez	San Juan	Lost	RSF–5
10 Mar 1979	B (WBC)	Mensah Kpalongo	Los Angeles	Won	KO–3
3 Jun 1979	B (WBC)	Lupe Pintor	Las Vegas	Lost	PTS–15
16 Oct 1987	JFe (WBC)	Jeff Fenech	Sydney	Lost	TKO–4
29 Feb 1988	JFe (WBC)	Daniel Zaragoza	Los Angeles	Lost	RSF–10

Fritzie ZIVIC

Born: Pittsburgh, USA, 8 May 1913
Died: Pittsburgh, 16 May 1984
World title fights: 3 (all welterweight) won 2, lost 1

DATE	WEIGHT	OPPONENT	VENUE	RESULT	
4 Oct 1940	W	Henry Armstrong	New York	Won	PTS–15
17 Jan 1941	W	Henry Armstrong	New York	Won	KO–12
29 Jul 1941	W	Freddie Cochrane	Newark, New Jersey	Lost	PTS–15

Juan ZURITA

Born: Guadalajara, Mexico, 12 May 1914
World title fights: 2 (both lightweight) won 1, lost 1

DATE	WEIGHT	OPPONENT	VENUE	RESULT	
8 Mar 1944	L (NBA)	Sammy Angott	Hollywood	Won	PTS–15
18 Apr 1945	L (NBA)	Ike Williams	Mexico City	Lost	KO–2

INDEX

THE CHALLENGERS

FELTZ, Tommy 82
FERNANDEZ, Florentino 86
FERNANDEZ, Francisco 162
FERNANDEZ, Jorge 98
FERNANDEZ, Jose 74
FERNANDEZ, Mark 160
FERNANDEZ, Vilomar 71, 120
FERRAND, Victor 91
FERRERI, Paul 260
FINCH, Bruce 136
FINNEGAN, Chris 83
FIRPO, Luis Angel 65
FISHER, Tony 204
FLORES, Elino 69
FLORES, Jesse 252
FLORES, Jose Maria 64
FLYNN, Jim 32, 117
FOGERTY, Jack 65
FOLLEY, Zora 5
FONTAINE, Ritchie 11
FORAN, Ginger 29
FORD, Al 84
FORD, Ernesto 87
FORD, Pat 192, 218
FORTE, Tommy 216
FOURIE, Pierre 83, 87
FOX, Billy 137
FOX, Tiger Jack 24
FRANCIS, Kid 30
FRANK, Scott 108
FRATTO, Rocky 160
FRAZIER, Marvis 108
FRAZIER, Tyrone 106
FREITAS, George 184
FRUSH, Danny 69, 122
FUENTES, Moses 217
FUENTES, Sammy 47
FUKUYAMA, Shig 128
FULLER, Sammy 212
FULLJAMES, George 65
FULLMER, Don 22
FURESAWA, Kimio 36, 76

FURLANO, Nicky 200
FURR, Phil 11
FURUYAMA, Tetsuo Lion 42, 80, 168
FUSARIO, Charley 27, 205

GAINER, Al 138
GALAXY, Sakda 256
GALENTO, Tony 144
GALLARDO, Jesus 189
GALVEZ, Ali 63, 195
GANIGAN, Andy 10
GANT, Johnny 75
GAONA, Alfredo 85
GARCIA, Agustin 44, 118
GARCIA, Cleo 57, 145, 231
GARCIA, Danny 135
GARCIA, Enrique 154
GARCIA, Jorge 'Rocky', 218
GARCIA, Lorenzo 32
GARDNER, Gus 88
GARDNER, Oscar 67, 149
GARDNER, Tony 176
GARRISON, Jimmy 11
GATTELLARI, Rocky 33
GAULT, Henry Pappy 40
GAYMON, Dorcy 171
GHNOULY, Joe 11
GIAMBRA, Joey 168
GIBBONS, Tommy 65
GILROY, Freddie 101
GIMENEZ, Carlos 42
GIMENEZ, Joan Jose 100
GIOVANNI, Nestor 102
GIRONES, Jose 161
GODOY, Arturo 144
GOLDBERG, Benny 184
GOMEZ, Pedro 214
GONZALEZ, Alonso 259
GONZALEZ, Manuel (Arg) 128
GONZALEZ, Manuel (USA) 53, 98
GONZALEZ, Paul 35

LAMPKIN, Kelvin 179
LAMPKIN, Ray 71
LANE, Kenny 30, 183
LANE, Larry 184
LANG, Bill 33
LANGLOIS, Pierre 181
LARA, Rogelio 6
LASISI, Joe 106
LaSTARZA, Roland 154
LEDOUX, Charles 92
LEDOUX, Scott 108
LEE, Dong-Chun 86, 197
LEE, Glen 8, 89
LEE, Jeung-Jai 126
LEE, Ki-Jun 15
LEE, Sam-Jung, 118
LEE, Sang-Ho 52
LEE, Seung-Soon 28
LEE, William 100
LELLO, Pete 115
LENNY, Eddie 67
LEON, Arturo 10
LEON, Casper 16, 82
LESLIE, Jock 194
LEVINE, George 133
LEWIS, Hedgemon 171, 231
LEWIS, Willie 187
LICATA, Tony 165
LIM, Jeung-Keun 95
LINDSAY, Kenny 183, 184
LIRA, Johnny 76
LITTLE, Steve 112
LOAYZA, Stanislaus 96
LOGGI, Juan Martin 202
LOMELI, Louie 251
LOMSKI, Leo 144
LONDAS, Daniel 162
LONDON, Brian 4, 190
LONG, Al 31
LOPEZ, Alvaro 54, 63, 87, 170
LOPEZ, Ernie 171
LOPEZ, Gerardo 173

LOPEZ, Joey 30, 73
LOPEZ, Jose Mario 185
LOPEZ, Juan Antonio 93, 94
LOPEZ, Leonardo 184
LOPEZ, Lucio 143, 196
LOUIS, Young Joe 170, 177
LOVERA, Rafael 78
LUCAS, Javier 259
LUCAS, Pretty Boy 225
LUDICK, Willie 53
LUMUMBA, Patrick 148
LUNNY III, Ray 74
LUPINO, Maurizio 54
LYLE, Ron 5

McAVOY, Jock 138
McCARTHY, Billy 65
McCARTHY, Cal 66
McCRORY, Steve 79
McDONALD, Jim 60, 228
McDONALD, Roddy 35
McDONNELL, Jim 162, 174
McGARVEY, Ron 74
MACHEN, Eddie 235
MACK, Marvin 189
McKEEVER, Charlie 226, 227
McMILLAN, William 69
McNEELEY, Tommy 191
McPARTLAND, Kid 133
MAGALLANO, Elmer 224
MAHACHAI, Montsayarm 99
MAIER, Dave 174
MAJORES, Vicente Saldivar 62
MAKHATHINI, Siza 131, 148
MAKIN, Olli 166
MAKLOUFI, Ould 223
MALDONADO, Orlando 182
MALINGA, Sugar Boy 206
MALVAREZ, Juan 142, 192
MAMAKOS, Steve 258
MANCA, Fortunato 158
MANFREDO, Al 11

Index of challengers compiled by Lyn Greenwood